Junkers Ju 87
STUKA

All marks and variants (1935–45)

COVER IMAGE: Junkers Ju 87 D-3.

(John Weal/Art Tech)

First published in February 2018
Reprinted August 2018

A catalogue record for this book is available from the British Library.

ISBN 978 1 78521 141 6

Library of Congress control no. 2017948599

Published by Haynes Publishing,
Sparkford, Yeovil,
Somerset BA22 7JJ, UK.
Tel: 01963 440635
Int. tel: +44 1963 440635
Website: www.haynes.com

Haynes North America Inc.,
859 Lawrence Drive, Newbury Park,
California 91320, USA.

Printed in Malaysia.

Commissioning Editor: Jonathan Falconer
Copy editor: Michelle Tilling
Proof reader: Penny Housden
Indexer: Peter Nicholson
Page design: James Robertson

Acknowledgements

I am indebted to fellow authors Chris Goss and Andy Saunders for kindly allowing use of photographs from their respective collections and for their welcome advice on the Stuka; also to my friend Dr Simon Trew from the Department of War Studies, RMA Sandhurst, for his guidance on some of the historical aspects of this book.

Photographers Claudia Weber-Gebert (Germany), Pierre Kosimidis (www. ww2wrecks.com) (Greece), Peter R. March, Richard Crockett, Ian F. Paterson, James Payne/Through Their Eyes and Wings Museum for permission to use copyright photographs.

Crécy Publishing for kindly allowing use of the extract from *Wings of the Luftwaffe* by Eric Brown.

Art Tech for their kind permission to reproduce the cutaway drawing of the Ju 87 D-3 by the talented John Weal.

Bundesarchiv, Getty Images, Alamy, SA-Kuva – Finnish Defence Forces Wartime Photograph Archive (www.sa-kuva.fi), US National Archives, US Navy, World of Warplanes, Fleet Air Arm Museum, Wikimedia Commons and Hellenic Air Force for permission to reproduce photographs in their collections.

Junkers Ju 87 STUKA

All marks and variants (1935–45)

Owners' Workshop Manual

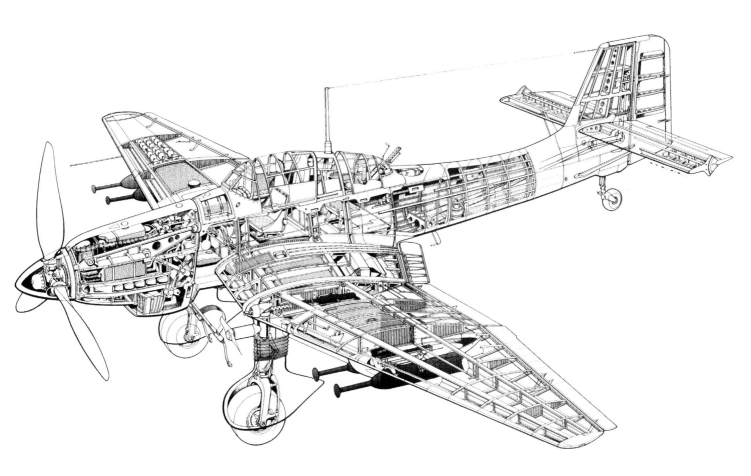

Insights into the design, construction and operation of the Luftwaffe dive-bomber that symbolised the terror of the German Blitzkrieg

Jonathan Falconer

Contents

OPPOSITE During a pause in operations, a Ju 87 crew from II. Gruppe of Stukageschwader 2 (II./StG 2) pose for a Kriegsberichter photographer in northern France during the summer of 1940. *(Copyright unknown)*

Introduction

BELOW The face of Blitzkrieg: Ju 87 B Stukas from the IIIrd Gruppe of Stukageschwader 77 (III./StG 77) fly in close formation over the Crimea after an attack on Sebastopol in 1942. *(Andy Saunders collection)*

If ever a sight and a sound came to symbolise the terror of the German Blitzkrieg then it was the Junkers Ju 87 – the Stuka. Even its name sounds aggressive, derived as it is from the word 'Sturzkampfflugzeug', which is the generic German term for dive-bomber. With its distinctive cranked wing and vulture-like looks, the blood-curdling shriek of a Stuka in a vertical power-dive was certain to strike fear and panic into the most battle-hardened soldiers as well as defenceless civilians.

In the early days of the war the Ju 87 certainly lived up to its fearsome reputation but later, when it came up against better-equipped adversaries and the war had changed in character, the Stuka finally met its match.

The first in a succession of prototypes of the Ju 87 flew in the spring of 1935 and in late 1936 a handful of pre-production aircraft were secretly shipped to Spain where they flew with the Legion Kondor in the Civil War. It was in Spain that the fledgling Luftwaffe gained

invaluable experience, testing and refining tactical air power and developing air-to-ground communications between its dive-bombers and armoured units. This 'dry-run' paid dividends, for by 1939 the Luftwaffe and its dive-bombers were ready to wreak havoc in Poland.

It was during the Spanish Civil War that the Ju 87 acquired a nickname that was to stick among the dive-bomber's air and groundcrews for the rest of its service life. The Stuka was named 'Jolanthe' by Oberstleutnant Günter Schwartzkopff, the Gruppenkommandeur of IV.(St)/LG 1's 11th Staffel, the Luftwaffe unit that supplied the clutch of Ju 87 A-1s ('Antons') to the Legion Kondor in Spain. His inspiration was a large pink sow called Jolanthe, the porcine heroine of the German blockbuster romantic comedy film, *Krach um Jolanthe* (*Trouble with Jolanthe*), released in 1934. The small group of Antons flown by the Legion Kondor became known as the 'Jolanthe Kette', sporting the unit badge of a pink pig on an oval disc emblazoned on their port undercarriage wheel spats.

On 1 September 1939 the Stuka was in the vanguard of the Blitzkrieg on Poland, where its banshee howl and terrifying accuracy set the benchmark for Germany's future conquests. Its campaigns in the West in 1940 saw France and Belgium, Holland, Denmark and Norway, fall hopelessly under the hammer-blows of Panzer and Stuka. In its Ju 87 B ('Berta') and R ('Richard', long-range) versions, the Stuka proved highly effective as airborne artillery,

moving swiftly through France and the Low Countries working in close cooperation with the Panzer columns, demolishing all opposition that lay in their paths.

When it came to the next phase in Hitler's plan for domination in Europe, the English Channel stood in his way before he could subdue Great Britain. It was this narrow stretch of water and the inherent flaws in the Stuka's design that saw the dive-bomber meet its match over southern England in the summer of 1940. Its limited range, slow speed and poor defensive armament saw the Ju 87 suffer at the hands of the RAF's fighters in the Battle of Britain. After 18 August the Stuka was withdrawn from the front line and the Stukagruppen were moved up to the Pas-de-Calais in anticipation of Operation Seelöwe (Sealion), where it was intended they'd support the airborne and amphibious invasion of England – which never came.

Germany's attention now turned to other theatres of operations in the Mediterranean, the Balkans and in North Africa. The 'Berta', 'Richard' (and later the 'Dora') marks were adapted for service in the heat and dust of North Africa where, during the early campaigns, they were very effective, but with the invasion of Russia on 22 June 1941 came a bitter war of attrition that the Germans had neither foreseen nor prepared for. From then until the end of the conflict most of the Luftwaffe's Ju 87 squadrons (as well as a handful of Stuka units operated by

ABOVE The Stuka received its baptism of fire with the German Legion Kondor during the Spanish Civil War of 1937–38. Nicknamed 'Jolanthe' after the porcine star of a popular film of the day, Ju 87 A-1s in Spain were called the 'Jolanthe Kette' and sported an emblem of a sow on their port undercarriage spats. *(Author's collection)*

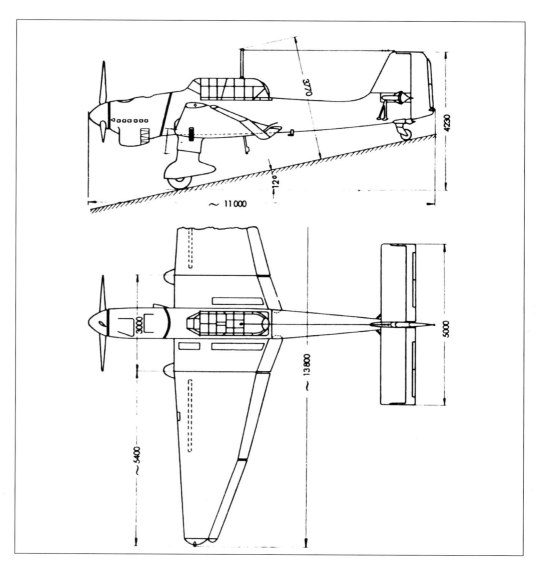

its allies) were heavily involved in the fighting on the Eastern Front.

It was primarily in the war with Russia that the role of the Stuka evolved from one of dive-bombing to embrace ground-attack and close air-support, but it should not be forgotten that the Ju 87 achieved remarkable success in the maritime strike role against the Royal Navy in the Mediterranean, and vessels of the Soviet Black Sea and Baltic Fleets. With the Ju 87 D-series (the Dora) introduced in January 1942 the wing-mounted fixed MG 17 7.92mm machine guns were replaced with a pair of 20mm quick-firing MG151/20 cannon to bolster the destructive power of the aircraft's bombload. Additional armour plating was bolted to the cockpit and around vital components to defend the crew and their aircraft from ground fire. New weapons

systems were also developed that added to the choice of firepower available to the Stuka: anti-personnel cluster-bomb dispensers and multi-gun pods were hung beneath the Stuka's wings to drive back the hordes of Russian infantry and soft-skinned vehicles on the exposed Steppes.

To counter the fast-growing numbers of Soviet tanks, a potent new weapon was added to the Stuka's arsenal in 1943. Twin 37mm auto-cannon were fitted to the Ju 87 G ('Gustav', a development of the Ju 87 D-5) in under-wing gun pods, which proved to be deadly tank-killers. Armed with the 'Panzerknacker' or 'tank cracker' (as they were nicknamed), Gustavs flew their first anti-tank operations on 5 July 1943, which was also the first day of Operation Citadel – the epic tank Battle of Kursk.

Several other variations on the basic Ju 87 design were either trialled or considered by the Luftfahrtministerium's Technisches Amt, the most notable among them being the Ju 87 C ('Cäsar') and the Ju 87 F ('Friedrich'). Intended for service on the *Graf Zeppelin* aircraft carrier, the Cäsar was essentially a navalised Ju 87 B with folding wings and an arrester hook. Delays in the carrier's construction caused a policy rethink and the Cäsar was cancelled in May 1940 after only five aircraft had been built.

The Friedrich was planned as a successor to the Ju 87 D, with enhanced aerodynamics and a retractable undercarriage, as well as a rotating vertical tail surface to give the rear gunner an improved field of fire. In the end it was deemed to offer little improvement over the Dora and so the idea was abandoned in 1943.

As a design, the Ju 87 was a survivor. In a steady succession of improved marks and variants, Stukas were in continuous action from the first day of war, right up until the very last throes of the Third Reich in early May 1945. They were always at the sharp end where the fighting was at its fiercest, and it is a testament to the bravery and tenacity of its crews that they fought on, even after the tide of war had turned against them.

Early in the war the image of the Ju 87 as a Teutonic harbinger of destruction was seized upon by Joseph Goebbels and his Nazi propaganda ministry to turn the Stuka and its crews into stylised figureheads of the invincible German war machine. The front covers of *Der Adler* and *Signal* magazines regularly showed artists' impressions of Stukas winning the war for Germany, while Karl Ritter's contemporary propaganda film, *Stukas*, commissioned by

ABOVE Ju 87 Ds of StG 5 on the Leningrad Front in 1943. The 'Dora' version of the Ju 87 saw extensive action on the Eastern Front between 1942 and 1945. *(Andy Saunders collection)*

RIGHT Scourge of the Red Army: when the Ju 87 G 'Kanonenvogel' (Cannon bird) was introduced into combat at the Battle of Kursk in July 1943, its pair of BK 37 'Panzerknacker' (Panzer cracker) auto-cannon decimated Russian tank formations. *(Andy Saunders collection)*

the Luftwaffe, followed the fortunes of three Stuka squadrons and their crews, incorporating authentic documentary footage of Ju 87s in action to lend credibility to the production. To a 21st-century audience the film is painfully jingoistic and propagandist, extolling the honour of dying for the Fatherland, but nonetheless after it was premiered in Berlin on 27 June 1941

it became a runaway success with wartime German cinema audiences, grossing 3.18 million Reichsmarks (RM) in its first six months, against production costs of 1.96 million RM.

Adding to the cult of the Stuka as the elite cavalry of the air, a 'Stuka Lied' (or song) was specially composed with a rousing refrain, 'We are the black hussars of the air, the Stukas, the

RIGHT The Ju 87 regularly graced the front cover of the Luftwaffe's bi-weekly propaganda magazine *Der Adler*. *(Author's collection)*

FAR RIGHT Released on 25 June 1941, three days after the launch of Operation Barbarossa, the Luftwaffe propaganda film *Stukas* tells the story of a dive-bomber squadron during the Battle of France in May and June 1940. *(Author's collection)*

Stukas, the Stukas!', which forms the finale of the film.

Many Stuka pilots were recipients of the Knight's Cross, but one in particular became the most famous and highly decorated Luftwaffe flier of the entire war. His name was Hans-Ulrich Rudel. He began his operational career in Greece in 1941 with StG 2, the 'Immelmann' Geschwader, which soon transferred to the Russian Front. It was there that Rudel quickly built a reputation as a skilled and daring dive-bomber and ground-attack pilot. By the war's end he had completed an unsurpassed 2,530 combat missions (mostly on the Eastern Front, mainly with the Ju 87) and included one Russian battleship, one cruiser, a destroyer and 519 tanks among his kills, making him the most successful ground-attack pilot of all time.

Hitler took a close interest in Rudel and awarded him the Knight's Cross with Swords, Oak Leaves and Diamonds on 29 March 1944, as only the tenth German serviceman to receive the honour. On New Year's Day 1945 he was further invested with the highest award made to any German serviceman in the Second World War, specially created for Rudel by the Führer, who pinned to Rudel's breast the Knight's Cross with Swords, Oak Leaves and Diamonds,

LEFT Ace Stuka pilot Hans-Ulrich Rudel was the most successful ground-attack pilot of the Second World War on any side, with 519 tank kills and 2,530 sorties on the Eastern Front to his credit. *(Author's collection)*

in Gold, during a ceremony in the Reich Chancellery.

The Stuka may have died in the flames of the collapsing Third Reich in 1945, but its legacy lives on in the 21st century as the inspiration behind the design of the American Fairchild A-10 Thunderbolt II ground-attack jet – the legendary 'Hog'.

BELOW The Stuka's child: the Fairchild Republic A-10 Thunderbolt II ground-attack jet is the modern-day successor to the Ju 87. *(USAF)*

Chapter One

The Junkers Ju 87 story

With an inverted gull wing that became its defining feature, the scream of a Junkers Ju 87 Stuka dive bomber in a vertical power dive has become one of the most enduring sights and sounds of the Second World War. Its dominance of European battlefields in the first years of the war was short-lived when changing fortunes and the introduction of modern fighter aircraft meant the hunter eventually became the hunted.

OPPOSITE Junkers Ju 87 Ds of StG 3, operating from their base at Dorpat in Estonia, overfly the frozen landscape of East Prussia on 9 March 1944. Images like this one exemplify the experience of hundreds of Stuka crews on the Eastern Front in the Second World War. *(Bild 101I-726-0224-15A)*

The origin of dive-bombing with aircraft remains somewhat obscure, but the British Royal Flying Corps has a strong claim to being the 'inventors' of the tactic. Towards the end of the First World War in March 1918, an 84 Squadron SE5a flown by Second Lieutenant William Henry Brown made a successful dive-bombing attack against enemy ammunition barges on a French canal. No 84 Squadron had been keen to test the effectiveness of dive-bombing against ground targets that were too big for machine-gun strafing and too small for conventional bombing. Brown's sortie was made more difficult by the presence of patchy fog, but he found his target and from a dive down to 500ft he released the bombs in turn, scoring a direct hit with his fourth and last bomb.

In the same year, dive-bombing trials using the SE5a and Sopwith Camel were also carried out at the RAE Armament Experimental Station at Orford Ness in Suffolk. Later, the RAF officially concluded (after its formation on 1 April 1918) that dive-bombing was an unsafe practice for pilots and aircraft alike, and it held firmly to this viewpoint for the next 30 years.

However, during the 1920s and '30s air arms and tacticians overseas in France and Germany, the USA and Japan were more sympathetic to the concept. In 1934 Wolfram

von Richthofen was in charge of aircraft procurement at the Technisches Amt (Technical Office) of the Reichsluftfahrtministerium (RLM – German Air Ministry). Richthofen was a German aristocrat and First World War fighter pilot with Jagdgeschwader 1 (JG 1), a unit which latterly flew the famous Fokker Dr 1 triplane. (His cousin was Manfred von Richthofen, the legendary 'Red Baron', who was also the highest-scoring ace of the war with 80 victories.)

Under Wolfram von Richthofen's supervision, the Messerschmitt Bf 109 fighter and the Heinkel He 111 and Dornier Do 17 bombers went from the drawing board to factory production in less than three years, which was a remarkable achievement. However, he was firmly against dive-bombers for similar reasons to the RAF (although there is a touch of irony to this fact because he was eventually to command VIII. Fliegerkorps in 1939, which included seven Stukagruppen).

As early as 1933 the aircraft manufacturer Junkers, under the leadership of Dipl.-Ing. Hermann Pohlmann, had begun work on its own design for a dive-bomber, which was to become the Ju 87.

When Hermann Goering, the head of the new Luftwaffe, set about recruiting former First World War fliers, among those with whom

RIGHT Ernst Zindel became design director and deputy head of Junkers Flugzeugwerke AG in 1933. Under his leadership the company developed the Ju 52, Ju 87, Ju 88, Ju 90, Ju 290 and Ju 388, but he was best known as the creator of the Ju 52 transport. *(BA 146-1972-004-24)*

BELOW Ernst Udet sits in the cockpit of Curtiss F11C Goshawk, D-IRIK, one of two examples brought to Germany from the USA in October 1933 by Hermann Goering. Udet flew this particular aircraft in aerobatic displays during the 1936 summer Olympics in Germany. He was a champion of the Ju 87 and influential in the adoption of dive-bombing as a tactic by the Luftwaffe. *(Chris Goss collection)*

ABOVE Although he was initially favoured by Goering, Udet was not alone among the Luftwaffe hierarchy in failing to see eye to eye with the Reichsmarschall. By 1939 Udet had risen to the position of Director-General of Equipment for the Luftwaffe, but the stress of the job led to alcoholism and this, combined with him falling out of favour with the Nazi Party hierarchy, ended with his suicide on 17 November 1941 at the age of 45. Udet is seen here (on the left) with Crown Prince William of Prussia (centre, son of the Kaiser) at Berlin-Tempelhof airport on 1 April 1934.
(BA 102-01591A)

he made contact was an old crony from his own fighter days, the ace Ernst Udet. Like Wolfram von Richthofen, both Goering and Udet had been invited to join the Red Baron's 'Flying Circus', JG 1 (Goering later became its commander in July 1918). While touring the USA in 1931, Udet's interest had been piqued by its development of the dive-bomber, which he saw demonstrated at flying displays by Curtiss F11C Gosshawk biplanes. He was quick to realise this method had a significant part to play in the emerging Luftwaffe.

Towards the end of 1935 the Junkers company's first design iteration for a dive-bomber had been completed and evaluated – the monoplane Ju 87 V1, which first flew on 17 September ('V' standing for Versuchsmuster, or prototype). The only major problem identified was the oil cooler, which caused the engine to overheat easily owing to its small size, but this was quickly rectified.

With an inverted gullwing that would later become the defining design characteristic of the Ju 87, the aircraft also featured a fixed trousered undercarriage, a square twin fin and rudder

RIGHT The first prototype – Ju 87 V1 (D-UBYR) – which made its inaugural flight on 17 September 1935, was powered by a 525hp Rolls-Royce Kestrel V engine because the planned Jumo 10 (later to become the Jumo 210) was unavailable. The twin-finned V1 crashed on a test flight on 24 January 1936, killing the pilot and engineer.
(US National Archives)

assembly and was powered by a Rolls-Royce Kestrel V water-cooled 12-cylinder 685hp engine driving a wooden two-blade fixed-pitch propeller. Its bombload was carried externally underneath the wings and along the fuselage centreline, while the Ju 87's defensive armament was limited to a single, moveable rearward-firing MG 15 machine gun and a pair of forward-firing MG 15s mounted on top of the engine

Tragedy was around the corner, for while undergoing evaluation at Erprobungsstelle (Experimental Station) Rechlin, the Ju 87 V1 crashed on 24 January 1936 at Kleutsch near Dresden, killing the Junkers chief test pilot, Willi Neuenhofen, and his engineer, Heinrich Kreft. The cause was attributed to the collapse of the twin fins during a test-dive, which resulted in the aircraft entering an inverted spin.

This led to a revised prototype, the Ju 87 V2, on which the twin fins were replaced with a single vertical stabiliser tailplane as well as hydraulically operated dive brakes, fitted under each mainplane leading edge and rotatable to 90°. The V2 first flew on 25 February 1936 and was powered by a Jumo 210A engine, since

ABOVE Together with Hanna Reitsch, Melitta Schiller was among the top test pilots in Nazi Germany. She was closely involved with test-flying the Ju 87 prototypes and, including flights in the Ju 88, she made more than 2,000 dives. *(US National Archives)*

BELOW Ju 87 V2, D-UHUH, first flew on 25 February 1936 and represented a major revision to the Ju 87's design with a single vertical stabiliser in place of the twin fins of V1. *(Andy Saunders collection)*

the RLM had no interest in procuring a bomber that used a British Rolls-Royce engine (this was later exchanged for a Jumo 210 in early 1937).

ABOVE The third prototype Ju 87 V3 (D-UKYQ) was first flown on 27 March 1936. Fitted with a Jumo 210A engine the aircraft went to Rechlin for performance trials.
(Copyright unknown)

In June 1936 Goering passed over von Richthofen to head up the Technisches Amt, instead offering the job to his crony Udet, which meant the latter was now in a strong position to advance his dive-bomber agenda. In exchange for Udet accepting the position, Goering brought two Curtiss Hawks (the export version of the F11C) to Germany for evaluation by Erprobungsstelle-Rechlin. Although these trials were not entirely successful, they prompted Udet to carry out more of his own, which only confirmed his initial belief that the Luftwaffe needed to have such a bomber. It was not long before the consummate professional von Richthofen became disenchanted with the incompetent Udet.

For some time (and off the record) Udet had been encouraging German firms that had already taken it upon themselves to develop further their own dive-bomber designs, among which was Junkers. In July 1936 performance trials were held at Rechlin to consider which of the four new dive-bomber designs would be chosen for the Luftwaffe. Vying for selection were the Arado Ar 81, the Blohm und Voss Ha 137, the Heinkel He 118 and the Junkers Ju 87 V2 – and it was the Ju 87 that was finally picked. This was due in some part to its rugged design and suitability for mass production.

The ultimate Versuchsmuster was the Ju 87

V4, the production prototype for the Ju 87 A-0 (zero series), which first flew on 20 June 1936, powered by a Jumo 210A engine. Aerodynamic improvements were made to the wing leading edge and the engine cowling was made flatter, which improved the pilot's forward view. It was fitted with a new bomb-release fork underneath the forward fuselage for use in dive-bombing. The contraption held the 250kg bomb in a cradle that swung down and out shortly before the bomb was released in order to clear the propeller arc. In the left wing a fixed MG 17 machine gun was added. Another unique feature of the Ju 87 was the inclusion of the newly available Askania auto-pilot (see page 40), a safety device that automatically pulled the aircraft out of its dive once the bomb had been released. This was to safeguard the pilot in the event of him blacking out during the high-g pull-out from the dive. It was first fitted to the ten pre-production models of the aircraft, designated Ju 87 A-0. Flight-testing at Rechlin led von Richthofen to conclude that the overall performance of the Ju 87 was still unsatisfactory and that a more powerful engine was needed.

When the Spanish Civil War broke out in 1936 the conflict was used by the Luftwaffe as a proving ground for its new aircraft designs, including a handful of Ju 87 V4s detached from IV.(St)/LG 1's 11th Staffel at Graz in Austria. Germany's Legion Kondor was sent to aid the Nationalist General Franco in his bid to subdue

the Republican elements in Spain. In November Wolfram von Richthofen left the Technisches Amt to become the Chief of Staff to the Legion Kondor, in which role he was to develop and establish the close air-support tactics that later became an essential trademark of the German Blitzkrieg in Poland and France. It was also in Spain that his attitude towards dive-bombing and the Ju 87 changed, cementing his belief in the aircraft.

By the end of the year three Ju 87s had arrived in Spain in conditions of great secrecy. These were Ju 87 V4s with a simplified wing design to facilitate mass production when the time came. By testing the aircraft and their crews under actual combat conditions, the Luftwaffe was able to hone its tactics and Junkers was able to improve the Ju 87's design based on its performance in Spain.

Initially, however, the Ju 87 was not a good performer. The pre-production Ju 87 A-0, with its 602hp Junkers Jumo 210A (non-fuel injected) engine was considerably under-powered, which restricted the aircraft to a top speed of 199mph at 12,000ft, unladen, and a maximum range of 620 miles. Its normal bombload was a single 250kg bomb, but a 500kg weapon could only be lifted by not carrying the second (radio operator/gunner) crew member.

Learning from the experience, Pohlmann and his team at Junkers redeveloped the design to create the Ju 87 B-0, which featured the slightly improved 661hp Jumo 210D engine with two-speed supercharger and three-blade variable pitch propeller that gave a top speed of 234mph at 15,000ft, and increased the payload to one 500kg bomb, or one 250kg and four 50kg bombs with both crew, and a range of 370 miles fully loaded. The trousered main undercarriage casing with its bracing struts was replaced with the more streamlined and unbraced spats that became the feature of all future Ju 87s. Defensive armament was improved with the replacement of the forward-firing fixed guns in the wings with MG 17 machine guns.

By the time war in Europe broke out in September 1939, the 986hp Jumo 211A-powered Ju 87 B-1 equipped most operational dive-bomber units of the Luftwaffe.

'Anton' – the Ju 87 A

Powered by the Jumo 210A, the **Ju 87 A-1** was the first true production version of the Ju 87, differing from the Ju 87 A-0 in several small ways: its length was 35ft 5.25in (10.80m), height 12ft 9.5in (3.90m), empty weight 5,104lb (2,315kg), max take-off weight 7,495lb (3,400kg), max level speed 199mph (320km/h) at 12,140ft (3,400m), a maximum cruising speed of 171mph (275km/h) at optimum altitude, a maximum range of 621 miles (1,000km), and a service ceiling of 22,965ft (7,000m).

ABOVE Ju 87 A-1 (52+C24) of 4./StG 165 'Immelmann', flying from Nuremberg in the Sudetenland crisis, summer 1938. Note the pre-war tri-colour splinter camouflage scheme. *(Author's collection)*

JUNKERS JU 87 A – TECHNICAL SPECIFICATION

Crew	2
Wingspan	13.8m (45ft 3.30in)
Length	11.00m (35ft 4.3in)
Height	4.16m (13ft 6.5in)
Engine	1 × Junkers Jumo 210D rated at 681hp at 2,700rpm for take-off; 690hp at 2,700rpm at 1,500m (4,920ft) first supercharger speed; 671hp at 2,700rpm at 3,700m (12,140ft) second supercharger speed
Empty weight	2,570kg (5,665lb)
Maximum take-off weight	3,400kg (7,495lb)
Maximum speed	320km/h (199mph)
Cruising speed	290km/h (180mph)
Service ceiling	7,000m (22,966ft)
Time to climb to 6,000m (19,685ft)	31min
Maximum range	600km (373 miles) at 4,000m
Armament	
Guns	1× 7.92mm MG 17 fixed machine gun in the wing, forward; 1 × 7.92mm MG 15 flexible machine gun to rear
Bombs	normal load, 1 × 250kg (550lb) bomb externally beneath fuselage, and 4 × 50kg bombs, two under each wing

Towards the end of 1937 the **Ju 87 A-2** replaced the A-1 on the Dessau production line, incorporating two significant changes over its predecessor. It was powered by a 680hp Jumo 210D with a two-stage supercharger driving a three-blade metal propeller with wider chord blades. By the summer of 1938 a total of some 200 Ju 87 A aircraft had been delivered, at which time the Ju 87 B started to come on stream in the factories. Once the war had begun all Ju 87 As were withdrawn from front-line service and relegated to use as advanced trainers.

'Berta' – the Ju 87 B

The main difference between the Anton and the **Ju 87 B-0** series (the 'Berta') was that the latter was almost completely redesigned as well as being fitted with the improved and more powerful Jumo 211A rated at 990hp.

A new engine cowling design was incorporated featuring an asymmetric air intake on the top for the oil cooler, a large 'chin' coolant radiator underneath the nose and an enlarged air intake for the engine supercharger on the right-hand side of the cowling. The rear fuselage structure was also strengthened and the tailfin redesigned and enlarged. Pilot and gunner benefited from a redesigned cockpit canopy, with a sliding hood over each crewman's position instead of the hinged canopies of the Anton.

Underneath the wings the heavy, braced and trousered main undercarriage legs were replaced by more streamlined spats covering part of the wheels and the shock absorber. The undercarriage was also host to that defining piece of dive-bombing terror equipment, the wind-driven noise-making propeller – or the 'Jericho trumpet', one on each undercarriage leg.

The Berta had two fixed forward-firing MG 17 machines, one in each wing, and a Revi 12/C reflector gunsight was installed above the instrument panel. In the rear cockpit the gunner's MG 15 machine gun was given greater freedom of movement when it was combined with an Ikaria-Linsen Lafette ball-mount instead of the simple slot in the canopy of the Ju 87 A.

Identical to the B-0, the **Ju 87 B-1** series was fitted with the Jumo 211D engine offering 1,184hp at 2,400rpm, which made it possible to increase the bombload to 1,000kg. The sub-variant Ju 87 B-1/U2 (the 'U' meaning Umrüst-Bausatz, or factory conversion kit) was

JUNKERS JU 87 B – TECHNICAL SPECIFICATION

Crew	2
Wingspan	13.8m (45ft 3.30in)
Length	11.00m (36ft 1.07in)
Height	4.23m (13ft 10.53in)
Engine	1 × Junkers Jumo 211A rated at 1,000hp (Ju 87 A-0); Jumo 211D rated at 1,184hp (B-1 and B-2)
Empty weight	3,205kg (7,086lb)
Maximum take-off weight	4,390kg (9,678lb)
Maximum speed	390km/h (242mph)
Cruising speed	340km/h (211mph)
Service ceiling	8,200m (26,903ft) with 500kg (1,100lb) bombload
Time to climb to 3,000m (9,843ft)	12min
Maximum range, normal	800km (497 miles) at 4,000m with 500kg bombload
Armament	
Guns:	2 × 7.92mm MG 17 fixed machine guns in the wing, forward; 1 × 7.92mm MG 15 flexible machine gun to rear
Bombs:	normal load, 1 × 250kg (550lb) bomb externally beneath fuselage, and 4 × 50kg bombs, two under each wing

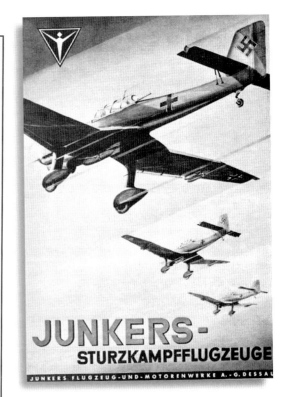

ABOVE Junkers advertised its Ju 87 as a modern warplane, although within months of the war beginning it became obsolete when pitted against faster and more modern designs. *(Author's collection)*

BELOW A Kette of Ju 87 B-1s on a training flight carrying cement practice bombs (Zement-bomben or 'Zebo') under the wings. *(Copyright unknown)*

also retrofitted with a FuG VIIa radio set in the rear cockpit.

By the end of 1939 some 557 Ju 87 B-1s had been delivered to front-line units of the Luftwaffe.

From late 1939 the **Ju 87 B-2** series began to appear on the Junkers production lines. It differed very little from the B-1 series except for the addition of individual exhaust ejector stubs (instead of open ports), electro-hydraulically operated radiator cooling gills and the addition of the Junkers VS-5 propeller with broad-chord blades.

There were four Ju 87 B-2 sub-variants: the B-2/U2 with improved radio equipment; B-2/U3 fitted with armour plating to protect the pilot and gunner; B-2/U4 fitted with a ski undercarriage instead of the usual spatted wheels; and the B-2 trop, intended for use in North Africa and fitted with engine air intake sand filters and a desert survival equipment pack. (The trop series of Ju 87 B-2 and later the R used a rectangular air intake with sand filter instead of the standard semi-circular intake.)

In spite of all these improvements, the Berta was still only suitable for restricted areas of operations, owing to its limited range and poor defensive firepower.

'Cäsar' – the Ju 87 C

Germany was very much the odd man out in the Second World War when it came to aircraft carriers. During this period the US Navy commissioned 112 aircraft carriers, Britain 72 and Japan 21, but Germany produced only one Flugzeugträger and it was never actually completed. Named *Graf Zeppelin* after the airship pioneer, her keel was laid down in December 1936 and she was launched two years later. Weighing in at 28,000 tons and with a length of 361ft from stem to stern, the carrier's air group was planned to include 20 obsolete Fieseler Fi 167 torpedo biplanes, 13 Ju 87 Stukas and 10 Messerschmitt Bf 109 fighters. Trägergruppe 186 (TrGr 186) was formed in August 1938 as *Graf Zeppelin*'s dedicated air unit. Initially the Stuka element was 4.(Stuka)/186 with Ju 87 Bs, but on 10 September 1939 Stab I.(Stuka)/186 was formed with 1 to 3 Staffeln, and 4./186 was renamed 3./186. TrGr 186 was disbanded on 5 July 1940 and I./186 became III./StG 1.

In the opening months of the war the Bf 109 was Germany's only possible choice for a carrier-based fighter, which was navalised as the Bf 109 T with folding wings. The Ju 87 B was chosen to fly reconnaissance and attack missions from the *Graf Zeppelin*, suitably modified as the navalised Ju 87 C or Cäsar variant. It featured wings that folded rearwards and parallel to the fuselage, an arrester hook beneath the tailplane and the fixed reinforced undercarriage was made jettisonable in the event of a ditching. Flotation bags were fitted inside the wings and fuselage and a fuel-dumping system was incorporated.

In early 1939 two initial production examples of the Ju 87 B-1 were converted as prototypes for the Cäsar series – D-IHFH (Ju 87 V10) and D-ILGM (Ju 87 V11). Simultaneously, ten pre-production **Ju 87 Cs** were built at Tempelhof incorporating the navalised features as well as a wingspan reduction from 13.8m (45ft 6in) to 13.2m (43ft 6in). These aircraft were issued to TrGr 186 alongside the standard B-1s for evaluation. Flight-testing of the Ju 87 C began in early 1939 and the Kriegsmarine ordered 170, but delays in the carrier's construction and the experience of war eventually caused a rethink. Production of the Cäsar ended in

BELOW Cäsar – the Ju 87 C-variant that was designed with folding wings for operation from the *Graf Zeppelin* aircraft carrier, which eventually never entered service. *(Copyright unknown)*

ABOVE Ju 87 V10
(TK+HD, formerly
D-IHFH), prototype
of the carrier-borne
C-variant, was
equipped with an
arrester hook and
catapult fittings but its
wings were fixed and
not capable of folding.
*(James Payne/Through
Their Eyes)*

May 1940 after only five had been built. These were eventually returned to B-2 standard and retained for other testing purposes.

TrGr 186 never launched its aircraft for combat, but many of its aircrews were to see action later, including in the invasion of Poland on 1 September 1939. Hanptmann Helmut Mahlke was awarded the Knight's Cross for sinking 3 warships and 29 cargo vessels. The unit badge of an anchor and winged helmet can be seen emblazoned on the fuselage forward of the cockpit in photographs of Stukas during the Battle of Britain period.

When the war began to turn against Germany's surface ships in 1943, Hitler cancelled all major warship construction. *Graf Zeppelin* was moved from one berth to another to avoid Allied bombing, but in April 1945 she was scuttled at Stettin by the Kriegsmarine to prevent her falling into Russian hands. Refloated after the war and used by the Soviets as a target in weapons tests, she was finally sunk for good.

'Richard' – the long-range Ju 87 R

Apart from when the Ju 87 was used for close-air support on the front-line, the limited range of the Ju 87 B-1 and B-2 had become apparent during the campaigns in Poland and western Europe in 1939 and 1940. Dive-bombing of enemy shipping at sea (rather

than in coastal waters) was also out of the question owing to range limitations of the B version with its total range of about 500 miles.

To extend the range of the Ju 87, the Jumo 211A-engined Ju 87 R-1 (the 'R' standing for Reichweitenausführung or 'long-range version') the fuel system was upgraded to include two 300-litre under-wing drop tanks, which effectively increased the total range to 780 miles at 13,120ft. As well as the external tanks, the tankage inside the inner wings was enlarged to two 240-litre tanks, giving the resulting Ju 87 R-series a total fuel capacity of 1,080 litres (238 gallons) and the enhanced range necessary for anti-shipping operations. An additional oil tank was also fitted in the forward upper fuselage to cater for the extended range.

The first unit to operate the Ju 87 R was I./StG 1 in the invasion of Norway in April 1940. Richards also flew in the French Campaign and during the Battle of Britain. Four versions of the Ju 87 R series were accepted for service: the Ju 87 R-1 (Jumo 211A), Ju 87 R-2 (Jumo 211D), Ju 87 R-2 trop (Jumo 211D), Ju 87 R-3 (Jumo 211D) and Ju 87 R-4 (Jumo 211J).

The Ju 87 R-1 was based on the airframe of the B-1 and in common with its progenitor it could be operated with either a wheeled or a ski undercarriage, but its use in southern Europe as well as over the sea precluded the use of the ski undercarriage option. The R-2 was modelled on the B-2 with an airframe that was

stressed for dive speeds of up to 370mph, but its increased weight meant its performance was not as good as the R-1. At sea level it could fly at between 177 and 190mph, while at 16,400ft it could reach 198–217mph. A maximum range of up to 1,200 miles was possible, depending on the bomb and fuel loads.

A tropicalised version, the R-2 trop, could be modified locally from the standard R-2 with a kit that included a tropical air intake filter for the carburettor and emergency survival equipment for the crew. A total of 471 Ju 87 R-2s was delivered to front-line units by the end of June 1941. Only a few examples of the R-3 variant were built as an experimental glider tug. The R-4 differed from the R-2 in being fitted with the Jumo 211J engine.

By the time that the last Ju 87 R rolled off the Weserflug production line in October 1941, a total of 972 of the R-series had been built, comprising 105 R-1, 472 R-2 and 144 R-4 aircraft.

'Dora' – the Ju 87 D

After a year of war the Luftwaffe High Command realised that despite its great achievements in the Blitzkrieg campaigns, the Ju 87 B no longer met the wider demands in many areas of its use. When it came up against enemy fighters its defensive armament proved woefully inadequate, just as its armour plating was found wanting against ground-based anti-aircraft fire; and the lacklustre performance of the Jumo 211D engine with only 1,200hp was also disappointing. The Stuka needed a complete upgrade and this found expression in the new Ju 87 D-1.

Although a significant improvement over the Berta, the Dora was still viewed as an interim version of the Ju 87 until the new ground-attack Henschel Hs 129 and Junkers Ju 88 P entered service. When the replacement aircraft failed to live up to expectations, the Dora became established in service, with the first aircraft arriving on the units in late 1941.

Differing externally from the Ju 87 A, B and R versions, the Dora was fitted with the more powerful Jumo 211J or P engine (1,479hp at 2,700rpm) with supercharger intercoolers.

A new propeller for the Jumo 211J offered increased engine power and could deliver 1,400hp at 2,600rpm. Bomb-carrying capability was raised dramatically from 500kg (1,100lb) in the Ju 87 B to a maximum of 1,800kg (4,000lb) over short range in the D-version (a more usual load would have been 500kg to 1,200kg – or 1,100lb to 2,600lb).

Internal fuel capacity was raised with the addition of two more fuel tanks inside the wings, with provision made for the carriage of two under-wing drop-tanks (like the Ju 87 R). Test-flights at Erprobungsstelle-Rechlin–Lärz concluded that with four tanks the endurance time was 2 hours 15 minutes, but with the pair of drop-tanks this was almost doubled to 4 hours.

The oil cooler was relocated from on top of the engine to the position formerly occupied by the big 'chin' coolant radiator, which in turn was replaced by two new coolant radiators underneath the inboard wing sections.

Aerodynamic improvements were made to the cockpit coupé, but the streamlining resulted in more cramped conditions for the crew and a reduction in the excellent all-round visibility of the Berta, and for this reason it was not popular. However, the addition of 50mm armoured glass

BELOW Ju 87 D-5s near completion on Weser Flugzeugbau's Lemwerder production line in 1942. *(BA 101I-642-4711-08)*

for the windscreen and improved defensive armour plate for the crew were welcome developments, together with the introduction of twin MG 81Z ('Zwilling') rear-firing machine guns in the gunner's position, with 1,000rpg.

The landing gear was strengthened, which made the alternative of a ski undercarriage possible, although in practice the new wheeled gear proved less robust than that fitted to the Berta. For emergency landings on water, the landing gear was jettisonable using an explosive cartridge. Dive brakes were omitted from some D models, and wing armament was upgraded with the powerful MG 151/20 cannon, replacing the existing MG 17 machine guns.

In January 1942 the first Ju 87 D-1s were tried in combat with I./StG 2 in Russia, but the extreme winter conditions quickly took their toll on the new Stuka. Initial deliveries of the D-1 were fitted with a Heine variable-pitch propeller with wooden blades, but these developed cracks in the freezing weather and they were replaced with a more stable Junkers VS 11 variable-pitch metal propeller. Problems were also encountered with the new undercarriage of the D series, so the undercarriage used on the Bertas was used on the first production aircraft,

but due to the reduced wheel size this led to a harsh reduction in the maximum take-off weight to 5,009kg. Changes were made to the new undercarriage design and it was fitted to later aircraft in the series. By the end of 1942 a total of 559 Ju 87 D-1s had been built.

Ju 87 D variants

D-1 – as with the B-2 trop, the D-1 trop was intended for use in North Africa and was fitted with engine air intake sand filters and a desert survival equipment pack.

D-2 – used as a glider-tug by converting older D-series airframes, it featured a strengthened rear fuselage and tailwheel unit incorporating a glider tow-hook. It was also fitted with flame-damped exhausts for dusk and night-time operations.

D-3 – the first D-variant to be fully equipped for close air-support, armed with twin MG 151/20 cannon under the wings and retaining its bomb-carrying capability. It had much-improved armour plating around the engine and the cockpit, the wind-driven propeller for the Jericho trumpets was omitted and the stubs were either removed or faired over. A total of 1,559 D-3s were built.

ABOVE Ju 87 D-3s from the 5th Staffel of StG 2 over the Crimea during the spring of 1943. The D-3, along with the D-1 and D-5, was a standard version of the 'Dora' from which a host of different variants were developed. *(BA 101I-453-1047-12)*

JUNKERS JU 87 D/G – TECHNICAL SPECIFICATION

Crew	2
Wingspan (G-2)	15.00m (49ft 2in)
Length	11.50m (37ft 9in)
Height	4.24m (14ft 6in)
Engine	1 × Junkers Jumo 211J rated at 1,420bhp for take-off
Empty weight	D – 3,550kg (7,826lb); G – 3,600kg (7,937lb)
Take-off weight	5,840kg (12,877lb)
Maximum weight	6,610kg (14,575lb)
Maximum speed	409km/h (254mph)
Cruising speed	319km/h (198mph)
Service ceiling	7,290m (23,900ft)
Time to climb to 5,000m (16,400ft)	19.8min
Maximum range, normal	820km (510 miles)
Maximum range with auxiliary tanks (D-version)	1,535km (953 miles)
Armament, normal	1 × SC1000 bomb under the fuselage, or 1 × SC500 or SC250 and 4 × SC50 or SC70. (On the D-3, 2 × MG 17s in the wing, removed on the D-5 for 2 × 20 mm MG 151/20 cannon.)
Armament, Ju 87 G	2 × BK 3.7cm, each with either 6 or 12 rounds.

BELOW The Stuka that never was – the Ju 87 F.

(World of Warplanes)

D-4 – a handful of D-1 and D-3 aircraft were converted for use as torpedo bombers, but eventually this option was not pursued.

D-5 – outer wing extensions were fitted to increase manoeuvrability resulting in a wingspan of 49ft 2½in (15m) and an aspect ratio of 6.67. The main undercarriage was also jettisonable, like that of the Ju 87 C. Dive brakes were removed from later aircraft of this variant.

D-6 – built in limited numbers to train pilots, but owing to shortages in materials it did not enter mass production.

D-7 – based on the D-1 airframe, upgraded to D-5 standard, the D-7 was optimised for night operations with flame-damped exhausts, night-flying cockpit instrumentation, two 20mm MG 151/20 cannon; powered by the 1,500hp Jumo 211P.

D-8 – essentially a conversion of the D-5 to daylight attack configuration, with long-span wings and MG 151/20 cannon.

Ju 87 F – the Stuka that never was

When Junkers submitted its design proposal for a Ju 87 F to the Technisches Amt in the spring of 1941 it was rejected because it offered few performance improvements over the existing Ju 87 D. The company worked on a more extensive redesign in which attention was given to aerodynamics and in particular the wing shape. It retained the Stuka's characteristic inverted-gull configuration but adopted a more simplified planform with a continuous taper applied to the leading and trailing edges. The span of the centre section was also increased. A fully retractable main undercarriage was introduced with the gear legs swivelling through 90° and retracting backwards into bays in the underside of the wing.

Serious thought was also given to a rotating vertical tail surface which, when rotated downwards, would have given the gunner in the rear cockpit a much improved field of fire. (It is not known how the aircraft would have handled in this configuration.)

At this point the RLM allocated the designation Ju 187 to the project since the Ju 87 F bore little more than a passing resemblance to the basic Ju 87 design. In its final iteration submitted to the RLM early in 1943, the use of a Jumo 213A engine was proposed for the Ju 187, rated at 1,776hp for take-off and 1,480hp for climb and combat at 18,375ft (5,600m).

It also featured a remotely controlled dorsal barbette mounting one 13mm MG 131 machine gun and one 20mm MG 151/20 cannon, with a fixed forward-firing armament that comprised two 20mm MG 151/20 cannon. The maximum bombload consisted of a 1,000kg bomb beneath the fuselage and four 50kg bombs on hard-points underneath the wing.

The maximum speed with a full external load was anticipated to be little more than 248.5mph (400km/h). With its performance assessed as being no better than that of the latest Ju 87 D variant, the Ju 187 project was abandoned in the autumn of 1943.

'Gustav' – the Ju 87 G

The last combat variant of the Ju 87 and successor of the Ju 87 D was the G-series – the feared Soviet tank hunters on the Eastern Front. Converted on the front line from older D-3 series airframes by groundcrews, the Ju 87 G-1 retained the smaller wing but the dive brakes were removed, making it the most unrepresentative among Stuka variants. The G-2 was derived from the Ju 87 D-5.

By adapting the 3.7cm Flak 18/36/37/43-series of ground-based anti-aircraft cannon for aircraft use, then mounting a pair of the weapons in under-wing gun pods outboard of the undercarriage legs (as the Bordkanone BK 37), the Stuka was transformed into the highly effective Ju 87 G 'Panzerknacker' or 'Kanonenvogel' ('tank cracker' or 'cannon bird'), which was flown with notable success by Hans-Ulrich Rudel of StG 2 'Immelmann'.

Plans had been drawn up as early as January 1942 for a cannon-armed Ju 87 tank-buster for use primarily on the Eastern Front, where it was hoped it could stem the growing tide of Soviet armour. The performance and survivability of the twin-engine Henschel Hs 129 and Junkers Ju 88 P-1 ground-attack aircraft was not living up to expectations and so preference was given to developing the tried and tested Stuka design.

JU 87F/JU 187 BASIC SPECIFICATION

Crew	2
Wingspan	18.06m (59ft 3.25in)
Length	11.80m (38ft 8.75in)
Height	3.90m (12ft 9.75in)
Engine	1 × Junkers Jumo 213A rated at 1,776hp for take-off
Fixed armament	2 × 20mm MG 151/20 fixed forward-firing cannon in wingroots, 1 × 13mm MG 131 machine gun and 1 × 15mm MG 151/15 cannon in the dorsal turret
Bombload	1 × 1,000kg bomb semi-recessed into a lower-fuselage weapons bay, or 1 × 250kg bomb carried ventrally and 4 × 50kg bombs on external wing racks

During early 1943 a Ju 87 D-1 with Flak 18 pods was tested at Rechlin and at the Briansk training area. Despite its lower speed owing to the increased drag from the gun installations (reduced by 30–40km/h) and its limited ammunition capacity (up to 12 shells per gun pod in two magazines), the first of the new Ju 87 G-1s fitted with the BK 3.7cm Flak 18 was delivered to StG 2 'Immelmann', which flew its initial anti-tank operation in the Bielgorod–Charkov area on 5 July 1943, the first day of Operation Citadel – the epic Battle of Kursk.

Hans-Ulrich Rudel led nine G-1s in support of the 3. SS-Panzer-Division 'Totenkopf' on this occasion, personally

BELOW With its twin BK 3.7cm auto-cannon, the Ju 87 G 'Kanonenvogel' (cannon bird) was a deadly adversary for Russian armour on the Eastern Front. This is a Gustav of the Panzerjägerstaffel of StG 1. *(BA 101I-353-1645-04)*

knocking out 12 Soviet tanks. He recalls the occasion in his autobiography:

The sight of these masses of tanks reminds me of my cannon-carrying aircraft of the experimental unit, which I have brought with me from the Crimea. With this enormous target of enemy tanks it should be possible to try it out. It is true the flak defences covering the Soviet tank units are very heavy, but I say to myself that both groups are facing each other at a distance of 1,200 to 1,800 yards, and unless I am brought down like a stone by a direct hit by flak it must always be possible to crash-land the damaged aircraft in our own tank lines. The first flight therefore flies with bombs behind me in the only cannon-carrying aeroplane. So the attempt is made.

In the first attack four tanks explode under the hammer blows of my cannons; by the evening the total rises to twelve. We are all seized with a kind of passion for the chase from the glorious feeling of having saved much German bloodshed with every tank destroyed.

ABOVE Romania was among several foreign air forces that operated the Ju 87. *(Copyright unknown)*

LEFT The Japanese were so impressed by the Ju 87's performance that they purchased two Ju 87 A-1s for evaluation. Coded 71+E11 and 71+E12, they wore standard German 'splinter' camouflage, but the Japanese national markings replaced the Luftwaffe's black Balkan cross. The Mitsubishi Aircraft Company assembled them in January 1938 with the first aircraft assigned to the Army Aviation Maintenance School at Tachikawa for detailed examination, while the second was sent to the Army Aviation Flying School at Hamamatsu for evaluation. *(Copyright unknown)*

The G-1 quickly established itself as a formidable tank hunter and destroyer, although its manoeuvrability had been noticeably impaired by the addition of the BK 37 gun pods which, when added to the Gustav's poor defensive armament, made it an almost perfect target for enemy fighters. Success on the battlefield for the Gustav, therefore, was often only possible if it was flown by an experienced pilot, and with minimal enemy anti-aircraft and fighter opposition.

Ju 87 H – dual-control trainer

A further variant that was created by converting aircraft of the Ju 87 D series was the Ju 87 H dual-control trainer. During the early days of Stuka operations a dedicated Ju 87 trainer aircraft had not been considered necessary, but with the greatly changed combat environment from 1943 onwards – particularly on the Eastern Front – the skills required for flying and surviving in the type were becoming more specialised and important that even experienced bomber and fighter pilots had to fly with a Ju 87 instructor before taking their places in the ranks of the depleted Stukagruppen.

Ju 87 K – the foreign Stukas

Although the Ju 87 K was not an actual mark of Stuka, the 'K' suffix was given to aircraft that were supplied to Germany's allies in the Second World War. Both Japan and the Soviet Union were given production prototypes for evaluation, while Ju 87s – ranging from the Ju 87 A, B, R, D and G – were operated by the air forces of Austria, Bulgaria, Croatia, Hungary, Italy, Slovakia and Romania for much of the war, primarily on the Eastern Front and in the Balkans. The emphasis of this book is on Luftwaffe use of the Ju 87 and so its operation by minor Axis allies has not been covered.

Endgame

Ju 87 production finally ceased during November/December 1944, when a grand total of more than 5,700 aircraft had been built at factories in Dessau, Tempelhof and Weserflug.

COMBAT COMPARISONS – THE STUKA AND OTHER DIVE-BOMBERS

The main difference between the Luftwaffe's Ju 87 and the dive-bombers of Britain, the USA and Japan, was that the Stuka was originally intended to attack land targets, whereas the others were all naval combat aircraft. Here is a comparison of the Junkers Ju 87 B-1 with its dive-bomber contemporaries from some of the other fighting powers in the Second World War.

Great Britain – Blackburn Skua

The British Blackburn Skua was a rather ugly-looking monoplane two-seat fighter and dive-bomber. Its low speed and lack of manoeuvrability saw it outgunned and outperformed when it came up against high-performance fighters like the Messerschmitt Bf 109.

When operating from the aircraft carriers HMS *Ark Royal* and *Furious* in the dive-bombing role, the Skua carried a single 500lb SAP bomb on a retractable ejector arm in a recess on the fuselage underside. The Skua's usual dive angle was 70° and its dive brakes, which were modified Zap-type trailing-edge flaps housed in recesses under the wing, proved very effective at holding a dive speed of 300mph.

The Skua's greatest success was when seven aircraft of 800 NAS flying off *Ark Royal* sank the German cruiser *Königsberg*

BELOW Blackburn Skuas of 803 Naval Air Squadron. *(Fleet Air Arm Museum)*

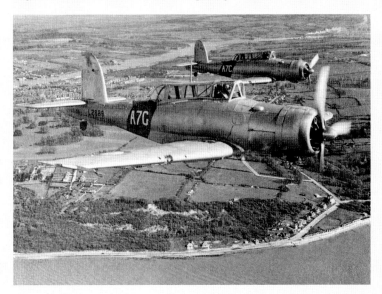

in Bergen harbour on 10 April 1940. Its effective but short-lived contribution to the war came to an end in March 1941 when it was replaced by the Fairey Fulmar and later that year the Hawker Sea Hurricane. As a result the Fleet Air Arm ceased to have a dedicated dive-bomber.

USA – Douglas SBD Dauntless

Introduced in 1940 to the US Marine Corps and the US Navy as a dive-bomber/scout, the two-seat single-engine Douglas SBD Dauntless went on to become the US Navy's standard carrier-borne dive-bomber of the Second World War. It was blessed with long range, good handling and dive characteristics, a worthwhile bombload and relatively good defensive armament. One 1,000lb or 1,600lb bomb was carried under the fuselage centreline, with a crutch to swing it clear of the propeller arc on release; and two 100-pounders under the wings.

The Dauntless played a crucial role in the war in the Pacific against the Japanese, with its finest hour during the Battle of Midway in June 1942 where Navy SBDs sank or fatally damaged all four Japanese fleet carriers present.

The Dauntless was stressed to 4g and could dive unbraked to reach a speed of 425mph, but in practice the brakes held the dive-speed to about 276mph. The dive brakes were large, perforated, split trailing-edge flaps, which were so designed to reduce tail buffeting during the manoeuvre. Attack dives were commenced from 15,000ft, with the peel-off starting from the aircraft at the top of the stack and following the formation commander down in turn, with a small gap in between each aircraft to divide the defences. The normal angle of dive was 70°. Unlike the Ju 87, there was no automatic pull-out device used by the US Navy and pilots

BELOW A US Navy Douglas SBD-5 Dauntless of VB-16 flies low over the battleship USS *Washington* (BB-56) en route to the invasion of the Gilbert Islands, 12 November 1943. The ship in the background is USS *Lexington* (CV-16), the aircraft's home carrier. *(US Navy)*

judged the correct moment at the bottom of the dive to commence their pull-out.

Like the Stuka's experience with the Henschel Hs 129 and the Ju 88 P-1, it was planned to replace the Dauntless with a newer and more capable design in the guise of the Curtiss Helldiver. However, delays in the development programme meant that the Dauntless remained in service until the end of the war, but in any case it also happened to be a better aircraft all-round than its intended replacement.

Imperial Japan – Aichi D3A 'Val'

In a reflection of the circumstances surrounding intended replacements for the Ju 87 and the SDB Dauntless, the successor for the carrier-borne Aichi D3A 'Val' was bedevilled with technical problems. The Yokosuka D4Y 'Judy' was not ready for service until 1943, by which time the writing was already on the wall for Japan.

As the Imperial Japanese Navy's principal dive-bomber, the two-seat single-engine Vals took part in most IJN actions, including the attack on Pearl Harbor on 7 December 1941, and they went on to sink more Allied warships than any other Axis aircraft.

The Judy shared a fixed undercarriage design with the Ju 87 and similar dive brakes in the form of rotating strips attached under the wing leading edges; and an elliptical wing inspired by the Heinkel He 70. Its regular bombload was a single 250kg bomb carried under the fuselage and swung out on a crutch to clear the propeller arc; two additional 60kg bombs could be carried on racks under each wing.

ABOVE Pearl Harbor, 7 December 1941: an Aichi D3A1 is caught by a US Navy photographer as it pulls up after dropping its bombs on the US Navy's base in the Philippines. *(US Navy)*

Type	Junkers Ju 87 B-1	Blackburn Skua Mk II	Douglas SBD-5 Dauntless	Aichi D3A2
Engine	1,184hp Junkers Jumo 211D	890hp Bristol Perseus XII	1,200hp Wright R-1820-60 Cyclone	1,300hp Mitsubishi Kinsei 54
Crew	2	2	2	2
Wingspan	13.20m (43ft 3in)	14.07m (46ft 2in)	12.66m (41ft 6in)	14.35m (47ft 1½in)
Length	11.00m (36ft 1in)	10.84m (35ft 7in)	10.06m (33ft 0in)	10.24m (33ft 6¾in)
Height	3.77m (12ft 3½in)	4.32m (12ft 6in)	3.94m (12ft 11in)	3.33m (10ft 11¼in)
Wing area	31.9m² (343sq ft)	28.98m² (319sq ft)	30.19m² (325sq ft)	–
Empty weight	2,760kg (6,084lb)	2,493kg (5,496lb)	3,028kg (6,675lb)	2,618kg (5,771lb)
Max weight	4,400kg (9,700lb)	3,733kg (8,228lb)	4,322kg (9,528lb)	3,800kg (8,378lb)
Max speed	350km/h (217mph)	362km/h (225mph) at 2,040m	407km/h (253mph) at 5,060m	428km/h (266mph)
Dive speed	600km/h (372mph)	483km/h (300mph)	445km/h (277mph)	–
Ceiling	8,100m (26,575ft)	5,820m (19,100ft)	8,075m (26,492ft)	1,0880m (35,695ft)
Climb	3,000m (9,842ft) in 8.8min	5,820m (19,094ft) in 43min	3,050m (10,000ft) in 8min	–
Range	800km (497 miles)	700km (435 miles)	2,084km (1,294 miles)	1,560km (970 miles)
Fixed armament	2 × 7.9mm MG17	4 × 7.7mm	2 × 12.7mm	2 × 7.7mm
Rear armament	1 × 7.9mm MG15	1 × 7.7mm	2 × 7.62mm	1 × 7.7mm
Bombload	1,000kg (2,200lb)	227kg (500lb)	815kg (1,796lb)	370kg (815lb)

Chapter Two

Anatomy of the Stuka

The Ju 87 was indisputably an ugly aircraft, whose Vulture-like looks underlined its deadly purpose. It was a classic example of function over form where its manufacturer Junkers succeeded in combining canny design with utility and ease of operation. The basic structure and systems of the Stuka were sound ones that remained virtually unchanged for the entire war.

OPPOSITE The RAF Museum, Hendon's Junkers Ju 87 G, with its port wing removed to show the Kugelverschraubung (ball joint) attachment points on the inner wing section and radiator coolant pipework. *(Author)*

To the casual observer the Ju 87 appeared as a robust aircraft capable of withstanding the stresses of dive-bombing and able to operate from rudimentary forward airfields. When writing about the aircraft in 1940, a *Flight* magazine journalist remarked that 'the Ju 87 has obviously been designed to be as simple as possible – the fixed undercarriage with its single leg attached to the wing spar is typical. It has been intended to do its job and then be thrown on the scrapheap of war – and no doubt many a pilot has been thrown with it.' It was a grudging appreciation of a rugged – and at first sight simple – aircraft that was built for a specific role, which it filled admirably.

However, the Ju 87 was anything but crude in the way its designers applied German engineering ingenuity and used the technologies and materials of the day. Yet, when compared to other German weapons of the period where over-complication by design took precedence over simplicity of operation – the legendary Tiger I tank is a prime example of this – the Stuka succeeded in combining clever design with utility and ease of operation.

General overview of the airframe

The Ju 87 was a single-engine low-wing monoplane of all-metal stressed-skin semi-monocoque construction, with flush riveting on all external surfaces except for the underside of the wing. It carried a crew of two and had two non-retracting undercarriage legs.

Fuselage (Rumpf)

The fuselage was generally oval in cross-section and was built up around four longitudinal stiffeners and Z-section vertical frames set against and riveted to the Duralumin skin. The stringers were of the 'bowler-hat' type and were attached to the skin by two lines of rivets. They were continuous through the frames and cut-outs were provided for them. At each junction a curved angle bracket was riveted to both stringer and frame. In the lower part of the fuselage, which was under high compressive loads in the dive, the stringer spacing was as close as 3½in, to which was riveted unusually thick metal skin.

The fuselage and the load-bearing centre section with anhedral inner wing sections (containing the fuel tanks) were a single unit, to which the outer wings were attached by distinctive Junkers universal ball and socket screw connectors.

Forward of the cockpit area was the engine bay containing a water-cooled inverted V-12 Junkers Jumo 211 engine mounted on two main support frames, augmented by three tubular struts. The cockpit was separated and protected from the engine by an asbestos mesh/Dural firewall and Frame 1.

BELOW Wing spars and fuselage framing, Ju 87 B. *(Junkers)*

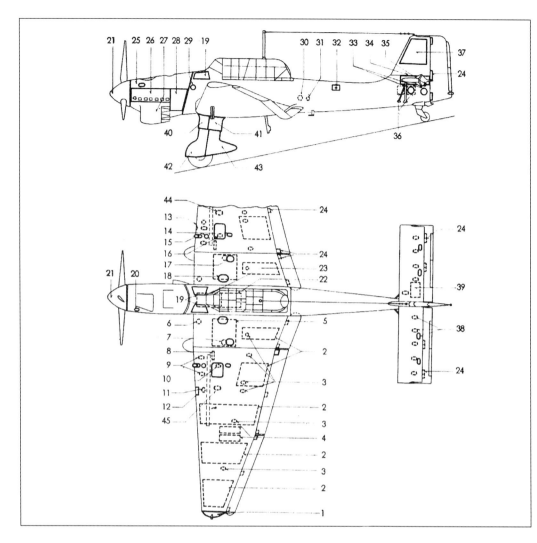

LEFT Cowlings and panels, Ju 87 B. *(Junkers)*

BELOW An unusual view of a partially dismantled Ju 87 B fuselage. This was the first Ju 87 (S2+LM) to fall intact into RAF hands on British soil. Belonging to 4./StG 77, the aircraft was shot down on 8 August 1940 by Pilot Officer Peter Parrott of 145 Squadron, causing it to force-land at St Lawrence, Isle of Wight. Its pilot, Unteroffizier Pittroff, was captured but his gunner Unteroffizier Schubert was killed. It is seen here at RAE Farnborough after evaluation. *(Andy Saunders collection)*

RIGHT Kugelverschraubung, inner wing section, male connector. The threads and spherical surfaces of the ball screw connections needed to be carefully cleaned before assembly and then regreased. *(Author)*

FAR RIGHT Ball joint, outer wing, female connector. When loosening the ball screw connections using a spigot wrench, it was necessary to begin with the lower ring nuts and then, with the wing slightly raised, loosen the upper ring nuts. Care needed to be taken during lifting the wing to maintain it level at all times because of the risk of buckling the skin. *(Author)*

JUNKERS UNIVERSAL BALL AND SOCKET SCREW CONNECTORS (KUGELVERSCHRAUBUNG)

By concentrating loads through a small number of large fittings compared to the alternative of dozens of small bolts and screws (as used, for example, on the RAF's Bristol Blenheim fighter-bomber), the Junkers universal ball and socket screw connector was a 'male and female' union that combined strength with ease of assembly and dismantling. The connectors were made out of steel with screw caps of chrome nickel steel. The 'male' ball joint was locked into the 'female' socket by a screwed coupling ring, which was turned by inserting a spigot wrench into the holes around its circumference.

For example, on the Ju 87 the wing attachment was achieved by uniting the 'female' socket and screw-ring attached to the outer wing with the 'male' ball joint and screw thread on the inner wing connection points. The two halves were locked together with the coupling ring.

There were different types and sizes of ball joint and screw connectors, each one addressing the stress requirements of a particular structure – for example, fuselage, wings and engine assembly. On the Ju 87 the load-bearing centre section and the wings, horizontal stabilisers and the engine attachments to the fuselage were joined by ball and socket screw connectors.

LEFT The wings have been removed from this Ju 87 D undergoing a major overhaul. Ball joints for the wing attachments and upper engine bearer are all visible in this picture. The complete structure weighed about 200kg and six men were required to safely remove the wing. *(BA 101I-642-4711-17A)*

Tailplane (Höhenleitwerk)

The tailplane comprised a pair of neutral dihedral rectangular planform horizontal tail surfaces with trimmable elevators, vertical stabiliser with balanced rudder equipped with automatic trim tabs and an auxiliary rudder. To aid maintenance of control cables, removable inspection panels were fitted in the upper and lower sides of the horizontal tail surfaces and in the left side of the fin.

Horizontal stabilisers (Höhenflosse)

The Ju 87 had an adjustable incidence horizontal tailplane that was attached to the fuselage with a rotatable front spar bearing and braced on opposite sides by reversed V-struts. A hydraulic push-rod actuated a pull-in strut at the extreme end of the fuselage that engaged on the underside of the tailplane. Adjustments to the tailplane incidence were made in the cockpit by the pilot moving a gear lever set in a switchbox on his left-hand side. Four notched positions could be selected using the gear lever – land, start, go and climb – each accompanied by an individual indicator light that illuminated beside the position selected.

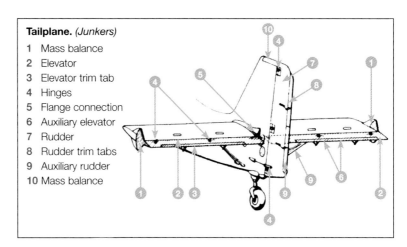

Tailplane. *(Junkers)*

1 Mass balance
2 Elevator
3 Elevator trim tab
4 Hinges
5 Flange connection
6 Auxiliary elevator
7 Rudder
8 Rudder trim tabs
9 Auxiliary rudder
10 Mass balance

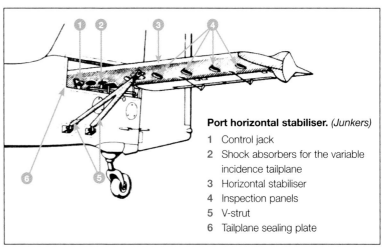

Port horizontal stabiliser. *(Junkers)*

1 Control jack
2 Shock absorbers for the variable incidence tailplane
3 Horizontal stabiliser
4 Inspection panels
5 V-strut
6 Tailplane sealing plate

VARIABLE INCIDENCE TAILPLANE

In comparison to the other flight controls on the Ju 87, the variable incidence horizontal stabiliser was very powerful in its effect. The large trim changes needed on entering and pulling out of a dive required substantial elevator deflections, but at these large deflections little more elevator movement remained in the same direction. Therefore, the variable incidence horizontal stabiliser was incorporated in the Ju 87 design to take out the trim changes. The stabiliser was larger than the elevator and consequently did not need to be moved through such a large angle, leaving the elevator streamlining the tailplane with a full movement up and down. The pilot trimmed the aircraft prior to entering the dive so that the horizontal stabiliser handled the bulk of the pitch control demand, with the elevator handling the rest. After pulling out, he trimmed the aircraft for level or climbing flight.

BELOW The single-piece variable incidence tailplane, minus the sealing plate and control jack. *(Author)*

The Ju 87 was fitted with a dive pull-out safety device, the Askania dive recovery mechanism (Stürzflug-Automatik), which worked in conjunction with the aircraft's dive brakes, horizontal tailplane and starboard elevator. It had been trialled by the Luftwaffe in the 1930s by test pilot Melitta Schiller on the ten pre-production Ju 87 A-0s. The device was fitted to most Ju 87s as a necessary safety precaution because the pilot was at risk of losing consciousness as a result of the high g forces experienced during the pull-out (flare-out) after bomb-release. The Askania dive recovery mechanism was designed to complete the pull-out automatically and initiate the climb back to altitude, during which time the pilot would have recovered if he had blacked out.

When the pilot lowered the dive brakes, a tab on the starboard elevator was hydraulically activated, cancelling out the resulting nose-up pitching moment and the aircraft automatically nosed into a dive.

At the same time the dive recovery mechanism and pilot safety control were enabled. The latter was a dedicated hydraulically actuated device that restricted control column movement to 5° forwards and backwards of neutral to relieve the pilot of the heavy stick forces that would otherwise have to be applied to keep the nose down, and mitigate the high g-loading on pull-out. Neither the rudder nor elevator trimmers were used during the dive manoeuvre.

As the height quickly unwound on the contact altimeter (pre-set by the pilot), a horn sounded in the cockpit when the aircraft reached a point 600m (2,000ft) above the pre-set bomb-release height. Some 4 seconds later, when the aircraft reached the bomb-release height (usually 700m – 2,300ft – above the ground) and the horn ceased, a signal light illuminated on the instrument panel and the pilot toggled a switch on the control column to release the bomb and disengage the Askania automatic pull-out device. This returned the starboard elevator trim tab to its normal position and the aircraft was eased out of the dive at a height of 450m (1,475ft) when the crew experienced a force of about 6g.

On the Ju 87 D-5 the functions of bomb-release and dive recovery were separated and individual push-buttons were fitted to the control column.

Should the pull-out device fail for whatever reason, the pilot was able to override the mechanism that limited the movement of the control column, but a stick force of about 65lb was needed to overcome the high g forces experienced.

Thus, even if the dive was vertical, the aircraft would not come into contact with the released bomb.

BELOW With dive brakes extended, this Ju 87 has just released its bombload and the Askania automatic pull-out device is about to flare the Stuka out of its dive. *(Author's collection)*

CONTACT ALTIMETER (KONTAKT-HÖHENMESSER)

The contact altimeter was located on the main instrument panel above the standard altimeter. It had two hands and two concentric knobs at the 6 o'clock position. The white hand indicated the aircraft altitude in kilometres and the outer knob adjusted for barometric pressure in millibars (shown as an inset at the 12 o'clock position). The second (red) hand was adjusted using the small centre adjusting knob marked with a 'K' to set a reference 'pull-out' height (in kilometres) for a dive-bombing attack on a target. At this height an electrical contact (hence the name contact altimeter) was made, which released the bomb and the Askania dive recovery mechanism proceeded to pull the aircraft out of the dive. The contact altimeter relieved the pilot of having to manually judge when to release the bomb and allowed him to focus on the target and flying the aircraft.

LEFT Contact altimeter.
(Author's collection)

Elevators (Höhenruder)

The divided elevator was in two halves, port and starboard, which were joined by a flange screw connection, and each elevator half was attached to the stabiliser on five ball hinges. Elevator travel (40° up, 30° down) was limited by control stops inside the fuselage and the cockpit (the control column range of movement was 16° forwards and 22° rearwards). Elevator trimming tabs on both elevators were manually adjustable by the pilot, but those on the right elevator could be automatically overridden by the Askania dive recovery mechanism and controlled by an electro-hydraulic unit fitted between the middle and rear frames of the horizontal stabiliser. This unit carried an actuator, a solenoid and a powerful spring-loaded angle lever and retraction strut linked to the trimming tab. Manual control of the trimming tabs on the right elevator were automatically disengaged when the aircraft entered the dive as follows.

Vertical stabiliser and rudder (Seitenflosse und Seitenruder)

The vertical stabiliser was trapezoidal in shape, consisting of a fin and rudder with automatic trim tab and auxiliary rudder. The tailfin was attached to the fuselage at its front end on Frame 13 with two stud bolts and its rear on Frame 16 with screw bolts.

The horn-balanced rudder was attached to the fin structure on three roller bearings/ball hinges, with 30° travel either side limited by stops on the fin and in the cockpit. A double trim flap extended the full height of the rudder;

BELOW The tailfin, horizontal stabilisers and variable incidence tailplane on a Ju 87 D-5. Note also the MG 81 Z 'Zwilling' rear gun. *(SA-Kuva)*

ABOVE This crash-landed Ju 87 B (A5+KL) of 3./StG 1 shows to good advantage the removable panel on the tailfin for access to control cable runs, and the variable incidence tailplane (again, minus the sealing plate) that shows it to be a single structure running through the tailfin construction from one side to the other. *(Chris Goss collection)*

the upper trimmer was adjustable by the pilot from the cockpit while a lower-placed trimmer could be used as an auxiliary rudder.

Wings (Flügel)

The three-section inverted gullwing mainplane was of all-metal construction and built around two main spars (Träger), covered with stressed sheet Duralumin skins. The wing was characterised by a flattened 'W' shape, achieved by attaching two dihedralled outboard sections with rounded wingtips to the anhedralled centre section. As already stated, each outboard wing section was attached to the centre section with four Junkers universal ball and socket screw connectors. The wing's centre section was permanently attached to the fuselage structure. Incorporated in each wing were ailerons, wing flaps and dive brakes.

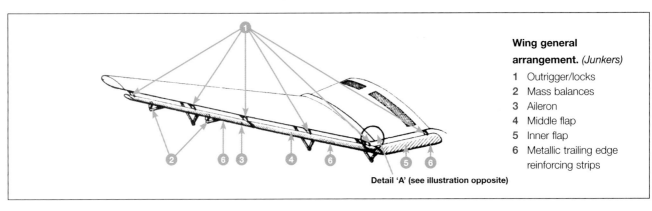

Wing general arrangement. *(Junkers)*

1 Outrigger/locks
2 Mass balances
3 Aileron
4 Middle flap
5 Inner flap
6 Metallic trailing edge reinforcing strips

Detail 'A' (see illustration opposite)

LEFT In this head-on view of an early Ju 87 B the characteristic inverted gullwing and the Doppelflügel trailing edge wing flaps are well illustrated. *(James Payne/Through Their Eyes)*

BELOW Port outer wing section of the RAF Museum's Ju 87 G, showing the aerofoil shape and the four ball-joint connectors. *(Author)*

Aileron and flaps (Querruder und Klappe)

The aileron and flaps were designed as part of a unique control system, the whole of which extended the full span of the wing. Created by Junkers who named it Doppelflügel, or 'double-wing', the single-piece aileron and two-piece flaps were interlinked and hinge-mounted together just below the trailing edge of the centre (inner) and outboard wing sections, fully exposing the entire control surface cross-section to the slipstream and forming a slot between the two surfaces.

In normal flight the ailerons were used for their intended purpose of roll control, but they could be lowered like flaps for landing while retaining the differential movement needed for lateral control.

The ailerons and flaps were attached to the wing by patented Junkers ball hinges and rotated about their forward edges. The trimmable ailerons were mechanically operated while the flaps featured hydraulic actuation.

The mechanically simple Doppelflügel was invented by Otto Mader at Junkers in the late 1920s and was mainly used on the ubiquitous 'Tante Ju' Ju 52/3m airliner/military transport and of course on the Ju 87. When not in use, the Ju 87's flaps created more drag than other types of flap system, but they were more effective at creating additional lift at low speeds than plain or split flaps.

Dive brakes (Sturzflugbremsen)

To reduce the aircraft's speed in a dive, dive brakes were fitted underneath each wing. They were flush-mounted against the inner half of the outer wing near the leading edge and attached to the front spar. Consisting of a pair of narrow span-wise slats, the dive brakes were carried on three hinged ball-joint fittings and for deployment they were turned hydraulically, edge-on, through 90°. The brakes were extended shortly before beginning a dive and in their extended braking position they limited the dive speed to approximately 335mph (540km/h). Extension and retraction was by

RIGHT **The dive brakes are evident in this close formation of Ju 87 D-5s of StG 2.** *(Copyright unknown)*

ABOVE **An early Ju 87 A shows the position of the wing flaps. Also note the upward-hinging cockpit canopy and the slit for the gunner's hand-held MG 17 machine gun.** *(James Payne/Through Their Eyes)*

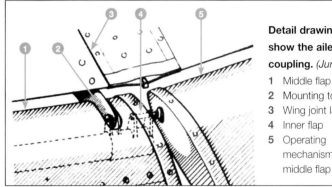

Detail drawing 'A' to show the aileron/flap coupling. *(Junkers)*

1. Middle flap
2. Mounting to wing
3. Wing joint lap plate
4. Inner flap
5. Operating mechanism for middle flap

Junkers Ju 87 D-3.

(John Weal/Art Tech)

1 Spinner
2 Pitch-change mechanism housing
3 Blade hub
4 Junkers VS11 constant-speed airscrew
5 Anti-vibration engine mounting attachments
6 Oil filler point and marker
7 Auxiliary oil tank, 26.8-litre capacity (5.9 Imp gal)
8 Junkers Jumo 211J-1 12-cylinder inverted-vee liquid-cooled engine
9 Magnesium alloy forged engine mount

10 Coolant (Glysantin-water) header tank
11 Ejector exhaust stubs
12 Fuel injection unit housing
13 Induction air cooler
14 Armoured radiator
15 Inertia starter cranking point
16 Ball-joint bulkhead fixing (lower)
17 Tubular steel mount support strut
18 Ventral armour, 8mm (0.315in)
19 Main oil tank, 45 litres (9.9 Imp gal)
20 Oil filling point

21 Transverse support frame
22 Rudder pedals
23 Control column
24 Heating point
25 Auxiliary air intake
26 Ball-joint bulkhead fixing (upper)
27 Bulkhead
28 Oil tank, 31 litres (6.8 Imp gal)
29 Oil filler point and marker (Intava 100)
30 Fuel filler cap
31 Self-sealing starboard outer fuel tank, 150 litres (33 Imp gal)

32 Underwing bombs with Dienartstab percussion rods
33 Signal flare tube
34 Spherical oxygen bottles
35 Wing skinning
36 Starboard navigation light
37 Aileron mass balance
38 Doppelflügel (double-wing) aileron and flap (starboard outer)
39 Aileron hinge
40 Corrugated wing rib station
41 Reinforced armoured windscreen
42 Reflector sight
43 Padded crash bar
44 Signal flare tube
45 Braced fuselage mainframe
46 Front spar/fuselage attachment point

47 Pilot's seat, reinforced with 4mm side and 8mm rear armour
48 Inter-cockpit bulkhead
49 Sliding canopy handgrip
50 External side armour
51 Pilot's back armour, 8mm
52 Headrest
53 Aft-sliding cockpit canopy (shown part open)

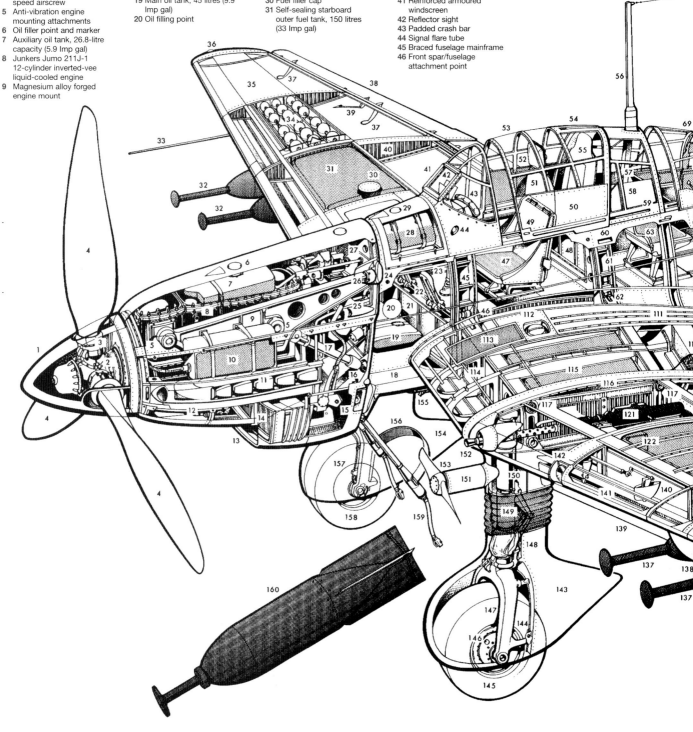

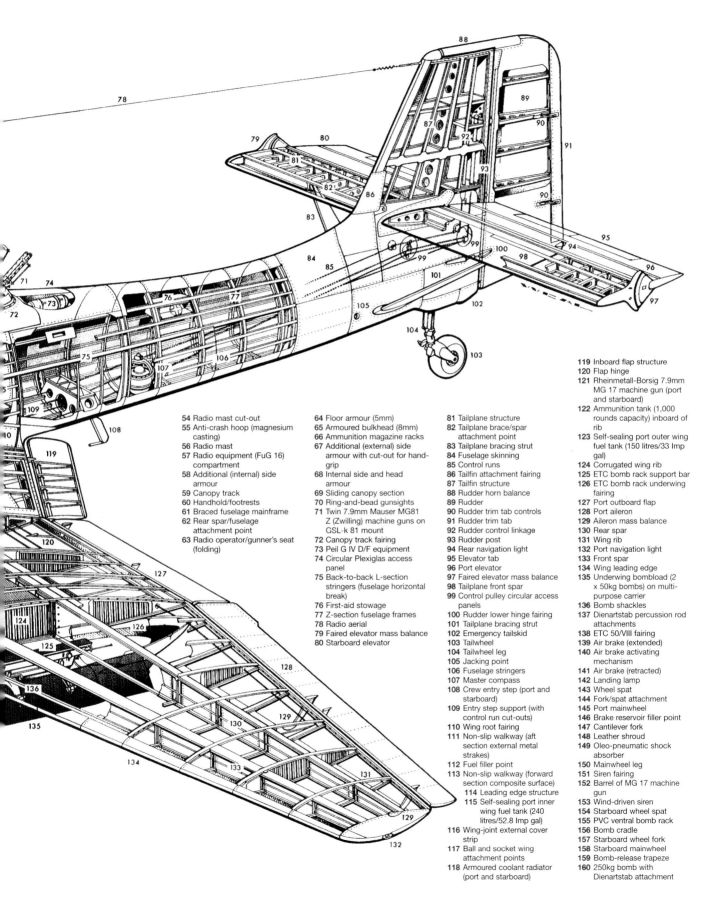

54 Radio mast cut-out
55 Anti-crash hoop (magnesium casting)
56 Radio mast
57 Radio equipment (FuG 16) compartment
58 Additional (internal) side armour
59 Canopy track
60 Handhold/footrests
61 Braced fuselage mainframe
62 Rear spar/fuselage attachment point
63 Radio operator/gunner's seat (folding)
64 Floor armour (5mm)
65 Armoured bulkhead (8mm)
66 Ammunition magazine racks
67 Additional (external) side armour with cut-out for hand-grip
68 Internal side and head armour
69 Sliding canopy section
70 Ring-and-bead gunsights
71 Twin 7.9mm Mauser MG81 Z (Zwilling) machine guns on GSL-k 81 mount
72 Canopy track fairing
73 Peil G IV D/F equipment
74 Circular Plexiglas access panel
75 Back-to-back L-section stringers (fuselage horizontal break)
76 First-aid stowage
77 Z-section fuselage frames
78 Radio aerial
79 Faired elevator mass balance
80 Starboard elevator
81 Tailplane structure
82 Tailplane brace/spar attachment point
83 Tailplane bracing strut
84 Fuselage skinning
85 Control runs
86 Tailfin attachment fairing
87 Tailfin structure
88 Rudder horn balance
89 Rudder
90 Rudder trim tab controls
91 Rudder trim tab
92 Rudder control linkage
93 Rudder post
94 Rear navigation light
95 Elevator tab
96 Port elevator
97 Faired elevator mass balance
98 Tailplane front spar
99 Control pulley circular access panels
100 Rudder lower hinge fairing
101 Tailplane bracing strut
102 Emergency tailskid
103 Tailwheel
104 Tailwheel leg
105 Jacking point
106 Fuselage stringers
107 Master compass
108 Crew entry step (port and starboard)
109 Entry step support (with control run cut-outs)
110 Wing root fairing
111 Non-slip walkway (aft section external metal strakes)
112 Fuel filler point
113 Non-slip walkway (forward section composite surface)
114 Leading edge structure
115 Self-sealing port inner wing fuel tank (240 litres/52.8 Imp gal)
116 Wing-joint external cover strip
117 Ball and socket wing attachment points
118 Armoured coolant radiator (port and starboard)
119 Inboard flap structure
120 Flap hinge
121 Rheinmetall-Borsig 7.9mm MG 17 machine gun (port and starboard)
122 Ammunition tank (1,000 rounds capacity) inboard of rib
123 Self-sealing port outer wing fuel tank (150 litres/33 Imp gal)
124 Corrugated wing rib
125 ETC bomb rack support bar
126 ETC bomb rack underwing fairing
127 Port outboard flap
128 Port aileron
129 Aileron mass balance
130 Rear spar
131 Wing rib
132 Port navigation light
133 Front spar
134 Wing leading edge
135 Underwing bombload (2 x 50kg bombs) on multi-purpose carrier
136 Bomb shackles
137 Dienartstab percussion rod attachments
138 ETC 50/VIII fairing
139 Air brake (extended)
140 Air brake activating mechanism
141 Air brake (retracted)
142 Landing lamp
143 Wheel spat
144 Fork/spat attachment
145 Port mainwheel
146 Brake reservoir filler point
147 Cantilever fork
148 Leather shroud
149 Oleo-pneumatic shock absorber
150 Mainwheel leg
151 Siren fairing
152 Barrel of MG 17 machine gun
153 Wind-driven siren
154 Starboard wheel spat
155 PVC ventral bomb rack
156 Bomb cradle
157 Starboard wheel fork
158 Starboard mainwheel
159 Bomb-release trapeze
160 250kg bomb with Dienartstab attachment

Actuating mechanism

for dive brake. *(Junkers)*

1 Wing rib
2 Spar 1
3 Upper bleed screw
4 Connector,
  16mm x 1.5mm
5 Retractable strut with
  lock
6 Hydraulic oil line
7 Connector,
  14mm x 1.5mm
8 Lower bleed screw
9 Adjustable rod end
10 Dive brake
11 Indicator jack
12 Spring
13 Bell crank
14 Cable
15 Panel cover in upper
   wing surface

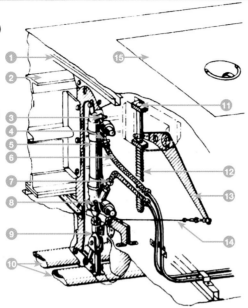

means of oleo-hydraulic pistons at opposite ends of the dive brake frame. The pilot could monitor the hydraulic oil pressure on a gauge located on the left side of the cockpit.

The pilot could visually check the position of the dive brakes from the cockpit by observing a pair of red-painted indicator jacks that popped above the upper surface of the wings when the brakes were lowered. Each jack was linked to the dive brake pistons by a cable and angle-lever. When the brakes were raised a spring action retracted them inside the wing.

Dive brake

schematic. *(Junkers)*

1 Dive brake twin profile tubes
2 Outer boom
3 Middle boom
4 Support bearing
5 Casing for the actuating jack

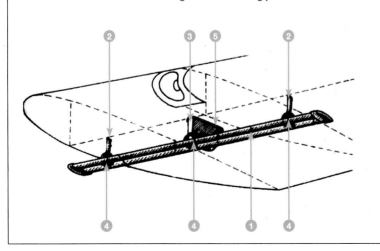

GERMAN SPECIALIST AERONAUTICAL ALLOYS

The main construction material for the Ju 87 was Duralumin and the external skin was made of Duralumin sheeting; Pantal alloy was used for airframe parts that needed to be of strong construction, such as the wing flaps; a strong and lightweight alloy called Elektronmetall was used in the manufacture of wheel hubs, for example. Other parts that were required to take heavy stresses were made from steel.

Elektronmetall

Elektronmetall is the generic name for a large group of different lightweight and high-tensile strength magnesium alloys that were first developed in Germany in 1908 by Gustav Pistor and Wilhelm Moschel at Chemische Fabrik Griesheim-Elektron. Their qualities made them ideal for use in aeronautical engineering applications. Alloys in the Elektron range contain some of the following elements in varying proportions: aluminium, yttrium, neodymium, silver, gadolinium, zinc, zirconium, manganese and other rare earth metals. Depending on the combination of elements added to the magnesium, the results are changes to the mechanical properties of the alloy that include creep resistance, thermal stability and resistance to corrosion.

Pantal

Pantal is another light but strong aeronautical alloy used in the construction of the Ju 87. It can be welded as easily as aluminium, but has a higher stability. Pantal is an aluminium–magnesium alloy containing titanium as a hardening element. It is made from aluminium with added silicon (0.7%), magnesium (1.4%) and titanium (0.2%). On the Brinell hardness scale it is rated at 40. (For comparison purposes lead is rated at 5HB, hardened aluminium 75HB and mild steel 120HB.)

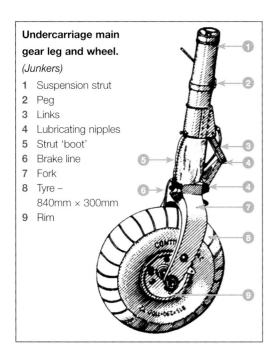

Undercarriage main gear leg and wheel. *(Junkers)*

1 Suspension strut
2 Peg
3 Links
4 Lubricating nipples
5 Strut 'boot'
6 Brake line
7 Fork
8 Tyre – 840mm × 300mm
9 Rim

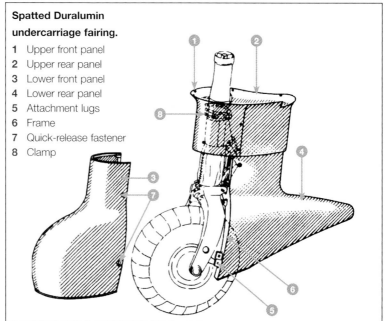

Spatted Duralumin undercarriage fairing.

1 Upper front panel
2 Upper rear panel
3 Lower front panel
4 Lower rear panel
5 Attachment lugs
6 Frame
7 Quick-release fastener
8 Clamp

Undercarriage (Fahrwerk)

Main gear (Laufräder)

The Ju 87's landing gear was designed as a pair of fixed, non-retractable single-leg units. An important reason for this choice in a dive-bomber was linked to the structural integrity of the wing, which was not weakened by the incorporation of a wheelwell for a retractable undercarriage. Another consideration was that even a slight twisting of the wing during a sharp pull-out from a dive might result in the failure of a retractable undercarriage to lower.

The landing gear units and their components were designed to be interchangeable. Each unit was enclosed inside a spatted Duralumin fairing comprising of upper and lower panels. The upper panel had a front and rear cap and was screwed to a supporting bracket fixed to the undercarriage leg. The lower rear chassis panel was attached to a frame, which in turn was fixed to the wheel fork with four bolts. The lower front chassis panel was fitted to the rear part of the rear panel with four quick-release fasteners. A mudguard was also incorporated inside the rear panel as a dirt trap.

RIGHT A general view of the main undercarriage on a Ju 87 B. *(Chris Goss collection)*

ABOVE This is the undercarriage of Oberleutnant Kurt Scheffel's Ju 87 B-1 of Stab I./StG 77 that was badly shot up in the Stuka attack of 18 August 1940 on Thorney Island. Although seriously injured, he nursed his aircraft back to France with his dead gunner on board. Of interest are the 0.303in bullet holes, wheel fork and oleo, and the attachment points for the spats. *(Andy Saunders collection)*

ABOVE A welded steel clamp attached the head of the sprung oleo strut to the front spar. Also seen in this photograph are two of the four ball connectors for the wing, as well as twin pipe runs for the coolant system. *(Author)*

Tailwheel general arrangement.

(Junkers)

1 Suspension unit head
2 Torque link
3 Suspension unit
4 Hull stock
5 Wheel tyre 380mm x 150mm
6 Bowden cable
7 Locking device
8 Wheel fork
9 Towing eye
10 Emergency spur
11 Clamp
12 Flanged bush

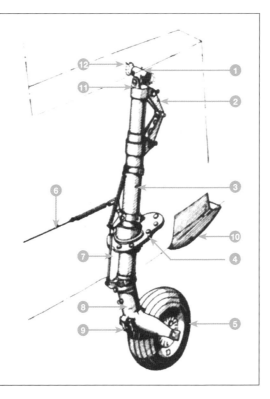

Each undercarriage leg was made up of a wheel with hydraulic brake, wheel fork and oleo strut shock absorbers with additional coil spring damping. The maintenance-free suspension unit was made by Kronprinz Ringfederbeinen (KPZ). In the crown of the fork the coil spring piston end was secured and tensioned by screws and a pair of hexagonal torque bolts.

Each leg of the fixed undercarriage was attached to the front (No 1) wing spar by a welded steel clamp fitting at the union between the inner and outer wing sections, close to the leading edge. The head of the sprung oleo strut was inserted into the clamp where it was tightly secured at top and bottom by double bolts. The strut was also secured to the upper wing structure with a metal cap and screw.

Tailwheel (Spornrad)

A non-retractable tailwheel unit was mounted to a horizontal frame located between fuselage Frames 15 and 16. It was attached to a

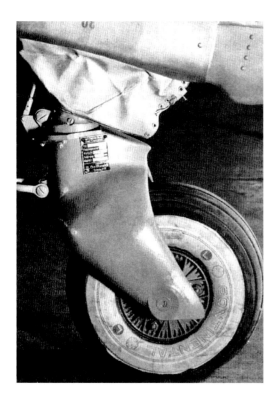

Kronprinz fork and spring-damped strut, which had a 360° free-castoring capability. The pilot could lock the tailwheel for take-off and landing to prevent shimmying, and in-flight, by means of a Bowden cable running from the cockpit.

Wheels and tyres

The mainwheels were cast in Elektronmetall (magnesium alloy) and fitted with 840mm × 300mm low-pressure tyres with a recommended operating pressure of 2.5atm (approx. 36psi). Each wheel had a servo-expanding drum brake unit operated by two hydraulic foot motors mounted behind the rudder pedals. The brakes could be operated individually by the pilot using foot pressure on the rudder control pedals.

The tailwheel hub was fitted with a 380mm × 150mm tyre with a recommended operating pressure of 3–3.5atm (44–51psi). It was unbraked.

Skis

For winter operations the aircraft's landing gear could be replaced with skis. Consisting of a set of three skis with plywood fairings, the main skis measured 3.78m (12ft 4in) long, 1.025m (3ft 4in) wide and 0.52m (1ft 7in) high (where they attached to the oleo). The tail ski was 1.005m (3ft 3in) × 0.44m (1ft 4in) × 0.2m (6in) respectively.

ABOVE LEFT Tailwheel of a Ju 87 B-1 on Junkers' Dessau assembly line. *(Junkers)*

ABOVE Mainwheel assembly and tyre of the RAF Museum's Ju 87 G with the front panel removed. *(Author)*

BELOW Ski-equipped Ju 87 B. *(BA 101I-392-1334-04)*

Cockpit (Kanzel)

The cockpit was located in the fuselage centre section between Frames 2 and 6 and contained all the instruments and controls necessary for flight. The two-man crew of pilot and gunner was housed in tandem beneath a fully glazed four-piece sliding canopy extending over both seats and affording excellent all-round visibility. The crew positions were separated from one another by a strong anti-roll-over frame made of cast magnesium, which was integral to the structure of the pilot's compartment roof.

Entry to the cockpit for both crewmembers was over the left wing, with the canopy sliding rearwards for the pilot, and the gunner's canopy sliding backwards. For ease of access, footholds and handgrips were used. Both canopies were opened by turning a handle on the left side of the fuselage and simultaneously pushing the canopy back. The pilot sat in front in a seat that could be adjusted manually by a lever. He operated the bomb-release as well as flying the aircraft. A padded bar in front of and above the instrument panel offered him some head protection should the forces in the dive pull-out or in a crash pull him forward off the seat.

Behind the pilot was the radio operator/rear gunner who occupied the back seat, which could be rotated (like an office chair). He had a wide and strong belt extending across the fuselage just in front of his seat, which served the same purpose for him as the pilot's padded bar. Both men's seats had the bucket recess designed to accommodate seat-type parachutes (Sitzfallschirm, Fl 30231).

Pilot's instruments and cockpit equipment

In front of the pilot the instrument panel spanned the full width of the cockpit. Sensitive instruments like the airspeed indicator and altimeter were rubber-mounted on the primary flight instruments panel in the centre to prevent damage through vibration. As might be expected in a dive-bomber, there was a sensitive (or contact) altimeter as well as a standard type. Other instruments included a pilot magnetic compass (Führerkompass), bank and turn indicator, rate of climb/descent indicator, rev counter, boost gauge, clock, oil temperature and pressure gauges, fuel gauge and radiator coolant thermometer. The master compass was housed in the rear fuselage with

BELOW Pilot's instrument panel, Ju 87 B. *(Copyright unknown)*

1 Radiator cooling gills on/off switches
2 Dimmer rheostat
3 Clock (missing)
4 Radio direction finder (missing)
5 Altimeter
6 FK 38 magnetic compass
7 Landing flaps oil pressure gauge
8 Oil pressure gauge for variable incidence tailplane
9 Volt-ampere meter
10 On/off power switch
11 Fuel tank supply switch left/right
12 Fuel low warning light, left tank
13 Fuel contents gauge
14 Fuel low warning light, right tank (hidden behind control column)
15 Combined oil/fuel pressure gauge (hidden behind control column)
16 Bomb selector panel
17 Electric combined oil temperature gauge
18 Pitot tube heater indicator
19 Electric coolant temperature gauge
20 Variometer rate of climb/descent indicator
21 Boost gauge
22 Engine rpm
23 Radiator cooling gills position indicator
24 Airspeed indicator
25 Turn indicator
26 'Patin' pilot slave compass
27 Contact altimeter
28 Shock-mounted panel
29 Solid panel
30 Control column
31 Rudder pedals
32 Oil cooler control
33 Fuel hand pump
34 Injection pump handle
35 Supercharger

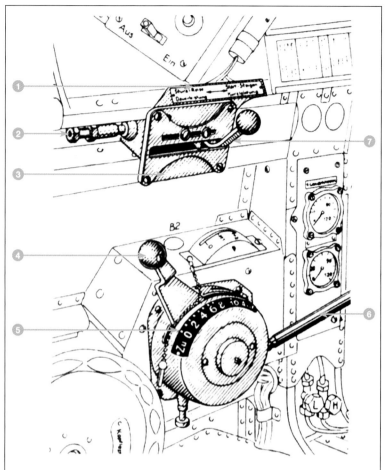

Propeller speed control and engine throttle. *(Junkers)*

1 Propeller speed adjustment settings 'Sturz-Reise–Start-Steigen'

2 Adjustment screw

3 Adjustment box

4 Throttle lever

5 Throttle lever settings 'closed–0–10–open'

6 Throttle push-rod to engine

7 Propeller speed adjustment lever

a pilot slave compass (Führertochterkompass) in the centre of the instrument panel.

The throttle control, propeller speed control, elevator and rudder trimmers, the adjustment levers for the tailplane, wing flaps and dive brakes were along the left fuselage sidewall. The remaining control levers for supercharger, injection pump and fuel hand pump were located on the instrument panel. In the upper centre of the panel was a movable ventilation nozzle to prevent the cockpit windows from misting up in the dive when the aircraft reached the more moist lower air. On the right wall of the cockpit was the electrical services panel.

A firing port for the Walther flare pistol was on the left fuselage sidewall into which the pistol could be clamped. A case containing six flare cartridges was attached to the right sidewall under the front windscreen. A rear-view mirror was located in the upper right corner of the windscreen.

For breathing at high altitude, oxygen apparatus with pressure gauge was installed on the right side of the pilot's cockpit, supplied from four 2-litre oxygen bottles located behind Frame 6. The bottles were filled on the ground via an external connector on the right fuselage wall behind the wing.

Flying controls (Flugsteuerungen)

The pilot's control column (Steuerknüppel) and rudder pedals (Seitensteuerung) were used to operate the elevators, rudder and ailerons by a combination of mechanical and hydraulic means; the wing flaps, dive brakes and variable incidence horizontal stabiliser were operated separately by a pair of shift levers contained in a switchbox on the left side of the cockpit. Also part of the switchbox was a hand wheel (for elevator trim) and a control knob (rudder trim) with incremental displays for both controllers.

Movement of the control column was transmitted mechanically to the elevators by means of a transverse shaft with levers, push-rods, swinging levers and cables, which was

BELOW LEFT Pilot's instrument panel, Ju 87 D-1. *(via Andy Saunders)*

ABOVE Pilot's instrument panel, Ju 87 G-2. This rare photograph was taken at RAF St Athan in 1964 and shows how the bomb selector panel common to the B, R and D variants was replaced on the Gustav with an operating panel for the BK 37 cannon. This aircraft is now on display at the RAF Museum, Hendon. *(Ian F. Paterson)*

limited in the cockpit to 16° forward and 22° backwards from the neutral position.

The ailerons, middle and inner flaps (Doppelflügel) were operated by means of hydraulic oil pressure via a shift slide and retraction strut to tie rods and control rods. To prevent structural damage to the flaps and the airframe, a safety device was incorporated in the flap control linkage that prevented them from being lowered above a certain speed.

The rudder had 30° of lateral travel in each

RIGHT Pilot's control column. *(Alamy D40R43)*

ABOVE Dive brake, flap and variable incidence tailplane controls in the cockpit of a Ju 87 G. Note how the propeller speed and throttle levers are located side by side in the same control unit on the Ju 87 D and G versions (on the B and R they were separate installations). *(Alamy E1DPGN)*

direction and was mechanically operated by a pair of foot pedals via bevel gears, levers and cables. Twin rudder cables ran aft on either side of the pilot's and gunner's cockpits inside red and white-painted ducting.

BELOW Landeklappensicherung mit Übersetzungsteil (landing flap safety device with translation unit). Operation of the aileron and flap push-rods was combined with the flap safety device, allowing the outer flap on each wing to be used independently as an aileron, and when circumstances required all three control surfaces could be used together as flaps. *(Junkers)*

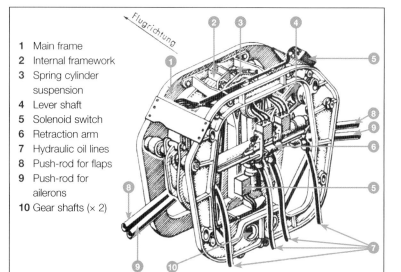

1 Main frame
2 Internal framework
3 Spring cylinder suspension
4 Lever shaft
5 Solenoid switch
6 Retraction arm
7 Hydraulic oil lines
8 Push-rod for flaps
9 Push-rod for ailerons
10 Gear shafts (× 2)

Dive brake, wing flap and tailplane controls (Schaltkasten für Klappen- und Flossen- verstellung)

A control box on the left side of the cockpit contained a pair of shift levers – one for operation of the dive brakes and the other (combined) lever for the wing flaps and variable incidence tailplane.

In order to adjust the flaps to the desired position the control lever was moved from its zero position into corresponding notched positions (start–0–travel/climb–0–land). When the corresponding signal lamp on the box lit up, the control lever had to be returned to one of the two '0' (zero) notches so that pressure in the hydraulic oil line could return to its resting level and recuperate.

If the flaps failed to extend when the lever was moved, then the airspeed was above the safe limit (the safety limiter device). With a corresponding reduction in speed the flaps would move automatically into the selected position.

If the engine-driven pump failed, the pilot could generate a working pressure to drive the flaps and tailplane by an emergency hand pump located on the right of his seat. Gauges for both pressure circuits could be found on the left-hand side of the fuselage.

Landeklappensicherung mit Übersetzungsteil

A mechanical translation unit (Übersetzungsteil) for the Doppelflügel ailerons and wing flaps was located in mid-fuselage between the wingroots. It was combined with the flap safety device (Landeklappensicherung) and allowed the third (outer) flap on each wing to be used either as an aileron or as a third flap (making all three wing trailing edge control surfaces as flaps together) when required. The advantage was that in low-speed flight and during landing the entire trailing edge of the wing could be devoted to flaps, providing better low-speed control.

Floor window (Bodenfenster)

For a better view of the ground below, especially before commencing an attack on a target, a window with anti-glare cover plate was installed in the bottom of the fuselage beneath the pilot's feet between Frames 1 and 2.

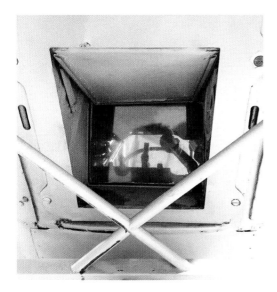

The floor window comprised a flat clear glass panel protected inside the fuselage by a Plexiglas window. The lower window was covered by a mechanically adjustable blind, which was operated by the pilot turning a small hand wheel mounted on the end of a guide tube counter-clockwise. Pressing a button to the right of the Revi gunsight activated the window washer system.

Cockpit canopy

The canopy framework was built from electro-etched profiles and steel tubing and glazed with Plexiglas. The windscreen was made of 25mm laminated armoured glass. The Ju 87 A variant had upward and sideways-hinging canopies over both the pilot's and gunner's cockpits. This feature was discontinued from the Berta onwards, for which the canopy structure

ABOVE LEFT A close-up underside view of the floor window. Through the glass panel inside can be seen the hand wheel for adjusting the blind, while in the top of the recess is the metal anti-glare cover plate in the open position. The cross-member in the foreground is part of the bomb trapeze mechanism. *(Author)*

ABOVE The hinging canopy design used on the Ju 87 A can be seen on this pre-war Anton (S17+M?), believed to have been serving with Luftnachrichten Schule 2. *(James Payne/Through Their Eyes)*

went through a thorough redesign with the incorporation of rearward-sliding canopies for each crewmember.

Pilot

From the Ju 87 B variant onwards, the pilot's canopy could be jettisoned from inside or outside by handgrips on the left-hand side. By

LEFT An Italian Ju 87 Picchiatello illustrates the revised cockpit canopy style fitted to the Ju 87 B and R variants. *(Copyright unknown)*

means of latching holes in the left running rail, into which a latch engaged when the handle was released, the canopy could be held in different intermediate positions. Emergency canopy release was achieved by pulling a red-marked cable in the top of the canopy, which released pins in the runners and the canopy was pulled away by the force of the slipstream.

Radioman/gunner

The radioman/gunner's canopy, like that of the pilot, was in two pieces with a fixed section and a sliding canopy. Located at the rear of the canopy was the machine gun in an Ikaria-Linsen Lafette Z10d ball mounting. The sliding canopy could be opened and closed from the outside by pressing the handle on the left side of the fuselage at Frame 4 and pushing back

BELOW **The radio operator/gunner's rearward-sliding canopy is well illustrated, together with the Ikaria-Linsen Lafette Z10d ball mounting and MG 17 machine gun.** *(Andy Saunders collection)*

the canopy. From inside it could be opened or closed by pulling or pressing a handle at the rear of the radioman/gunner's cockpit. When the handle was pulled, a pair of bevel gears meshed with a toothed rack that guided rollers located in running rails on each side of the canopy.

Armour-plating

In response to injuries sustained by Stuka crews during the early stages of the war, in particular while operating at low level, armour plating was added during the Battle of Britain period behind the pilot's seat on the Ju 87 B as well as rear armour for the gunner. Later, when the Ju 87 became more active in close air-support and ground-attack roles, particularly in Russia, it became increasingly vulnerable to damage from ground fire. This led to greater use of armour plating to protect the crew and vital systems, but the extra steel added to the Stuka's gross weight, which of course affected performance.

Ju 87s from the B-2 onwards benefited from both factory-fitted and local (field) modifications to accept additional armour plating – the 'U' standing for Umrüst-Bausätze or factory-supplied modification kits. Field modification kits (Rüstsätze) were also produced and were usually supplied to Luftwaffe units direct from the aircraft manufacturer (in this case Junkers). Such changes to an aircraft's airframe were usually denoted in the type designation with a '/R' suffix.

The Ju 87 B-2/U-3 was fitted with Umrüst-Bausätze and Rüstsätze additional armour,

which was also retrofitted inside the rear cockpit on the Ju 87 D-1, comprising angle-armour plating extending up both rear corners of the gunner's windows. From the D-5 onwards this was factory-fitted. From mid-1943 an armoured seat for the pilot was fitted to D-series aircraft, with additional armour protection of between 4 and 10mm underneath the fuselage, in the cockpit and attached to the sides of the fuselage, as well as around the coolant pipes from the under-wing radiators. Further armour plating was added around the cockpit on the Ju 87 G to protect the crew.

Communications

Located inside the cockpit midway between the pilot and radioman/gunner's positions was the communications equipment. It was operated by the gunner and consisted of a two-way Telefunken FuG (Funkgerät) VIIa radio transmitter/receiver set mounted in the rear cockpit for air-to-ground and aircraft-to-aircraft communication, operating at frequencies between 2,500 and 3,750kHz. The FuG VIIa set included an S6b (Sender) transmitter and an E5a (Empfänger) receiver, each with a large tuning dial and a U4b 24V power inverter (changing DC power from the aircraft's battery to AC power to operate the radio equipment).

RIGHT The wireless installation in an early Ju 87. The upper set is the S6 transmitter and the lower is the E5a receiver. (Copyright unknown)

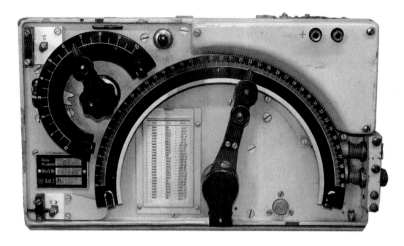

ABOVE **The Telefunken Type S6 transmitter set.** *(Copyright unknown)*

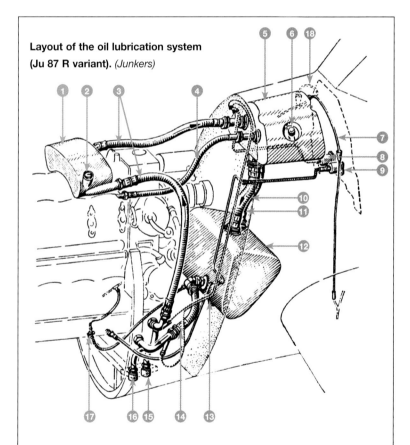

**Layout of the oil lubrication system
(Ju 87 R variant).** *(Junkers)*

1 Oil cooler	**7** Breather pipe (only	**11** Intake line
2 Pressure relief valve	on the Ju 87 R-1)	**12** Main oil tank
3 Return line	**8** Dual temperature	**13** Drain valve
4 Breather pipe from	gauge for oil inlet/	**14** Main oil line
engine	outlet	**15** Oil drain valve
5 Supplemental oil	**9** Dual pressure gauge	**16** Oil filler/drain valve
tank	for oil and fuel	**17** Cold start cock
6 Tank filler with	**10** Breather pipe from	**18** Breather pipe (only
dipstick	main oil tank	on the Ju 87 R-2)

Air-to-ground range was between 60 and 80km, aircraft-to-aircraft 40 and 60km and ground-to-air 80 and 120km.

A copper antenna wire ran from a mast on the canopy to the top of the tailfin. Pilot and wireless operator/gunner communicated using the Eigenverständigungsanlage (EiV) 1a intercom between crew stations.

The aircraft was also equipped with a FuG 25 Erstling IFF set with a dedicated blade antenna beneath the fuselage. Frequency reception range was 125 plus or minus 1.8MHz, with a transmitting frequency of 160MHz. It could be received at up to 100km (62 miles).

On the Ju 87 D and G versions, a Peilgerät (*PeilG*) IV, V or VI long- and medium-range radio ranging device (direction-finding or D/F) with a rotating PRE 4 goniometric antenna was fitted dorsally behind the rear cockpit inside a 10cm-deep 'tub'. The transparent Plexiglas® cover 'lid' featured a sunburst-shaped laminated metal antenna sitting flush with the aircraft skin. This installation was a 'flat' equivalent of a D/F loop and caused no air resistance, unlike the earlier loop antenna. The frequency range was 150–1,200kHz.

Systems (Anlage)

Lubricating oil (Schmierstoff)

The Ju 87 B's lubrication system featured a main oil tank located in the forward, lower section of the fuselage, behind Frame 1 and to the rear of the firewall. It had a capacity of 55 litres, but was usually only filled to 47 litres. An oil cooler with air scoop in the engine cowling was mounted on top of the crankcase and connected to the compressor intercooler. On the Jumo 211A engine, the oil-circulating volume at 2,400rpm was between 3,500 and 4,000kg/hr.

In addition to the main oil tank the Ju 87 D and G had an additional 36-litre tank in the upper part of the fuselage behind the firewall and an auxiliary 26.8-litre oil tank above the engine. The D had its oil cooler and armoured radiator relocated from the top of the engine to the position underneath formerly occupied by the coolant radiator.

The Ju 87 R had an additional 31-litre oil tank in the upper part of the fuselage behind the firewall.

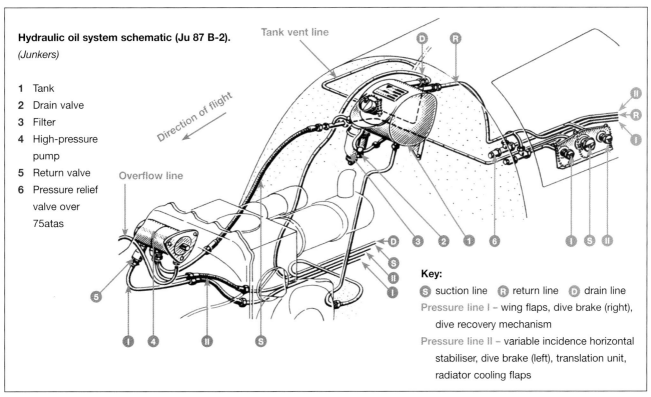

Hydraulic oil system schematic (Ju 87 B-2).
(Junkers)

1　Tank
2　Drain valve
3　Filter
4　High-pressure pump
5　Return valve
6　Pressure relief valve over 75atas

Tank vent line

Direction of flight

Overflow line

Key:
Ⓢ suction line　Ⓡ return line　Ⓓ drain line
Pressure line I – wing flaps, dive brake (right), dive recovery mechanism
Pressure line II – variable incidence horizontal stabiliser, dive brake (left), translation unit, radiator cooling flaps

A choice of three oils was used for lubrication: Aero-Shell-mittel, Intava or Mobilöl-Rotring, or Intava 100, with the oil being circulated by an engine-driven, geared oil pump.

ARGUS PIPE COUPLING (ARGUS–ROHRKUPPLUNGEN)

Engine changes of the Jumo Kraftei (power-egg, see page 82) were made simpler by the use of Argus-Rohrkupplungen (Argus pipe couplings) made by Argusfluidtechnik. The Rohrkupplung was a self-sealing connection system for fluid-carrying pipes and hose assemblies that assured an easy manual separation and a leakage-free coupling of filled hoses without using any tools. Both coupling parts had spring-loaded ball valves that were closed manually before separation. When the two halves were reconnected there were no problems with air pockets, which meant that bleeding of the system was unnecessary. Under pressure, the coupling could be made manually up to 20 bar.

Hydraulic oil (Drucköl)

The 2.4-litre collection tank for the pressurised hydraulic oil system was mounted to Frame 1 behind the engine. It was filled with approximately 2.25 litres of Ate Bremsöl hydraulic oil. The system operated the radiator cooling gills, dive brakes, flaps, variable incidence tailplane and starboard elevator trim tabs.

Fuel (Kraftstoff)

The Ju 87 B was fitted with two self-sealing 240-litre fuel tanks, one inside each inner wing cavity between the two wing spars. Fuel was supplied to the engine from the twin fuel tanks at a rate of 1,000 litres/hr at 2,600rpm by an electrically driven low-pressure–high-volume immersed pump inside each tank (a Jumo 2017 piston, or 2135 gear), and a double engine-driven high-pressure–low-volume accelerator pump mounted on the right-hand cylinder head (the Bosch injection pump) sucking the fuel into the pressure lines to feed the injection nozzles in each cylinder head.

With the long-range Ju 87 R, the two internal 240-litre fuel tanks were augmented with a pair of 300-litre drop tanks (Blechbehälter) mounted under the outer wings. The D-variant was also able to carry these.

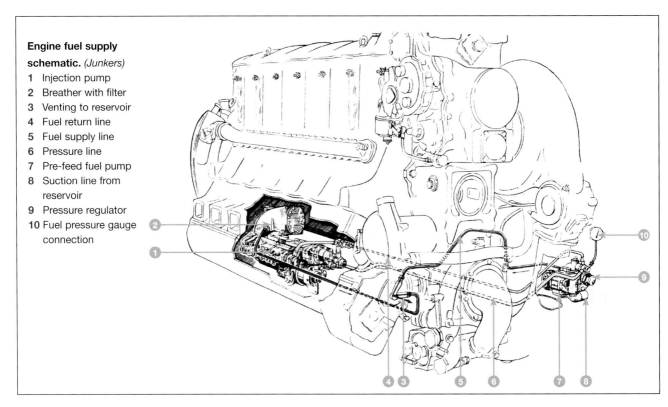

Engine fuel supply schematic. *(Junkers)*

1 Injection pump
2 Breather with filter
3 Venting to reservoir
4 Fuel return line
5 Fuel supply line
6 Pressure line
7 Pre-feed fuel pump
8 Suction line from reservoir
9 Pressure regulator
10 Fuel pressure gauge connection

The Ju 87 D and G had two additional self-sealing 150-litre fuel tanks, one each in the outer wing sections, making a total of four internal fuel tanks with 780 litres between them. It was necessary to fuel each tank separately.

Using B4-type 87 octane ethyl petrol, fuel consumption for the Jumo 211F and J at take-off (2,600rpm) was 430 litres/hr; in the climb and at combat power (2,400rpm) 345 litres/hr; and at maximum power (2,250rpm) 255 litres/hr.

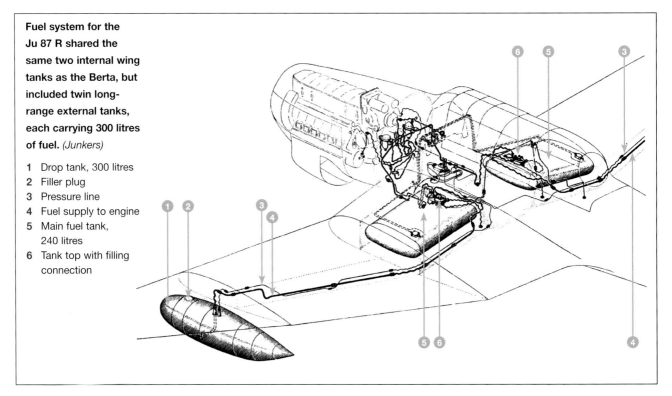

Fuel system for the Ju 87 R shared the same two internal wing tanks as the Berta, but included twin long-range external tanks, each carrying 300 litres of fuel. *(Junkers)*

1 Drop tank, 300 litres
2 Filler plug
3 Pressure line
4 Fuel supply to engine
5 Main fuel tank, 240 litres
6 Tank top with filling connection

Based on a fuel capacity of 780 litres, an endurance of 2 hours 15 minutes was possible; the use of drop tanks increased total fuel capacity to 1,370 litres and extended the aircraft's endurance to over 4 hours.

Coolant (Kühlerstoff)

Early marks of Ju 87 used an unpressurised open-cycle engine-cooling system, but with the Jumo 211E a pressurised closed-circuit system was introduced. Cooling was provided by a 1:1 mixture of water and ethylene glycol with 1.5% addition of Schutzöl 39 anti-corrosive fluid. In winter 25–30% Glysantin as an anti-freeze was added to protect the engine against temperatures down to -15°C.

A Behr-Lamellar radiator was positioned underneath the engine, attached by a suspension bracket and supported by an adjustable elastic cuff to the underside of the exhaust trough. Two support struts secured the radiator matrix to the rear frame. With a cooling area of 51m^2 and a content of approximately 20.5 litres, the coolant was circulated from a U-shaped expansion tank (on the Ju 87 A, B and R) wrapped around the underside of the reduction drive casing. Heated coolant from the engine flowed back into the expansion

tank from where it entered the radiator via two pipelines and was sucked back into the cooler at its lowest point.

Air-cooling of the radiator was achieved by a flap arrangement attached to the lower cowling frame with six splayed and rotatably mounted cooling flaps situated behind the radiator. These were adjusted electrically from the cockpit by means of two push-buttons ('open' and 'close') on the upper left instrument panel and were actuated by means of hydraulically controlled push-rods.

The coolant system was repositioned on the

ABOVE Close-up of one of the two external long-range tanks on a Ju 87 R-2 in May 1941. *(Copyright unknown)*

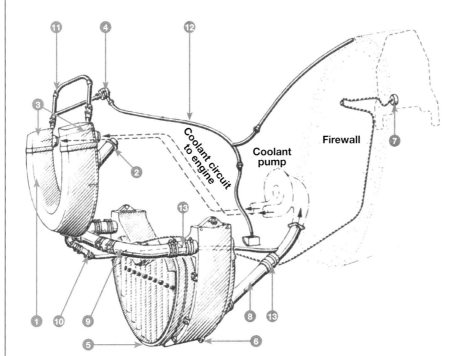

Radiator assembly and coolant system as used on the Ju 87 B and R variants. *(Junkers)*

1 Coolant header tank
2 Filler neck
3 Steam separator
4 Pressure relief valve
5 Radiator
6 Drain valve
7 Distant reading temperature gauge
8 Suction line
9 Line to radiator
10 Power line
11 Connecting line
12 Vent line
13 Rubber sleeve connector

RIGHT Early Ju 87 B, without cooling flaps. *(Chris Goss collection)*

FAR RIGHT This is a Ju 87 D-5 with oil cooler radiator underneath the nose and engine coolant radiators under each wing. *(SA-Kuva)*

BELOW Later Ju 87 B, with cooling flaps. This is possibly a 1./StG 3 aircraft in Crete in 1941. *(BA 101I-435-1008A-20)*

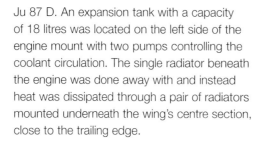

Ju 87 D. An expansion tank with a capacity of 18 litres was located on the left side of the engine mount with two pumps controlling the coolant circulation. The single radiator beneath the engine was done away with and instead heat was dissipated through a pair of radiators mounted underneath the wing's centre section, close to the trailing edge.

Electrical (Elektrisch)
The Ju 87 featured a Varta-Akku 24V electrical system powered by a 7.5Ah lead-acid battery and a 2,000W Bosch engine-driven generator. The battery was positioned on the floor of the wireless man's compartment and secured with tensioning straps. The system powered all radio equipment, directional compasses (Mutter und Tochter – 'mother and daughter', or main and slave), fuel tank content measurement, temperature gauges, bomb sight and cockpit illumination, instrument panel lights, navigation lights and an external landing light mounted between Ribs Id and Ia of the port wing. The system was protected by a set of circuit breakers on a control panel on the right side of the pilot's cockpit.

Oxygen (Sauerstoff)
Oxygen was stored in two pressurised (150 atu) 2-litre steel cylinders between Frames 5 and 6 and dispensed through demand regulators via flexible hose to the crew oxygen masks in the crew stations to the pilot and gunner. All oxygen tanks were refilled through a single-point filling valve in the port side of the fuselage.

For later marks of the Ju 87, the D and G versions, the crew's oxygen supply system was fed from 18 spherical tanks with separate regulators, which were grouped into six sets of three tanks inside the starboard outer

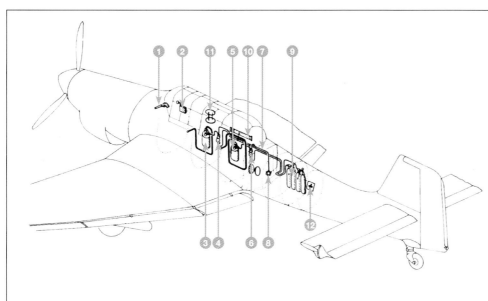

Oxygen and safety
equipment, Ju 87 B-2.
(Junkers)

1 Flare pistol
2 Flare storage
3 Compressed air breathing
  apparatus with tube (pilot)
4 Non-return valve
5 Compressed air breathing
  apparatus with tube (gunner)
6 Regulator valve
7 Oxygen supply line
8 External filling connector
9 Alloy oxygen bottles
10 Backrest
11 Gas mask installation
12 First-aid pack

wing. The breathing mixture was regulated depending on the altitude. All oxygen tanks were refilled through a single-point filling valve under the wing.

Armament (Rüstung)

Guns (Gewehr)

Rheinmetall-Borsig MG 15 machine gun

Designed and manufactured by Rheinmetall-Borsig during the 1930s and intended for hand-operation as a defensive weapon for combat aircraft, the 7.92mm MG 15 was used in the Ju 87 A, B and R series as a single rear-firing machine gun operated by the radioman/gunner. Capable of firing 900 rounds from 12 double-drum magazines stowed in the gunner's compartment, the MG 15 was installed in a Linsen-Lafette flexible mounting. The weapon was widely used in many Luftwaffe aircraft types of the early war years but by 1941 it had become obsolete in air combat terms and was replaced by other, newer machine-gun types like the MG 81.

BELOW FAR LEFT
Interior view of the gunner's position in a Ju 87 B, showing the MG 17 machine gun located in the Ikaria-Linsen Lafette Z10d ball mounting. In the foreground is storage for the 7.92mm double-drum ammunition magazines. Sadly, the blood spatters on the Perspex are from the gunner who was fatally injured in combat on 18 August 1940.
(Andy Saunders collection)

LEFT **The pilot of this StG 51 Ju 87 B hands the MG 15 machine gun to his gunner to install in its flexible mounting. The pilot wears a seat-type Sitzfallschirm (parachute). The single flexible-mount MG 15 machine gun was not much of a deterrent to any would-be attacker. Its arc of fire was seriously hampered by the Stuka's large tailplane.**
(Copyright unknown)

Rheinmetall-Borsig MG 17 machine gun (Ju 87 A, B, R)

The fixed-mounting partner to the MG 15, Rheinmetall-Borsig's 7.92mm machine gun was mainly used as forward-firing offensive armament, which is how it equipped the Ju 87 with one weapon mounted inside each wing. Pneumatically fired by the pilot from a button on top of the control column using compressed air from rechargeable bottles located inside the wing, the MG 17 was belt-fed with 1,000 rounds per gun from ammunition boxes inside the wing.

Mauser MG 81Z (Zwilling) machine gun (Ju 87 D and G)

Introduced on the Ju 87 D-1 from 1942, a pair of MG 81Z (Zwilling) 7.92mm Waffenfabrik-Mauser machine guns offered increased protection and a high rate of fire. They were mounted on the rotating metal turret ring of the GSL-k 81Z (Gleitschienenlafette, klein, 81Z). Weighing 12.9kg, the guns were manually operated by the gunner from either a seated or standing position and could be traversed through 40° to the left and right, elevated by 70° and depressed by 15°. They were sighted using the Visiereinrichtung VE 42. The installation was enclosed in a metal-framed Plexiglas cupola with an armoured cap on the top. Inside the cupola were sliding armoured shutters (Panzerschilde) on each side to give further protection to the gunner. The MG 81Z was fed with 1,000 rounds of belt-fed ammunition per barrel and had a theoretical rate of fire of 3,200 rounds/min, with a muzzle velocity of 705 to 875m/sec.

BELOW Mauser MG 81Z (Zwilling) twin machine gun installation in a Ju 87 D with armoured shutters and cap. *(Copyright unknown)*

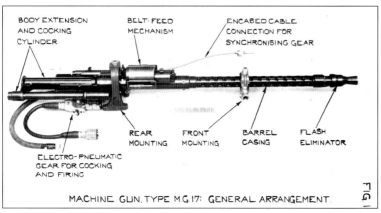

MACHINE GUN, TYPE M.G.17: GENERAL ARRANGEMENT.

FIG. I

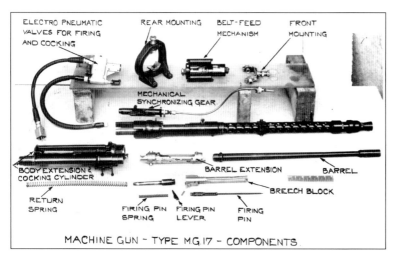

MACHINE GUN - TYPE M.G.17 - COMPONENTS

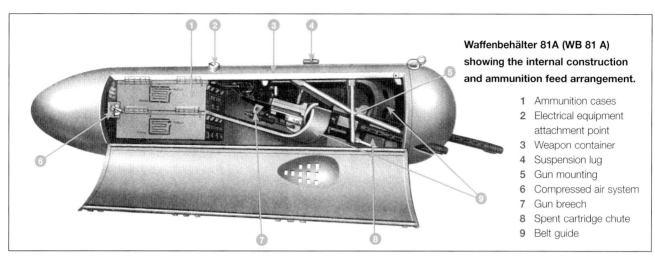

Waffenbehälter 81A (WB 81 A) showing the internal construction and ammunition feed arrangement.

1 Ammunition cases
2 Electrical equipment attachment point
3 Weapon container
4 Suspension lug
5 Gun mounting
6 Compressed air system
7 Gun breech
8 Spent cartridge chute
9 Belt guide

Mauser MG 151/20 20mm cannon (Ju 87 D)

Manufactured by Waffenfabrik-Mauser, the MG 151/20 cannon was used widely by the Luftwaffe on its fighters, fighter-bombers and ground-attack aircraft including later versions of the Stuka. From early 1943 onwards Ju 87 Ds carried a pair of MG 151/20s, one in each wing. The single-barrel automatic cannon with its electric priming and 20mm rounds could penetrate 10–12mm of armour at 300m and at an attack angle of 60°. With its metre-long barrel and a rate of fire of 740 rounds/min, the MG 151 had an effective range of 1km. When fitted to the Stuka in the ground-attack role it was a formidable weapon with a muzzle velocity of 805m/sec (with M-Geschoss – high-explosive shells) and 705m/sec (with HE-T – HE plus incendiary, AP – armour-piercing).

Waffenbehälter WB 81A and WB 81B weapon containers (Ju 87 D)

An effective weapon against the masses of Russian infantry on the open Steppe of the Eastern Front was the Waffenbehälter (WB) 81A or B weapon container (or gun pod) mounted on the Ju 87 D's under-wing bomb racks. The WB 81 was the same shape and dimensions as a 500kg bomb.

Six MG 81Z 7.92mm Mauser machine guns were carried in two WB 81A or WB 81B pods. Nicknamed the Gießkanne or 'watering can', each pod held three twin MG 81Z machine guns (making a total of six guns per pod) aligned to fire downwards at different, set, angles for low-level ground strafing.

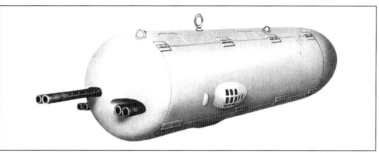

ABOVE Waffenbehälter 81B (WB 81B) with mounting eyelet. *(Junkers)*

BELOW Internal views of the WB 81B showing the location of guns and ammunition feeds. *(Junkers)*

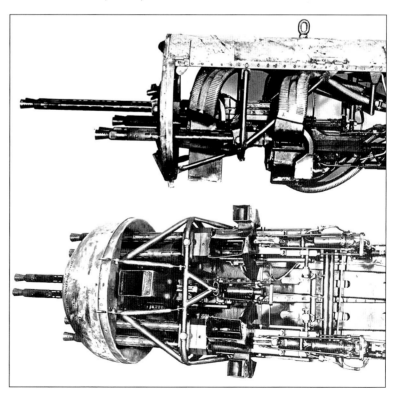

'Kanonenvogel': a Ju 87 G-1 of 10.(Pz)/ SG 3 Panzerjäger carrying a pair of BK 37 'Panzerknacker' underneath its wings.
(Bundesarchiv)

The guns in the WB 81A pod had a 15° inclination downward (relative to the aircraft's longitudinal axis), while those in the WB 81B were parallel to the aircraft's axis (that is, they had neutral inclination). They could be attached to fire either forward or behind the direction of flight. Each pod carried 250 rounds of ammunition per gun (total 1,500 rounds) and weighed 140kg (empty) and 180kg with a full supply of ammunition. The guns were fired electro-pneumatically using compressed air from two air bottles.

Bordkanone (BK) 37 auto-cannon (Ju 87 G)

With a pair of the formidable Bordkanone (BK) 37 slung beneath its wings, as a specialised tank hunter on the Eastern Front the Ju 87 G assumed what many would consider to be the dive-bomber's ultimate – although unrepresentative – form. It was known by its nickname, the 'Panzerknacker', or 'tank cracker'.

Although used in relatively small numbers, the BK 37-armed Ju 87 G achieved notoriety in the air on a par with the Tiger I tank on the ground, and it remained in action by day until the end of the war.

In May 1942, Inspector General of the Luftwaffe Erhard Milch ordered that ground-attack aircraft, including the Ju 87 D, should receive more powerful fixed armament. Owing to the narrow internal dimensions of the Stuka's wing, any heavier weapons would have to be carried underneath the wings. But re-equipment was slow and it took almost a year for the

first 25 Ju 87 G-1s to be fitted with the BK 37 cannon – a potent weapon, but too few in number when pitted against the massive resurgence in Soviet armour and its rapid advance westwards.

Based on an earlier design by Rheinmetall-Borsig (the 3.7cm Flak 18 anti-aircraft gun) the BK 37 auto cannon weighed in at over 355kg (800lb) and was attached to the under-wing bomb stations as a self-contained gun pod. It was a recoil-loading automatic weapon with an equivalent rate of fire of 160 rounds/min and a muzzle velocity with armour-piercing (APHE) ammunition that exceeded 840m/sec (2,790ft/sec). The gun was fed by 2 clips of 6 rounds each (there was also the option for clips of 8 and 12 rounds).

The weapon was electrically operated from the cockpit and the firing mechanism in each gun was controlled by compressed air. Electrical wiring of the previously installed MG 17 was reused in the first 12 Gustavs fitted with the BK 37, but all subsequent aircraft benefited from a brand new wiring installation.

Both guns were switched on together at the dedicated control panel on the lower right-hand side of the instrument panel (which replaced the bomb panel of the B, R and D variants), their live status indicated by the display of two symbols on the panel, and both weapons were fired simultaneously by the pilot pressing the fire button on the control column. However, in the event of a weapon failure it was still possible to fire the one independently of the other.

RIGHT Electrical and pneumatic system connections from the aircraft to the gun pod can be seen on the left. On the right above the gun barrel is the fairing containing the air heater for the gun.

To prevent frozen snow and ice from causing stoppages in the low-slung BK 37, an air heater was incorporated into each gun pack to warm the gun mechanism. A streamlined fairing containing a heater and combustion chamber was fitted underneath the wings inboard of each gun pod, which was fed with air and fuel. Cool air was drawn in through an intake on the front of the fairing where it entered the combustion chamber and was combined with fuel and the mixture was ignited by an electronic spark plug. The hot gas was then piped to the gun mechanism.

Used in top attacks against the relatively thin upper turret and engine compartment armour of Soviet tanks, the BK 37 scored devastating hits with its Panzergranatpatronen (armour-piercing high explosive – APHE) and Hartkernmunition (hard core) shells. The most effective ordnance was the latter (usually referred to as armour-piercing composite rigid – or APCR), which had a penetrating core of tungsten carbide sheathed in a light alloy shell with a sharply pointed profile. Hartkernmunition could penetrate up to

ABOVE BK 37 barrel with streamlined nose fairing removed revealing the recoil mechanism and electrical firing connections.

BELOW The BK 37 without its fairings.

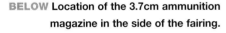

BELOW Location of the 3.7cm ammunition magazine in the side of the fairing.

'PANZERKNACKER' IN ACTION – LEUTNANT ERICH WITTOR, PANZERGRENADIER REGIMENT 'KURMARK'

On 2 February 1945 Leutnant Erich Wittor's armoured reconnaissance battalion received orders to take Trettin, a village east of Frankfurt an der Oder, but it was found to be occupied by Soviet tanks. To attack across open ground, without artillery support and in their lightly armoured vehicles, was suicidal. But, as Wittor commented, 'a soldier has to have luck', and this was forthcoming in the guise of Stukas equipped with BK 37 'Panzerknacker' cannon.

Suddenly we heard aircraft approaching. 'Stukas!' I shouted. 'Get out the identification panels!' We did not want to be attacked by our own aircraft.

They flew at medium height over us and banked round over Trettin. The village was flown over once more and then, with the next flight, we witnessed a unique display with deadly results for the enemy. From medium height the first machine flipped over on its wings and dived down with an ear-splitting noise. Was it the rush of air, or a switched-on siren, or both?

The dive was aimed straight at the village, the pilot only pulling up again just short of the rooftops. One would have thought he

ABOVE Leutnant Erich Wittor of Panzergrenadier Regiment 'Kurmark' witnessed the 'Panzerknacker' in action in the final months of fighting on the Eastern Front. *(via Tony Le Tissier)*

would crash into the houses, he was so close. Shortly before pulling up again he fired a single shot from his cannon, but the result was devastating.

A stab of flame shot up like an explosion and black smoke rose up into the sky between the houses. 'He's got a T-34!' we cried, for we were quite certain. Meanwhile, the other two aircraft had done the same, diving and firing their cannon, and two more Soviet tanks were on fire.

Once they had climbed up again, they banked round once more and dived down on Trettin. The T-34s stood no chance against this attack from the air. They were not camouflaged from above and insufficiently armoured, and so could be destroyed one after the other by our Stukas. We were particularly impressed by the accuracy of the leading aircraft, which only fired one shot each time and each time scored a hit. Our delight was indescribable.

Meanwhile, the Stukas had destroyed eight or nine enemy tanks . . . after their last attack the Stukas flew over us waggling their wings. That was the signal they had finished their job and now it was up to us.

BELOW The Ju 87 'Kanonenvogel' in flight was a slower and less manoeuvrable aircraft than its predecessors from the Ju 87 stable, but it was arguably the most deadly when it came to close air-support on the battlefield. *(Copyright unknown)*

BELOW With its engine compartment well ablaze, this Russian T-34 was caught in the open and destroyed, possibly the victim of a 'Kanonenvogel's' lethal BK 37 cannon. *(Bundesarchiv)*

140mm of armour at a striking angle of 90°, or 70mm at 60°.

As with the MG 151/20 cannon, Minengeschosspatronen (mine shells) high-capacity shells were also used with the BK 37. These had thinner walls than conventional HE ammunition shells and contained much larger quantities of explosive filler. After the war several countries copied the design for their own aircraft armament, including shells for Britain's ADEN cannon.

Also effective when used against non-armoured ground targets were Brandsprenggranatpatronen (high-explosive/incendiary) HE rounds with an incendiary filling.

The greatest exponent of the BK 37-armed Ju 87 G-1 was Hans-Ulrich Rudel, who had this to say about how the cannon affected the Stuka's performance:

The Ju 87, which is not any too fast of itself, now becomes even slower and is unfavourably affected by the load of the cannon it carries. Its manoeuvrability is disadvantageously reduced and its landing speed is increased considerably. But now [1943] armament potency is a prior consideration over flying performance.

Gunsights (Reflexvisier)
The 'Revi'
Located on top of the instrument panel coaming, the Carl Zeiss Revi C/12C gunsight was the standard German fighter reflector gunsight during the early to mid-war period and was used on the Ju 87 in conjunction with the fixed forward-firing armament. Early Ju 87 As used the Revi 2B; Ju 87 B and R the Revi C/12C; Ju 87 D the C/12C or D. Gun firing was achieved by the EPAD 17 electrical trigger mechanism.

For night operations later in the war the Ju 87's standard Revi C/12D gunsight was replaced with the Nachtrevi ('Nightrevi') C/12N. On some Ju 87 Ds and Gs the Revi C/16D, suited for low-trajectory gun firing, was exchanged for the Nachtrevi C/16D.

Bombs (Bomben)
German bombs were designated according to their weight in kilogrammes; for example: SC 50 was the 50kg version of the Sprengbombe-

ABOVE Revi C/12C gunsight in a Ju 87 B during the Battle of Britain period. *(Andy Saunders collection)*

BELOW
Schwarzmänner prepare to load a 250kg bomb on to a Ju 87 B-2 during the Battle of France in May 1940. Centreline bombs always had the suspension band fitted before being loaded. This provided a 'lug' on either side, which engaged with the swing-down bomb trapeze mechanism. *(Andy Saunders collection)*

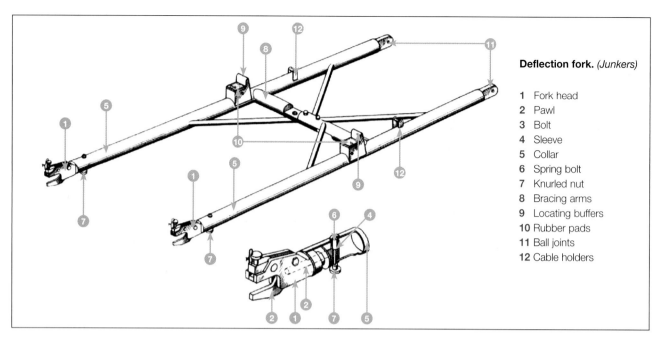

Deflection fork. *(Junkers)*

1 Fork head
2 Pawl
3 Bolt
4 Sleeve
5 Collar
6 Spring bolt
7 Knurled nut
8 Bracing arms
9 Locating buffers
10 Rubber pads
11 Ball joints
12 Cable holders

Cylindrisch. For heavier bombs in the Luftwaffe's arsenal names were also applied, such as the 1800 SC 'Satan'. They came in the following weights: 10, 50, 250, 500, 1,000 and 1,800kg.

On all marks of Ju 87 dive-bombers the largest bomb was always carried under the fuselage. It was provided with a displacement apparatus (also known as a deflector fork or 'trapeze') that engaged with lugs on the cylindrical body of the bomb in order to swing it away from the fuselage and so ensure clearance of the propeller arc during a diving release.

If forced to abort an attack, it was possible for a Stuka pilot to safely pull his aircraft out of a dive with the bombload still in place, but when carrying heavier weapons like the 1,000kg bomb the flare-out was limited to 3g.

The deflector fork or 'trapeze' apparatus under the fuselage was designed to accommodate different sizes of bomb. It was marked along its side with the locating positions for particular weapons. The following table lists those for the Ju 87 B-1, B-2, R-1 and R-2:

The Ju 87 could carry up to 1,800kg of bombs externally in various load configurations that varied, depending on the aircraft mark, aircraft role, theatre of operations and the year of the war. This was the choice available to Stuka units in the Battle of Britain in 1940:

- 1 × 1800 SC
- or 1 × 1400 PC
- or 1 × 1000 SC and 2 × 250kg
- or 1 × 1000 SC and 4 × 50kg
- or 1 × 500kg and 4 × 50kg
- or 1 × 250kg and 4 × 50kg

Key SC Sprengbombe-Cylindrische
Thin-cased general-purpose bomb
SD Sprengbombe-Dickwandig
Thick-cased semi-armour-piercing fragmentation bomb
PC Panzerbombe-Cylindrisch
Armour-piercing bomb

During 1940, Stuka crews were advised to observe the following minimum safety heights when dropping bombs armed with Type 5 and Type 15 impact fuses. This was to stop the aircraft from getting caught in the blast from the exploding munitions:

- SC 50 – not below 600m
- SC 250 – not below 825m
- SC 500 – not below 1,090m.

Fork position	1	2	3	4
Fork width	420mm	524mm	540mm	628mm
Fits for	SC 250	SC 500	PC 1000	SD 1000
	PC 500	SD 500	–	–
		Flam C 500		

PC 500 RS, PC 1000 RS – the 'Raketen-Panzerbomben'

The armour-piercing PC 500 ('Pauline') and PC 1000 RS ('Paul') Raketen Satz (rocket-propelled) bombs were designed for use primarily against shipping targets, with the rocket motor increasing the terminal velocity and armour penetration qualities of the bomb.

Using a standard AP bomb, a coupling attached the rocket container to the bomb's tail. A time fuse delayed the start of the solid fuel rocket motor to prevent any damage to the aircraft. The bomb could reach speeds of up to 345m/sec on impact when dropped from 2,000m, making it possible to smash armour plate on tanks and ships. Most of these weapons were used in 1941 against shipping in the Mediterranean.

Bomb-release gear (Abwurfgeräte)

The Ju 87 B-1, B-2 and R versions carried a single ETC 500/IX rack on the fuselage underside with electrical or mechanical release for either a 250kg or 500kg bomb; under each wing was a pair of ETC 50/VIII racks, each rack carrying a single 50kg bomb. The release mechanism was electrically operated by a push-button (Auslösedruckknopf KG-12A on Ju 87 B) on the pilot's control column, but in the event of a failure the bombs could be released mechanically.

For the Ju 87 D it was a slightly different arrangement. On the fuselage underside was a universal Schloß 1000/500 XI B bomb rack that could accept either a 500/XII C bomb ejector for 250kg or 500kg bombs, or a 2000 XIII type ejector for 1,000kg or 1,800kg weapons. Underneath the wings the two weapons stations carried either a Schloß 1000/500/IX B bomb rack with a 500/XII C ejector for a 250kg bomb, or two ETC 50/VIIIe ejectors for 50kg bombs. Each weapon station was contained inside a streamlined fairing.

Ju 87 Ds were fitted with electric bomb-selector switches. Bomb fusing and salvo pattern were controlled from a switching panel on the right side of the pilot's instrument panel. The options were for a full load release, single or combinations of bombs.

ABOVE ETC 50/VIII under-wing racks were each able to carry one 50kg bomb. *(Chris Goss collection)*

LEFT Detail of the Schloßlafette fairing on a Ju 87 D-5, loaded with 50kg bombs fitted with tail-screamers. *(SA-Kuva)*

RIGHT
Jericho trumpet,
which was powered
by the small propeller
attached to the
undercarriage leg.
(Copyright unknown)

If the scream of the Stuka's Jumo engine at full throttle and the crump of exploding bombs was not enough to make enemy troops break and run in panic, then the addition of 'Jericho trumpets' and bomb 'tail-screamers' added two more layers of terror to the cacophony.

The Stuka legend was inextricably linked to the dive-bomber's banshee howl, which was recognised early on by Luftwaffe General Ernst Udet who came up with the idea of fitting a wind-driven siren to each undercarriage leg. Powered by a small propeller attached to a bullet-shaped fairing, the siren added to the psychological distress and fear created by a Stuka attack. The pilot turned the propellers on or off via an electric switch in the cockpit, switching them on before the dive commenced and before the dive brakes were extended. They were turned off after the pull-out and once the aircraft had slowed to 200mph.

Another layer of terror was added with a simple cardboard whistle, or 'tail-screamer', which was attached to a bomb's tailfins. These were open-ended tubes shaped like organ pipes or tin whistles, measuring approximately 350mm × 38mm (14in × 1.5in). Air entered the tube as the bomb fell, creating a screaming noise as it passed across the lip.

BELOW A collection of 50kg and 250kg bombs ready for loading on to Ju 87s at Kemijärvi airfield in Lapland on 15 September 1941. Note the small 'tail-screamer' whistles on the smaller bombs. Some 1,800 years earlier Roman troops used a similar device to strike fear into their enemies with 'whistling' sling bullets drilled with 5mm holes. Researchers believe they were designed to give the soaring missiles a sharp buzzing or whistling noise in flight. *(SA-Kuva)*

Dive-bombing sight (Sturzvisier)

The Sturzvisier dive-bombing sight (commonly abbreviated to Stuvi) was an electrically operated analogue optical sighting device that was designed especially for use in dive-bombing. It was fitted into the roof of the pilot's cockpit in the upper front windscreen above the instrument panel in most versions of the Ju 87, from the B-series through to D. On some Doras the Stuvi was hinged up into a small Plexiglas bubble at the top of the windscreen.

Manufactured by Zeiss-Ikon, it calculated the angle between the longitudinal axis of the aircraft and the sight-line to the point of impact of the bomb. To compute the correct moment of bomb-release, it used manually input data for bombing height, angle of dive, airspeed, wind speed, air pressure above sea level (ASL) of the target and target height ASL.

When it was needed, the pilot hinged the Stuvi sight into its operational position, switching it on to activate the internal light and gyroscope. The aiming reticle appeared on the rectangular ground glass screen following data input and was placed on target. When not in use the site was rotated 90° to the right to avoid blocking the pilot's forward view.

(The Stuvi was also used in twin-engine aircraft like the Ju 88, Do 217 and Me 410 in conjunction with the Bombenziel-Anlage (BZA) analogue computer when they were operating in the dive-bombing role. The BZA was not fitted in the Ju 87 owing to its size and weight.)

Despite such sophisticated sighting equipment the Ju 87 also had a belt-and-braces aid to help the pilot calculate his dive angle. Lines (similar to those on a mathematical protractor) were marked on the pilot's section of the Plexiglas cockpit canopy. This usually took the form of four short intersecting lines on the side canopy next to the pilot's head, with each angle identified by colour: 40° in red, 50° in black, 60° in white, 70° in brown. The pilot put the aircraft into a dive and aligned the selected angle marking with the general horizon.

Anti-personnel fragmentation bombs

With the retreat of the German Army on all fronts after 1943 the close air-support of

LEFT The Sturzvisier (or Stuvi) optical dive-bombing sight. *(Author's collection)*

ABOVE LEFT AND LEFT Location detail for the Stuvi dive-bombing sight showing the device in its stowed position (left) and the Plexiglas bubble in the top of the windscreen (above left) to accommodate the sight's body. *(SA-Kuva)*

Sturzvisier targeting schematic. *(Junkers)*

1 Bomb release point
2 Flight path
3 Vertical plane
4 Line of sight
5 Bomb path
6 Aircraft's longitudinal axis
7 Flight path
8 Target in the sights

about 6°

Sight

Bomb release point

Sighting angle

Direction of flight

ground troops became ever more vital. During the winter of 1943/44 the role of supporting German tank-hunters on the Eastern Front (which included the Ju 87 G alongside the Hs 129 and Fw 190) assumed a growing importance and it fell to the Ju 87 D-5 armed with anti-personnel weapons. The use of small hollow-charge bombs like the SD 4 HL dropped on tank assembly areas, and lethal SD 2 'Butterfly' bomblets released from low level to suppress enemy flak positions, were strikingly effective.

Splitterbombe SD 2 'Butterfly'

As an anti-personnel weapon the 2kg ground-attack 'bomblet' was dropped in a steel Abwurfbehälter (drop container) that held 23 or more of these deadly little bombs. Abwurfbehälter came in a range of sizes – AB 50 (50kg), AB 70 (70kg), AB 250 (250kg) and AB 500 (500kg). The number suffixes were for the weight in kg of the filled container.

The containers were carried on the Stuka's under-wing bomb racks and fitted with an air-

LEFT Schwarzmänner winch an AB 250 bomblet container into position under the fuselage of an StG 3 Ju 87 D-5 at Dorpat on 9 March 1944. *(BA 101I-726-0224-26A)*

LEFT A Ju 87 B of
StG 77 carrying under-
wing 50kg bombs
fitted with 'Dinortstab'
percussion rods. *(Chris
Goss collection)*

burst fuse that blew them open at a pre-set
height, releasing and scattering the bomblets,
which became armed as they fell by a pair
of rudimentary hinged wings that hinged out
and rotated in flight like a sycamore seed.
The bomblets could be fused to explode on
or before impact, while others were fitted with
delayed action or anti-disturbance fuses.

fuse touched the ground it detonated the
bomb. Because of the risk of the rod fouling
the propeller, Dinortstäbe were seldom fitted
to the main under-fuselage 500kg bombs.
A development of the Dinortstab was later
used by the Americans in Vietnam where
it acquired the nickname 'daisy cutter' for
obvious reasons.

Splitterbombe SD 4 HL

With its super-fast impact fuse the 4kg SD
4 HL hollow charge bomb was vastly more
effective than larger conventional free-fall
weapons and proved highly effective against
troop concentrations and vehicles. As with
the SD 2, the SD 4 HL was carried in under-
wing containers – 74 bombs in the AB 500-1
container, 40 bombs in the AB 250.

Dinortstab percussion rods

The brainchild of one of the earliest members
of the Stuka arm, 'Onkel Oskar' Dinort,
veteran Kommodore of StG 2 'Immelmann',
the Dinortstab was a fuse designed to
detonate a bomb at or above ground level
(for maximum scatter effect) to prevent it from
burying itself in the ground before exploding.
The fuse itself was a long rod-like probe
fixed to the nose caps of under-wing and
under-fuselage bombs. When the tip of the

LEFT Oskar Dinort,
inventor of the
'Dinortstab'. He was
the first dive-bomber
pilot of the war to
receive the Knight's
Cross with Oak
Leaves. *(Copyright
unknown)*

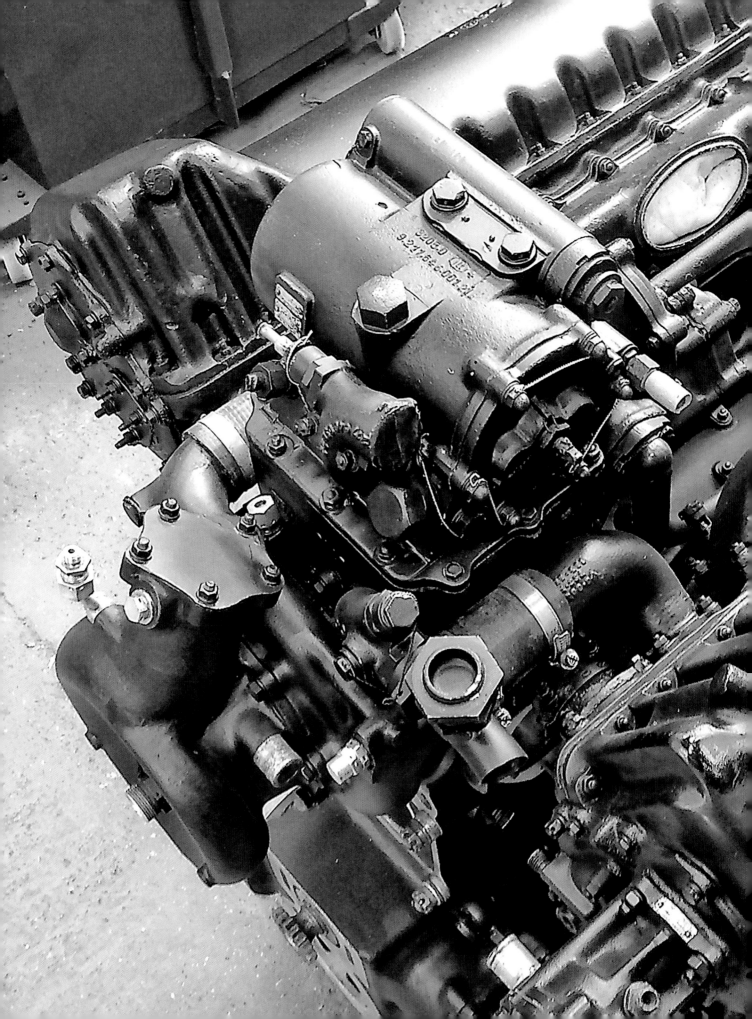

Chapter Three

Junkers Jumo 211 series

Built in greater number than any other German aero engine of the Second World War, the Jumo 211 was a robust and dependable power plant in the Ju 87. A succession of upgrades in the early war years resulted in the 211 being able to operate at much higher power settings, but its increased weight led to a reduction in the Stuka's operating performance.

OPPOSITE The Junkers Jumo 211J powered the Ju 87 as well as its stablemate the Ju 88. This rare example was recovered from the wreck of a Ju 88 D-1 that crashed in Norway in 1943. It has been restored by the Wings Museum at Redhill, Surrey. *(Wings Museum)*

ABOVE Fitters inspect the Jumo 211 engine of a Ju 87 B on 22 December 1939. Note the engine bearer, oil tank installation on top of the engine and the hose connected to the lubricating oil filler.
(BA 101I-378-0037-16A)

Between the wars both Junkers and the Bosch company had amassed large amounts of experience building diesel engines and injection pumps respectively. Junkers was alone among aero engine builders to have mass-produced diesels – the Jumo 205 (600–880hp) and the turbocharged 1,000hp 207. The two companies honed their skills in the precision engineering that was required for making diesel engines and injection pumps with the consequence that, when war came in 1939, they were already set up for mass production.

RIGHT The Daimler-Benz DB 601 engine as fitted in the Messerschmitt Bf 109.
(Black 6 Team)

Moreover, their experience enabled the German aircraft industry to select direct petrol injection for the Luftwaffe's other high-power aero engines. During the Battle of Britain in 1940 the outcome of this choice is well documented when it came to negative g manoeuvres in dogfights. The fuel-injected Daimler-Benz DB 601 engine of the Bf 109 was immune to the effects of negative g when pitted in combat against Spitfires and Hurricanes with their float carburettors, when their Merlin engines cut out in dives owing to momentary fuel starvation.

Paradoxically, while the Germans had mastered the craft of designing and building high-quality aero engines, they conservatively rated them so that when compared to the British Rolls-Royce Merlin installations in the Hurricane and Spitfire they gave the impression of being unwieldy and heavy. However, German liquid-cooled engines never quite matched the performance of the smaller Merlin.

The Jumo 211 engine described

The Junkers Jumo 211 was the principal German bomber engine of the Second World War, being used in the company's Ju 87 and Ju 88 aircraft, as well as in the Heinkel He 111 H-series of bombers. It became the most-produced German aero engine of the war with 68,248 examples built between 1937 and 1944 at factories in Magdeburg, Köthen, Leipzig, Stettin and Strasburg. Wartime production reached a peak in autumn 1942 with 1,700 engines a month.

In common with the other main aero engine series built by the Germans, the Daimler-Benz (DB) 601, 603 and 605, the Jumo 211 and its derivative the 213 were both inverted liquid-cooled V-12 engines with cast blocks and poppet valves (two inlet and one exhaust per cylinder). The coolant mixture was fairly standard at 47% water, 50% Glysantin (the German trade name for ethylene glycol) and 3% anti-corrosion oil. Like the Daimler-Benz engines, the Jumos had direct fuel injection and a supercharger mounted on the (right) side driven by a transverse shaft located at the rear of the engine. Most Jumos had a two-speed geared drive, unlike the DB engines with their variable hydraulic drive.

A succession of upgrades began in 1940 in a move to make the Jumo 211 engine more competitive with the DB 601 that was the main contender to power the Luftwaffe's aircraft. With a pressurised cooling system the resulting 211E proved to be able to run at much higher power settings without overheating and was

BELOW With its 1,400hp Jumo 211J engine warmed up to operating temperature, the pilot of this Ju 87 D-5 prepares to climb into the cockpit and strap in before taking off on a ground-attack mission on the Eastern Front during December 1944. The new design of the 211J allowed an aerodynamically cleaner installation than with the 211A and D models of the Anton and Berta, doing away with the big chin coolant radiator and replacing it with a pair of under-wing radiators. In its place was a small oil cooler fitted in a much neater and smaller chin. Note the 250kg under-wing bombs with Dinortstab and the weapon container under the fuselage centreline. *(BA 101I-665-6814-07)*

Jumo 211B and D –
front view.

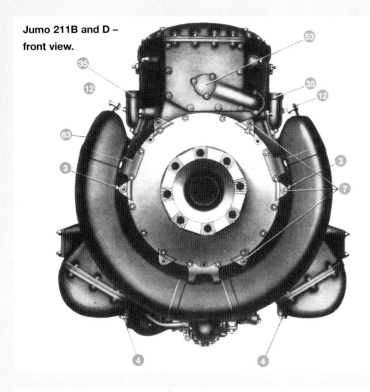

Jumo 211B and D –
rear view.

The Junkers Ju 87 B-1, R-2 and R-3 were fitted
with the Jumo 211D engine. *(Junkers)*

1 Engine bearer mounting points
2 Engine support points
3 Levelling points
4 Stop-feet on rocker box covers
5 Stop foot on fuel filter
6 Hoisting eye
7 Threaded holes on gearbox cover
8 Auxiliary eyes on engine housing (rear)
9 Auxiliary eyes on engine housing (middle)
10 Airscrew attachment point
11 Coolant system pressure gauge attachment point
12 Pressure relief valves
13 Filler pipe
14 Oil supply line inlet
15 Temperature gauge connection and oil supply line inlet
16 Oil return line
17 Temperature gauge connection and oil supply line inlet
18 Oil pressure gauge connection
19 Oil drain valve
20 Hydraulic oil connection for airscrew constant speed unit
21 Return oil flow from airscrew constant speed unit
22 Lubrication and pressure relief valve
23 Non-return valve
24 Ratchet for oil filter
25 Oil filter for reduction gearbox
26 Oil reservoir breather pipe
27 Swivelling high pressure connector
28 Fuel filter plug
29 Vacuum connector for pre-feed fuel pump
30 Pressure regulator on pre-feed fuel pump
31 Fuel pressure gauge
32 Fuel pressure relief valve
33 Junkers dual-injection pump
34 Exhaust openings

35 Pressure relief ducting for engine housing
36 Throttle control
37 Throttle stop screw
38 Manual control lever on automatic gearbox
39 Stop device
40 Supercharger intake with protective mesh
41 Bleed valve on boost pipe
42 Auxiliary outlet from supercharger
43 Air bleed connection
44 Connection for Bosch inertia starter
45 Bosch high-tension magneto GE12 (exhaust side spark plug connections)
46 HT cable
47 Power take-off with rubber drive belt
48 Power take-off for pressure or vacuum pump
49 Drive for engine rpm counter
50 Rotational speed sensor
51 Unused auxiliary drive
52 Power take-off for airscrew governor
53 Crankshaft cover attachment for dead-centre measuring device for ignition timing
54 Tie rod for engine housing (x 8)
55 Coolant injection holes (one for every cylinder on either side of the engine)
56 Oil filter for gearbox
57 Mounting flange for engine-mounted cannon or airscrew regulator
58 Lever adjustment switch
59 Lever adjustment
60 External access to automatic gearbox
61 Rocker arm for rich mixture
62 Plug lead harness
63 Coolant header tank
64 Boost pipe

**Jumo 211B and D –
left side view.**

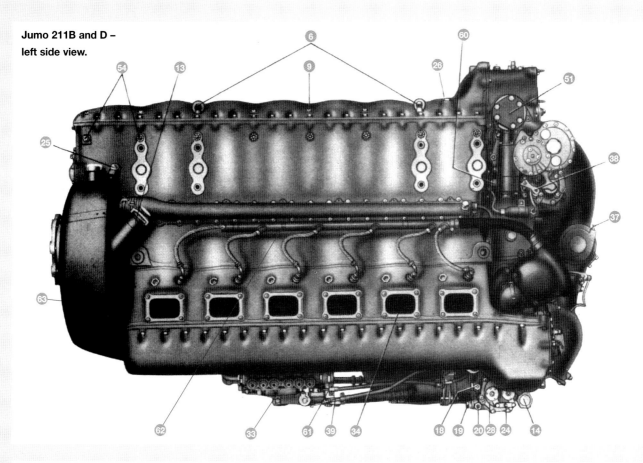

**Jumo 211B and D –
right side view.**

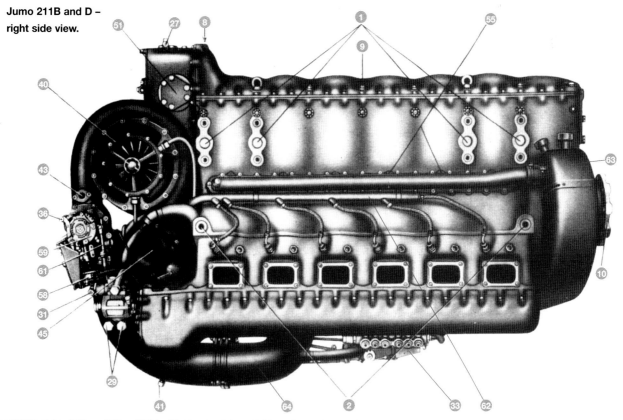

ABOVE Jumo 211F,
side view. *(Wikimedia*
Commons/Kogo)

BELOW Jumo 211F,
front view. *(Wikimedia*
Commons/Kogo)

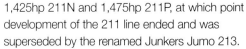

soon followed by the 211F, which featured a strengthened crankshaft and more efficient supercharger, while the 211J built on these improvements by adding an intercooler. Running at 2,600rpm the 211F and similar J engines delivered a much-improved 1,350hp. Further improvements to the 211 design led to the

1,425hp 211N and 1,475hp 211P, at which point development of the 211 line ended and was superseded by the renamed Junkers Jumo 213.

The downside to the heavier and more powerful Jumo engines was that they added to the Ju 87's gross weight and led to a reduction in its operating performance – rising from 4,300kg with the B-1 to 5,600kg (R-2) and 6,450kg with the D-1. Time to climb to 3,000m increased from 7 minutes with the B-1 to 16 minutes (R-2) and 22 minutes with the D-1, while the service ceiling and range dropped from 7,200m/850km to 5,800m/1,210km and 4,200m/800km respectively.

Kraftei – the power-egg

The Jumo was probably the first German aero engine to apply the Kraftei (power-egg) concept, which was a fully unitised modular engine installation that included the engine and all its ancillary equipment and systems. A Kraftei engine could be quickly and easily removed and replaced on compatible aircraft using standardised quick-change attachment points and connectors. There were two versions of the Kraftei – the Motoranlage, using additional specialised components depending

on the airframe it was to be fitted on; and the Triebwerksanlage, which was a more comprehensive unitisation that often included exhaust and oil cooling apparatus.

Britain was also an innovator and user of the power-egg. Both the Bristol Aeroplane Company and Rolls-Royce developed their own unitised installations to receive the Hercules and Merlin engines respectively. The United States aero engine industry was not so involved and only the Pratt & Whitney Twin Wasp radial engine power-egg was developed, but this was not in use until 1945.

General description

The liquid-cooled 12-cylinder 60° inverted-V Jumo 211A engine powered the first Ju 87 B-series aircraft in 1939. It was fitted with a two-speed supercharger, with direct-fuel injection into the cylinders and spark ignition. The three-bladed Junkers VS11 propeller was driven through spur reduction gearing, with both driving and driven gears splined to the shafts and centralised by split bronze cones. The driven shaft was mounted on a roller race at the rear, and on a combined roller and thrust race at the front housing cover. Auxiliaries and

ABOVE The Jumo Kraftei or 'power-egg'. Utilising a unitised modular installation reduced the amount of time that was needed for a complete engine change, a particularly important consideration when a Stuka unit was on campaign and operating away from airfields with full engineering facilities. *(Alamy D40PRJ)*

LEFT Auxiliary gearbox. *(Wings Museum)*

LEFT A Schwartzmann hand-cranks the Jumo 211J on a Ju 87 D in Finland, June 1944. *(SA-Kuva)*

accessories were driven through a train of gears in a wheelcase at the rear of the engine. A combination of hand-cranking Bosch inertia starter or an electric starter using a ground power source via the outboard connector was also fitted. The dry weight of the engine (ie with no fluids) was 640kg (1,408lb).

Engine housing

The engine housing was cast in light alloy as one single piece and consisted of the crankcase and two cylinder blocks in an inverted-V shape. The reduction gear housing was bolted to the front face; at the rear the wheelcase and supercharger casing were flanged to the engine.

The upper part of the crankcase was enclosed with a light alloy cover plate. The crankshaft bearing eyes were located on the two long sides of the crankcase, of which the first two and the last two were designed as engine mounts. The four mounting points were

THE INVERTED-V

Why did the German aero engine industry favour the inverted-V configuration? Ian Craighead, Head of Corporate Heritage and Chief Executive of the Rolls-Royce Heritage Trust, reviews some possible explanations:

Cyril Lovesey, the chief development engineer on the Rolls-Royce Merlin in the late 1930s, claimed that during a German Air Ministry visit to Derby in the early '30s the delegation saw a wooden mock-up of the PV12 (precursor to the Merlin), which was originally intended as an inverted V-12. They concluded that if Rolls-Royce were contemplating their next high-power engine to be an inverted vee then the new German engines would be built the same way. It has never been conclusively proven, though. It may also just have been a directive from the German Air Ministry that inline engines should be inverted.

The main advantage with an inverted-V is that the configuration allows a better view over the nose for the pilot – as in the Messerschmitt Bf 109, for example – but it doesn't explain why the Bf 110 and Heinkel

He 111 engines were also inverted. With the inverted configuration there are oil scavenge issues as well as oil temperature problems, but heat transfer to the oil does help with piston cooling.

The Rolls-Royce Kestrels that were supplied to Messerschmitt and Junkers for the first prototypes must have infuriated their designers, but once the DB 600 and Jumo motors were fit to fly they retained the configuration without reversing the arrangement to an upright vee.

Ironically, the Hispano Buchon version of the Bf 109 never received sufficient Daimler engines before Germany's defeat and so it was fitted with Merlin engines after the war, which made the Buchon look ungainly without the inverted engine.

Argus Motorenwerke also designed and built a series of inverted-V engines that were used in a number of German military aircraft types – the Argus As 10 V-8 powered the Fieseler Storch, while the As 410 and 411 V-12s were used in the Arado Ar 96, Focke-Wulf Fw 189 and Henschel Hs 129.

arranged in pairs on each side between the upper and the horizontal heads.

Wheelcase

The wheelcase was an aluminium casting bolted to the rear of the crankcase. It housed 18 accessory drives including two camshafts, one generator, two magnetos, one supercharger, three oil scavenge pumps, one oil pump, one vacuum pump, one tachometer, one starter, one injection pump, one fuel pump, one coolant pump and two unused auxiliary drives. All drives were taken from the end of the crankshaft through a short driveshaft and all gears had both their bearings contained inside the wheelcase so that alignment was not disturbed when the case was removed.

Engine mounting

The engine bearer was removable and was bolted to the fuselage firewall with five ball screw connections allowing easy removal of the engine, complete with its mounting. It consisted of left and right magnesium alloy forgings attached to the engine at two points on each side and supported under each lower

ABOVE Jumo 211 engines on the build line in the Junkers factory at Dessau in 1940. On the example in the foreground the crankshaft and its reduction gear drive can be seen in place inside the crankcase assembly. *(BA 146-2005-0015)*

LEFT The fuselage firewall on a dismantled Ju 87 B at RAE Farnborough, showing the four ball screw connection points and the apertures through which essential controls and services linked the engine, cockpit and the fuel system. *(Andy Saunders collection)*

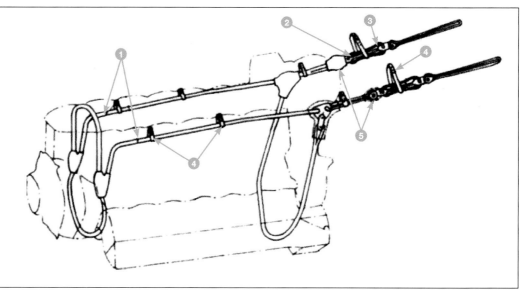

**Engine safety harness,
Ju 87 B-2.** *(Junkers)*

1 Engine safety harness
2 Cable
3 Expansion rod
4 Strap fasteners
5 Quick-release
connectors at engine
mounting

connection point by a steel support strut and a diagonal strut. Bearer plates were bolted and dowelled to the sides of the engine crankcase, and connected to the cantilever arms through rubber bushes that absorbed engine vibration and provided a flexible support.

In the event of the engine bearers failing, the engine was held securely by a safety harness. This was made of leather-covered wire cables which were looped around the engine and fastened to the fuselage behind Frame 1.

Engine cowling frame

The framework to which the engine cowlings were attached consisted of the front ring frame, which was screw-fastened to the reduction

drive casing of the engine, the left and right exhaust troughs and the rear and lower frames. The upper rear frame was bolted to each side of the engine and in turn the lower frame was attached to the upper by two bolts and supported by a pair of struts.

The radiator cowling was installed below the engine cowling, with radiator cooling flaps arranged at the front and controllable 'spreader' flaps to the rear. The spreader flaps were attached to the lower engine cowl behind the coolant cooler and were adjusted by pressure oil. The adjustment was made by means of two electromagnetic changeover valves, which controlled the expansion flap cylinder by pressure oil via a blocking system. The six spreader flaps

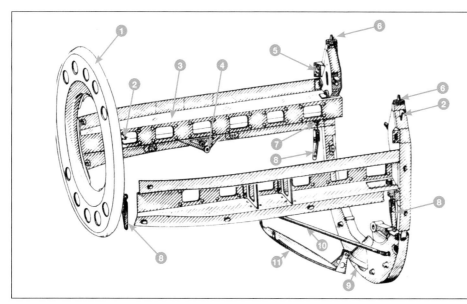

**Engine cowling framework,
Ju 87 B-2.** *(Junkers)*

1 Ring frame
2 Locking catch for top
cowling
3 Exhaust trough
4 Suspension lugs for radiator
5 Upper rear frame
6 Guide pins for top cowling
7 Guide pin for radiator fairing
8 Lock-down fastener for
radiator fairing
9 Lower rear frame
10 Strut
11 Metal cover

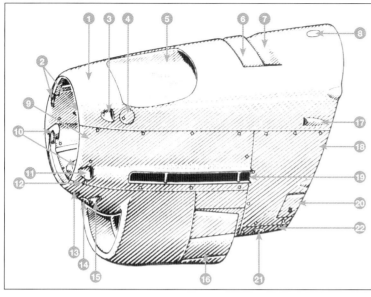

Engine cowling assembly, Ju 87 B-2. *(Junkers)*

1 Upper cowling hood
2 Lever latch for upper cowling hood
3 Air vent
4 Coolant filler cover
5 Cooling air intake for oil cooler
6 Split flap to regulate oil temperature
7 Cooling air vent from oil cooler
8 Lubricating oil filler cover
9 Left-side cowling
10 Lever latch for radiator fairing
11 Cooling air to engine exhausts
12 Quick-release fastener
13 Radiator fairing
14 Cover for warm air duct for winter starting
15 Air vent
16 Split flaps
17 Air vent for generator
18 Left rear cowling
19 Exhaust gas outlet
20 Cover for hand crank inertia starting handle
21 Outboard connection for electric starter
22 Rear cowling section

LEFT Junkers factory engineers work on the engine of a newly completed Ju 87 B. In the foreground can be seen the under-slung coolant radiator with feeder pipe connecting it with the header tank (out of view). *(BA 183-2004-0819-500)*

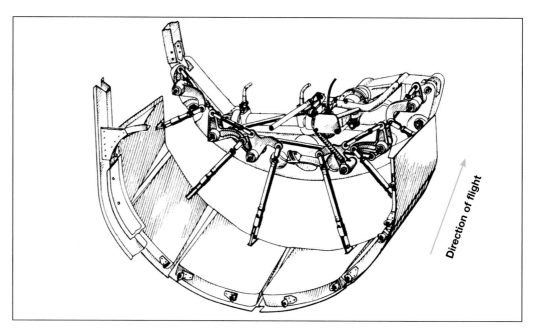

RIGHT Adjustable spreader flaps to the rear of the radiator cowling. *(Junkers)*

Direction of flight

RIGHT Steel cylinder liners. *(Wings Museum)*

were rotatably mounted at two points on Frame 3 of the lower shroud, and were actuated by means of push-rods controlled by 'open/close' push-buttons in the pilot's cockpit.

Cylinder block and heads

The cylinder banks were set at 60° and for each bank the cylinder head was a single-piece aluminium-alloy casting in which the camshaft bearing pedestals were cast integrally. Liners of 45-ton steel were bolted to the cylinder head by

RIGHT The stripped crankcase with block studs fitted, mounted on a roll-over stand for ease of working. *(Wings Museum)*

JUMO 211A – GENERAL DATA

Four stroke		
Bore	150mm	
	165mm	
Cylinder capacity	2.914 litres	
Firing order	1-9-4-11-2-7-6-10-3-8-5-12	
Valve timing and crank angle		
Inlet open	11° top dead centre	
Inlet closed	42° bottom dead centre	
Outlet open	52° top dead centre	
Outlet closed	30° bottom dead centre	
Valve clearance (cold)		
Open	0.8mm	
Closed	1.0mm	
Oil filter	Knecht filter.	
Petrol	Leaded petrol, knocking strength 87 octane, in accordance with CFR (Cooperative Fuel Research) engine procedures.	
Lubricant	Aero Shell 'Mittel' or Gargoyle-Mobilöl 'Rotring'.	

ABOVE Rocker arms before fitting the camshaft. *(Wings Museum)*

four long studs of 60-ton steel, the head itself being secured to the cylinder block by 14 studs. A bore of 150mm and a stroke of 165mm gave a capacity of 34.97 litres, with a compression ratio of 6.5:1.

Valves

The underhead camshaft with rocker arms operated two inlet and one exhaust valve per cylinder. Bronze valve guides were inserted into the flat-topped combustion chambers. The exhaust valve guide passed through the water space and was a press-fit in the opening into the combustion chamber, with the pressure joint made on an aluminium washer under the shoulder of the guide. Water leakage at the camshaft end of the guide was prevented by a rubber ring sitting in an annular groove. The steel valve seating rings were conical externally and were pressed into the head and rolled into a taper at the inner end. Intake valves were

made of chromium matensite steel, while the hollow exhaust valves were made of austenitic stainless steel with sodium-cooled stems. Rings were Stellite-faced to resist wear.

Camshafts

The camshafts were on seven aluminium iron alloy bearings driven by bevel and spur gears from the lower end of the auxiliary gearbox. The rockers oscillated on short spindles that were bolted to bosses on the cylinder head, thereby dispensing with bearing caps. Contact between the cams and rockers was on rollers.

Pistons

The pistons were made from forged aluminium alloy with slightly dished crowns ribbed on the

RIGHT Cylinder liners with crankshaft on a Jumo 211 engine on display at the Tangmere Military Aviation Museum in Sussex. It is believed to be from a Ju 87 shot down by Hurricanes of 43 Squadron in the English Channel off Selsey Bill in 1940. *(Author)*

BELOW Crankshaft and final drive reduction gear. *(Author)*

inside. Three compression rings and two oil scraper rings were fitted, one of the latter being above the gudgeon pin. Oil return holes were drilled behind and below these rings. Fully floating gudgeon pins were located by light alloy end caps and spigoted with a sliding fit into the pins.

Connecting rods

One forked and one plain connecting rod were clamped to the outer diameter of the big end bearing for each pair of cylinders. The main connecting rod had a double cross-section and was fork-shaped at the foot; the adjoining (plain) rod was located between the fork of the main connecting rod and worked in the same way. The big end bearings were steel-backed 80/20 copper/lead, while the little end bearings had floating cast-iron bushings.

Crankshaft

Another unusual feature of the Jumo 211 lay in the design of the crankshaft, in which all webs were in the form of flat plates and were extended to form balance weights, the shape of the pair of webs on each side of each main bearing being similar.

The six-throw one-piece crankshaft ran on eight leaded-bronze steel-backed bearings, with the additional bearing placed on the forward side of the airscrew reduction gear. The fourth bearing from the rear was flanged to take the crankshaft end thrust.

The crankshaft received a supply of lubricating oil through a sleeve at the front end and all bearings were lubricated through holes drilled in the journals and crankpins. Short tubes were fitted in each oil hole, which, in addition to preventing sludge entering the bearing, may have been intended to act as bushes to reduce the stresses in the shaft around the holes.

Ignition system

There were two Bosch high-tension magnetos, one supplying the exhaust side spark plugs and the other the inlet plugs (GE12 BRS 162 am – left bank; GE12 BRS 163 am – right bank).

Although four sparking-plug holes were provided on each side of the cylinder head, only two spark plugs (Zündkerzen) per cylinder were fitted. Twenty-four radio-shielded Beru F220/a

19 m (mica plugs) were located on the outer and inner sides of the cylinder head.

Supercharger

A transverse-mounted two-speed single-stage centrifugal supercharger was attached at the rear starboard side of the engine, with a forward-facing air intake. It was driven off the rear of the crankshaft by a two-speed gear housed in the auxiliaries gearbox with clutches and a layshaft rotated by a bevel drive, and coupled to the crankshaft by a splined shaft. The impeller housing and impeller were magnesium alloy forgings, with the impeller shaft carried on hardened-steel bushes, which rotated in self-aligning aluminium-alloy bearings and were set at 90° to the centreline of the engine. A low-ratio intermediate gear (7.85:1) was coupled to the shaft by roller clutch, and a high-ratio gear (11.37:1) by mechanically operated friction clutch.

Air was drawn into the supercharger through an intake manifold attached to the side of the impeller housing, protruding through the right-hand side engine cowling. A coarse mesh filter in the mouth of the intake prevented the ingestion of foreign bodies.

A barometric capsule-operated automatic two-speed gear-change was driven through a hydraulic servo incorporating an automatic override to prevent operation in high ratio below 3,050m (10,000ft). This modification overrode

the pilot's control and prevented the use of the high-speed gear below a safe altitude. Between the supercharger and the engine was a barrel-type throttle with automatic boost control.

Injection pump

A Junkers fully automatic dual-injection pump was located in the V of the cylinder heads on flexible metallic mountings. The pump drew fuel from the feed tanks through a de-aerator

ABOVE The two-speed supercharger was mounted at the rear of the engine.
(Copyright unknown)

LEFT The fuel sender unit was located in the V of the cylinder heads on flexible metallic mountings. It had a centrally disposed camshaft with six cams that actuated the twelve injection plungers.
(Wings Museum)

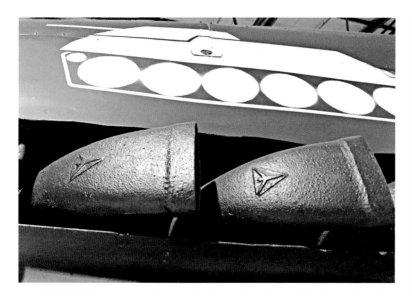

ABOVE Exhaust stub pipes on the Ju 87 G at the RAF Museum, Hendon.
(Author)

BELOW Exposed propeller dome and blades on Hendon's Gustav. *(Author)*

JABLO AND JICWOOD

Both the British and Germans used 'Jablo' propellers – Jablo Propellers Ltd being a brand as well as a generic name for a laminated wooden blade manufacturing process. Polish Jew Bruno Jablonsky worked in the German aircraft industry for Hugo Heine Propellerwerke in the early 20th century before emigrating to England in the 1930s and establishing Jablo Propellers and Jablo Plastics Industries.

The Schwarz wooden blade was made of specially manufactured 'hardwood' scarfed on to spruce, while the Heine wooden blade (Jablo in Britain) was made from so-called 'reinforced wood'.

DIN STANDARD COLOUR CODING OF TUBES, HOSES AND PIPELINES

On Luftwaffe aircraft, to avoid confusion all tubes, hoses and/or their ends were colour-coded in accordance with DIN L5.

Fuel	yellow
Oil	brown
Coolant/water	green
Oxygen/air	blue
Vent or bleed lines	blue with a single ring in the relevant colour

For example:

Fuel breather pipe	blue with a yellow ring
Hydraulic oil system	Brown with red ring
Hydraulic oil system for flap adjustment	brown with two red/black rings
Exhaust gases	black
Balancing pressure line	blue with a single black ring
Steam and condensation lines	green with red ring
Oxygen/compressed air	blue with two white rings
Boost pressure line	blue with two yellow rings

(The direction of flow is indicated by a red arrow on the line.)

to the Junkers 12-injector pump (one injector per cylinder) for squirting fuel into each cylinder through open nozzles screwed into the insides of the cylinder heads. Petrol bleeders for complete venting of the petrol pressure line and the injection pump were fitted at the apparatus housing above the left-hand magneto.

Fuel-injection nozzles

Single-orifice, centrifugal-type injection nozzles were situated on the centreline, at right angles to the crankshaft, and sprayed horizontally across the cylinders. The nozzle was screwed into the cylinder head and was liquid-cooled. On the Jumo 211D engine, the fuel-control limiter was modified and fitted with a second capsule to correct the fuel delivery for varying exhaust back pressures, thereby maintaining a more consistent mixture strength.

Exhausts

Early examples of the Ju 87 A and B-1 were fitted with simple exhaust openings in the cowling, although more efficient swept back exhaust ejectors were introduced on late production B-1s. This design principle continued in use for most subsequent marks of the Ju 87, with improvements.

From mid-1942 onwards Junkers made available B-2s, R-2s and R-4s with flame-eliminator pipes (Flammenvernichter) fitted over the exhaust ejectors for night operations; from late 1943 existing aircraft could be modified on their units to take these attachments. For night ground-attack and bombing sorties, Doras and Gustavs were fitted with flame-eliminator pipes.

Propeller

Junkers Verstell-Luftschraube (VS) 11 variable-pitch propeller

The Ju 87 was fitted with a constant-speed electrically operated variable-pitch Junkers VS 11 three-bladed clockwise-rotating airscrew. The laminated wooden blades (resin impregnated compressed wood veneer) were manufactured by either Schwarz (Propellerwerke Gustav Schwartz of Berlin) or Heine (Hugo Heine Propellerwerke, also of Berlin) with brass leading-edge strips. Wooden propeller blades were broader chord, while those made from metal were narrower and more pointed.

MAINTENANCE INSTRUCTIONS – JUNKERS JUMO 211F TO J

On the Jumo 211F, provision was made to provide supercharging, the rpm was increased to 2,600 and power raised to 1,340PS (985kW). An intercooler was provided on the 211J and power was boosted to 1,420PS (1,044kW).

After first test-flight:
- Clean the lubricant filter.
- Clean oil filter for gearbox.
- Clean fuel filter in the breather/filter.
- Clean small filter in lubricant pressure line for injection pump.
- Clean small filter in lubricant pressure line for supercharger boost controller.
- Tighten the nuts on the supercharger casing while the engine is still warm.
- Clean the oil pressure relief valve on the airscrew constant speed unit (CSU).

Every 12½ hours:
- Remove mesh filters by means of the pull-tabs/release-screws and clean through with benzene from the inside outwards. Blow through and reinstall. Note that the sludge drain hole for pressure relief is clean.
- Clean the fuel filter in the breather filter.
- Clean the lubricant filter for the injection pump.
- Clean the lubricant filter for the gearbox.
- Use a wrench to remove and reinstall the small filter element.
- Clean the oil pressure relief valve on the airscrew CSU.
- Check the coolant pressure relief valve.

Every 50 hours:
- As 12½ hours.
- Clean spark plugs.
- Check ignition magneto in accordance with manufacturer's instructions (Bosch).
- Tighten injection nozzle lines.
- Carry out compression test.
- Check the inertia control linkage.

100 hours:
- Remove the engine for partial overhaul.
- Drain fuel from the injection pump.

Chapter Four

Stuka at war

The heyday of the Ju 87 was in the Blitzkrieg campaigns of 1939 and 1940, where it was the undisputed king maker for Adolf Hitler. Stukas were in the vanguard of virtually every campaign fought by the German Army in the Second World War and their appearance over a battlefield could quickly turn a desperate situation into a victory for the troops on the ground.

OPPOSITE This formation of Ju 87 Ds follows their leader into a banking turn over a Russian city (possibly Stalingrad in 1943) having just dropped their under-fuselage bombs. Each aircraft still carries four 50kg bombs beneath its wings ready for delivery onto the next target. Kriegsberichter Werner Opitz of Luftwaffe Kriegsberichter Kompanie 7 (KBK Lw 7) took this dramatic photograph from the rear cockpit of an accompanying Stuka. *(BA 101I-646-5188-17)*

Beginning with its baptism of fire in the Spanish Civil War in 1938, followed by a brief interlude of less than a year before the outbreak of the Second World War, the Ju 87 and many of its crews experienced an unbroken run of front-line service right up until the end of the war in Europe in 1945. This was combat at the sharp end, operating in support of the German armies wherever the fighting was fiercest. The Stuka's timely intervention regularly turned around a desperate tactical situation and enabled the troops on the ground to snatch victory from out of the jaws of defeat.

Spanish Civil War

When the Spanish Civil War broke out in 1936 as a result of an attempted military coup against the elected government of the Second Spanish Republic, the country became a battleground for opposing Nationalist and Republican ideologies. The war took on an international flavour with volunteers from different countries flocking to Spain to fight. Ideology also prompted intervention by communist Russia, fascist Italy and Nazi Germany, because the European powers could not ignore what was happening in an area of vital interest for them.

Hermann Goering urged Hitler to give support to General Franco to help prevent the spread of communism in Spain and as a chance for him to test his young Luftwaffe. As a result Nazi Germany contributed its Legion Kondor, composed of aircraft, tanks, artillery and personnel from the Luftwaffe and Heer, which served alongside Nationalist forces. Commanding the Legion was Generalmajor Hugo Sperrle with Oberstleutnant Wolfram Freiherr von Richthofen as his Chief of Staff – the latter becoming a champion of close-air support.

Spain became the combat proving ground for German aircraft like the Heinkel He 111 medium bomber, the Messerschmitt Bf 109 fighter and the Junkers Ju 87 Stuka dive-bomber, all of which went on to become mainstays of the Luftwaffe's war machine in the Second World War. The air component of Legion Kondor comprised at its most some 140–150 aircraft and over the course of the whole Civil War it lost 232 machines. Overall, the Legion attained a maximum strength of 5,600 men and lost about 355.

In great secrecy, the first Ju 87 was shipped to Spain in November 1936 where the Civil War became the live trials arena for the Stuka prototype. This was Ju 87 V4, the fourth prototype aircraft. Between early December and 15 January 1937 Ju 87 V4 flew some 40 hours of operational combat trials with the Legion's experimental unit, VK/88, making six drops of an SC 250 bomb. A vast amount of

BELOW In late December 1936, Germany sent the first of four Ju 87s to fight with the Legion Kondor in Spain. By the end of the conflict in February 1939 the Nationalist air component stood at 491 aircraft, of which 126 were German- and 192 Italian-manned. Spaniards piloted 173 aircraft, of which about two-thirds were Italian and one-third German. *(Chris Goss collection)*

important data was gathered covering flying characteristics, equipment performance and tactics, among which was recognition that a more powerful engine was urgently required and the dive brakes needed improving. The valuable lessons from Spain were applied during further testing of Ju 87 V4 after its return to Germany.

Soon after this four Ju 87 A-1s were sent to Spain where they joined the Legion Kondor, with the intention of testing every tactical and technical possibility on the new dive-bomber. Presented with the opportunity of tactical experience for its crews in real combat conditions, Goering wanted as many of his pilots and radio operators as possible to take advantage of this, so new crews were rotated through at regular intervals.

The Ju 87's first taste of combat was during the advance on the city of Teruel in Aragon in eastern Spain, which eventually fell to Franco's Nationalist forces on 17 February 1937 after two months of bitter fighting. Ju 87s went on to be used in most battles during the Spanish Civil War, including the last major Republican offensive of the war in the Battle of the Ebro between July and November 1938 where they provided close-air support.

Thanks to the supremacy of the Messerschmitt Bf 109 over anything the Russians could supply to the Republican forces, the Stuka crews had little to worry about when it came to being intercepted by enemy aircraft, but they still had to look out for flak.

Although the Ju 87 A-1 suffered from poor performance when it came to top speed, operating height, bomb-carrying capability and maximum range, its use in Spain by the Legion Kondor proved a tremendous success. In October 1938 the Ju 87 A-1s were withdrawn from Spain and replaced by seven Ju 87 B-1s. Between 17 November and 1 December the fighting units of the Legion Kondor were stood down temporarily to rest and reorganise before Franco's planned offensive in Catalonia.

Ju 87 B-1s successfully bombed an ammunition dump near Mayals in Catalonia on 23 December and from mid-January 1939 onwards the Stukas assigned to 5.K/88 flew close-support operations during the Catalonia Offensive to back up the Nationalist advance on Tarragona, which had been in Republican hands

since the beginning of the conflict. Sorties were not always successful as shown on 4 March when three Ju 87s attacked the road bridge at Salvacañete, but their heavy bombs missed the target and detonated harmlessly some distance away. On the 16th, two Ju 87s joined with 20 He 111s in bombing bridges at Meco and Fuentidueña de Tajo (Madrid) and the road junction at Los Santos. When Stukas operated in support of the advance on Madrid on 27 March it was their swansong in Spain because in early April they were withdrawn from operations and shipped back to Germany.

While the Germans learned much in Spain about the applications of tactical air power in support of ground troops, where they refined their approach to warfighting at the tactical level – which paid dividends in the future campaigns in Poland, France and the Low Countries – its commanders thought of the Luftwaffe only in these terms and failed to consider the wider picture in developing an air force that also included strategic bombers.

Blitzkrieg Poland – 'Fall Weiss' (Case White)

As part of his plan to dominate Europe, Hitler was resolved to crush Poland. With the Nazi–Soviet Pact that was signed in August 1939 he was relieved of the danger of a war on two fronts, and he set out to destroy Poland.

Shortly before moving up to its jumping-off position in preparation for the impending attack on Poland, Hauptmann Walter Sigel and 1./StG 76 had been ordered to provide a demonstration of precision dive-bombing at the Neuhammer training ground to Luftwaffe top brass including Wolfram von Richthofen (commanding Fliegerkorps VIII), Hugo Sperrle (commanding Luftflotte 3) and Bruno Loerzer (Inspector of Fighters). The weather forecast for 15 August was for 7/10ths cloud between 2,500ft and 6,000ft, but clear below that level. Sigel briefed the 30 crews of the three Staffeln to approach the target at 12,000ft and dive through the cloud to release their smoke bombs at 1,000ft. Unfortunately the weather changed in the hour before the Ju 87 formation arrived over the target, where a thick ground mist had developed, the news of which had not

RIGHT Stukas of StG 1 take off for a dive-bombing sortie during the Polish campaign in September 1939. *(BA 101I-320-0946-32A)*

BELOW Stuka groundcrew of the 'Immelmann' Geschwader gather their personal kit before moving on to another operating base during the Polish campaign. In the background is 8/StG 2's Ju 87 B-1, T6+WF. *(Chris Goss collection)*

been passed on to Sigel and his Gruppe. They commenced their dives as planned, but Sigel realised at the last minute what had happened and pulled out with only feet to spare. He shouted a warning to his comrades as he did so, but it was too late to prevent many of them from flying one after the other straight into the ground at high speed. Thirteen Stukas and 26 crew were lost on that fateful day in what was a terrible accident. Sigel was cleared of any negligence at a subsequent court of inquiry

and the Ju 87 suffered no restrictions on its operational use.

Two weeks later, in the early hours of 1 September, 3./StG 1 carried out the first combat mission of the Second World War when two Ketten of Ju 87s (six aircraft) commanded by Oberleutnant Bruno Dilley, Staffelkapitän of the 3rd Staffel, attempted to destroy destructive charges fixed to the twin bridges at Tczew (Dirschau to the Germans) over the River Vistula in Poland. Where they

crossed the Polish border to Tczew, the bridges were a crucial rail link in the German plans to subdue Poland, supplying the twin thrust of the German armies attacking east from Germany and south from Prussia. The Poles had recognised the strategic importance of these bridges and had planted explosive charges to destroy them if war came.

The six Stuka pilots underwent meticulous training and German Intelligence made careful reconnaissance of the bridges in the days before the attack. When the time came, Dilley's Ketten took off at 04.26hrs on 1 September to make the short flight to the bridges, picking up the snaking line of the Vistula and following it north. Flying at very low level they arrived over the target at 04.35hrs and released their bombs from only 30ft with an accuracy that cut the detonator wires running along the railway embankment leading to the bridge. A massed force of 45 Stukas from I./StG 1 had left its jumping-off base at Elbingen one minute before Dilley's Ketten, heading for the same target where they dropped their bombs on Tczew railway station. However, none of this managed to prevent the defenders from repairing the circuits and blowing up the bridges, although

one of them was later repaired by German engineers and made serviceable again. Dilley's six Stukas made it back to their base unscathed.

Lesser known is a Stuka attack based on faulty intelligence on the town of Wieluń. In a mistaken belief that a Polish cavalry brigade was holed up there, 62 Ju 87s of I./StG 76 (led by Walter Sigel) and I./StG 77 (commanded by Oberst Günter Schwartzkopff, who was nicknamed the 'Stuka father') bombed the town twice on 1 September, killing 1,200

LEFT Stukas twice dive-bombed the town of Wieluń on 1 September in what became an atrocity against its civilian population. *(Copyright unknown)*

ABOVE After the end of the Polish campaign, Stukas of 8./StG 2 stop over at Olmütz-Neredin airfield, a pre-war Czech Air Force base occupied by the Germans in 1939. In the background can also be seen the Junkers Ju 52s used for transporting the Staffel's equipment and ground staff. Of note on the Ju 87 in the foreground are the unit code (T6+MS), the Staffel badge on the nose, and the aircraft's (early) Werk Nummer (446).
(Chris Goss collection)

RIGHT Major Frank Neubert, I./StG 2.
(Author's collection)

civilians and razing most of Wieluń, home to a population of 16,000.

At 04.45hrs the German battleship *Schleswig-Holstein* opened fire on the Polish garrison of the Westerplatte Fort at Danzig (Gdansk), while inland 62 German divisions supported by 1,300 aircraft surged forward across the Polish land borders. At 06.00hrs the capital, Warsaw, was struck by the first in a series of bombing raids. The invasion of Poland had begun.

Later that day elements of I./StG 2 under the command of Oskar Dinort launched an attack against the Polish Air Force and struck at the Polish Navy at Hela in the first of several attacks. The naval base was heavily defended with anti-aircraft guns and two Stukas were shot down – the first Ju 87s lost to enemy action. Command of the air was achieved on the first day after most of the Polish Air Force had been caught on the ground.

Pilot Frank Neubert (I./StG 2) and his gunner Franz Klinger claimed the first air-to-air victory of the Second World War that day when they shot down a Polish Air Force PZL P.11 fighter flown by the CO of 122 Squadron, Kpt Mieczysław Medwecki, as they returned from a sortie.

Flying ahead of the advancing columns of Panzers the Stukas acted as aerial artillery, destroying resistance in their path and putting into practice their new warfighting techniques, based upon rapid advance and the prevention of a static front line being formed that would allow enemy forces time to regroup.

The Polish government asked for the immediate military assistance of Britain and France at 08.00hrs on 1 September, but it took until noon on the 3rd for Britain to declare war on Germany, followed by France at 17.00hrs.

On 3 September Stukas were in action again over the port city of Gdynia where Ju 87 Bs and Cs from 4th Staffel Trägergruppe 186 (4./TrGr 186) – the Specialist Carrier Air Group formed to operate from the *Graf Zeppelin* carrier (see pages 23-24) – sank the Polish destroyer *Wicher* and the minelayer *Gryf*. By the 6th the two German

LEFT The major action
fought in the Tucheler
Heide between 1 and
5 September 1939
saw Stukas help
German ground forces
break through the
Polish Corridor and
reconnect Germany
with East Prussia.
Tucheler Heide was
a large forest near
the town of Tuchola
in northern Poland.
Before 1919, Tuchola
was originally in
West Prussia but the
Versailles Treaty saw
it incorporated in
the so-called Polish
Corridor. *(Getty Images)*

Army groups had linked up at Łódź in the centre
of Poland and driven a wedge down the middle
of the country, trapping most of the Polish Army
against the German border. Retreating in the path
of the relentless Blitzkrieg, on 8 September Polish
forces were hemmed into five isolated pockets
around Pomerania, Pozna , Łódź, Kraków and
Carpathia, when more than 150 Stukas arrived
overhead to bomb the troops into submission.
After four days of relentless bombardment and
dive-bombing, they surrendered.

West of Warsaw, near the town of Piątek
along the River Bzura, the Polish Army made
a valiant stand against the German 8th Army.
Their intention was to shield the remnants of
their army fleeing the defeat at the Battle of
Piotrków, to protect Warsaw, and to buy some
time before the promised French invasion of
Germany (which never came). Army Poznań,
which outnumbered the German 8th Army,
launched its attack on 9 September and routed
General Johannes Blaskowitz's forces, but the
Germans regrouped with the help of 10th Army
reinforcements pulled from across Poland and
proceeded to encircle the Army Pozna in the
Bzura Pocket.

Meanwhile, the capital, Warsaw, was
subjected to relentless and merciless air
attacks. At dawn on 15 September some 400
aircraft began round-the-clock bombardment
of the city, where Stukas comprised the bulk
of the attacking force – some 240 from eight
Gruppen. Wave upon wave of Ju 87s flew over
the burning city, dropping their high-explosive
bombs to stoke the inferno below.

On the following day, 16 September, the
Luftwaffe joined in squeezing the life out of the
Polish Army at Bzura, its Stukas helping to
crush the encircled Polish forces. Two days later
resistance collapsed and more than 120,000
prisoners were taken – roughly a quarter of the
Polish Army.

The Battle of Bzura marked the collapse of
Polish resistance. It encouraged Stalin to join
Hitler in the partition of Poland and on
17 September Soviet forces were quick to
move west and claim their share. Warsaw
finally fell on the 27th and the last major Polish
Army group capitulated on 6 October, caught
between two powerful enemies.

The Polish Campaign had been a total
success for the Germans and a vindication
of the Blitzkrieg tactic in which the Ju 87 was
largely responsible for shaping the victory. It had
also firmly established the fearsome reputation
of the Stuka, which was to strike fear into its
future opponents in the battles of 1940.

There was a lull in activity after the fall
of Poland. In March 1940, StG 1 was
re-equipped with the longer-range Ju 87 R in
anticipation of the next German adventures in
Norway and Denmark.

The Norwegian Campaign

Both Britain and Germany recognised that
control of Norwegian coastal waters was
essential for the transport of Swedish iron ore
via Narvik to feed the blast furnaces of the
industrial Ruhr. Maintaining the flow of this vital

RIGHT The long-range
Ju 87 R with its twin
drop-tanks made
its first appearance
with StG 1 during the
Norwegian Campaign
in April 1940.
(Bundesarchiv)

BELOW Generaloberst
Erhard Milch greets
Stuka crews of I./StG 1
at Drontheim, Norway,
on 23 April 1940.
Behind him is (A5+H?)
one of the unit's newly
delivered Ju 87 Rs. *(BA
101I-760-0165N-26)*

commodity to the Nazi war effort as well as breaking the Allied naval blockade of Germany would be that much easier if the Germans secured control of Norwegian waters. Depriving the British of the chance of securing the ports of Bergen, Narvik and Trondheim for the use of the Royal Navy was also a strong enough reason to beat Britain to the punch and invade Norway before they did.

Accordingly, at 04.15hrs local time on 9 April 1940 the Kriegsmarine landed strong amphibious forces at six locations up the Norwegian coast – Oslo, Kristiansund, Egersund, Bergen, Narvik and Trondheim – supported by airborne troops to capture other key sites such as airfields. Supporting the operation was Fliegerkorps X with some 400 bombers, including the long-range Ju 87 Rs of I./StG 1 (the only Stuka Gruppe to take part in the Norwegian Campaign), which flew from its base at Kiel-Holtenau to attack Oscarsborg Fortress on the approaches to Oslo. Within days British and French forces came to the aid of Norway with an expeditionary force.

Denmark was invaded simultaneously on 9 April, to secure Germany's communication lines to Norway during Operation Weserübung. In the longer term it was to provide the Germans with naval bases and help protect supplies of iron ore from Sweden. Danish resistance quickly crumbled and the government sued for peace within hours of the invasion.

In Norway, StG 1 operated initially from airfields at Stavanger-Sola and Oslo-Fornebu, as well as the frozen surface of Lake Jonsvatnet near Trondheim, until a temporary runway could be laid at Trondheim-Vaernes airfield. The unit was used mainly in the anti-

shipping role and achieved a number of successes. On 30 April 1940, the Gruppe sank anti-submarine trawlers *Siretoko*, *Jardine* and *Warwickshire*, and Oberleutnant Elmar Schaefer (1 Staffel) seriously damaged the sloop HMS *Bittern* (later sunk by HMS *Janus*) in Namsos harbour. They also badly damaged HMTs *Aston Villa* and *Gaul* (both were later scuttled on 3 May) and HMT *St Goran* (sunk 1 May). On 1 May the Gruppe failed to hit HMS *Ark Royal* but the Staffelkapitän of 2./StG 1, Oberleutnant Heinz Böhme, claimed a hit on the carrier HMS *Glorious* (in fact a near-miss).

Further success came the way of the Stukas on 3 May when Hauptmann Paul-Werner Hozzel led the Gruppe in sinking the French destroyer *Bison* and later that day sank HMS *Afridi* during the evacuation from Namsos. On the same day Leutnant Martin Möbus was credited with sinking a 9–12,000-ton vessel off Namsos. The following day the Gruppe sank the Norwegian steamers *Blaafjeld I*, *Sekstant*, *Pan* and *Aafjord* in Namsfjord.

The first signs that Stukas were vulnerable to fighter attack if faced with well-trained pilots came on 27 May when Feldwebel Kurt Zube was shot down off Bodø by a Gloster Gladiator flown by Flight Lieutenant Caesar Hull of 263 Squadron; Oberleutnant Heinz Böhme and Unteroffizier Horst Schamp (2 Staffel) were shot down and killed on 2 June by Sergeant Herbert Kitchener and Flight Lieutenant Alvin Williams of 263 Squadron; and Leutnant Klaus Kübel and Unteroffizier Rudolf Tribulowski (also of 2 Staffel) were shot down at Fagernes by Hurricane pilot Sergeant Bernard Taylor of 46 Squadron. Last to fall over Norway was Feldwebel Hans Ott and his gunner Sonderführer Günther Brack (3 Staffel), who were shot down by Flying Officer John Drummond of 46 Squadron.

BELOW A Ju 87 R of StG 1 waits for its next mission at a forward airfield near Trondheim during April or May 1940. *(BA 101I-761-0233-10)*

Blitzkrieg France and the Low Countries – 'Fall Gelb' (Case Yellow)

On 10 May 1940, Hitler launched his western offensive (Fall Gelb – 'Case Yellow') with the invasion of Belgium, Holland, France and Luxembourg. Once again the Luftwaffe played a pivotal role and Belgium and Holland fell within days, but France – with the help of the British Expeditionary Force (BEF) and the RAF – held out until early June.

Stukas helped to subdue quickly the Belgian fortress of Eben Emael in support of a daring glider-borne assault. Its spectacular capture delivered a body blow to Belgium from which it never recovered; a pinpoint dive-bombing attack destroyed the HQ of the commander responsible for the destruction of the bridges over the Albert Canal, saving two out of three and allowing the German Army to continue its rapid advance.

On 11 May the armoured units of the German 12. Armee thrust westwards towards the River Meuse at Sedan with Stukas flying missions from their German bases against French troops and artillery positions, preventing them bringing up reinforcements. The following day

ABOVE
Fallschirmjäger (paratroops) wave to an over-flying Stuka during the invasion of Holland in May 1940. *(Copyright unknown)*

RIGHT Ju 87 Rs of III./StG 2's 7th Staffel flying in close formation during the spring of 1940. *(Chris Goss collection)*

LEFT Stripped to the waist in the spring sunshine, III./StG 2 groundcrew prepare an 8th Staffel Ju 87 B (T6+AB) parked under its camouflaged hide for the next sortie over France, sometime in May 1940. Stuka units moved airfields almost daily to keep up with the rapid advance of the Panzers. *(Chris Goss collection)*

Ju 87s were used as flying artillery to lay down preliminary bombardments to cover the crossing of the Meuse by the Panzers and shock troops.

Wherever Allied forces – be they artillery, tanks or infantry – held up the advancing Panzers, a Flieger Verbindungsoffizier (the 'Flivo', a Luftwaffe liaison officer, see page 130) attached to the Panzer units would call up the Stukas to smash the opposition and allow the advance to continue.

Mindful of the fact that without an escort the Stukas were vulnerable to enemy fighter attacks, the Fliegerführer Close Air-Support messaged the Stukagruppen that in the event of them encountering enemy fighters they were to abort their mission and return to base. In an incident on 12 May near Sedan, six French Curtiss H-75 fighters from Groupe de Chasse I/5 attacked 12 unescorted Ju 87s, shooting down 11. Hauptmann Helmut

LEFT Luftwaffe top brass inspect a Stuka Gruppe in 1940. Generalfeldmarschall Albert Kesselring, commanding Luftflotte 2 (right), with his Chief of Staff Generalleutnant Wilhelm Speidel (centre), and Generalmajor Wolfram von Richthofen, commanding VIII Fliegerkorps (left). Von Richthofen was an early supporter of dive-bombing as a tactic and recognised the importance of effective air-to-ground communications, which became the norm in Luftwaffe operations by 1941. *(BA 183-B24129)*

Mahlke, Staffelkapitän of 3.(St)/186 (T), recalls an incident during a mission on 14 May 1940 involving French fighters:

A flight of four French Morane fighters came barrelling in fast. Obviously aware of the limited traverse of the Stuka's rearward-firing armament, they attacked our Staffel from behind and below, letting fly with everything they had. Our rearmost Kette was blown apart. The three machines dived

away from the formation, a couple of them already trailing thin banners of smoke. The Kommandeur's voice sounded over the R/T: 'Abort mission! Return to base!' Suiting the action to his words, the Kommandeur went into a wide right-hand turn. But by this time a second group of enemy fighters was bearing down fast on what remained of my Staffel out on the exposed left-hand flank. We were already over the scene of the ground fighting going on below and it was now that

something entirely unexpected happened. Behind the Staffel, between us and the rapidly approaching fighters, a few bursts from the enemy's heavy flak guns suddenly speckled the evening sky. The fighters immediately broke off their attack. Climbing away, they quickly disappeared from sight.

The breakthrough at Sedan and crossing over the River Meuse on 13 May had been made possible by Ju 87s flying more than 300 missions with StG 77, commanded by Günter Schwartzkopff, flying 200 sorties alone (Schwartzkopff was killed the following day after his Ju 87 was shot down at Le Chesne by AA fire). Efforts by the RAF's Advanced Air Striking Force and the French Air Force to wipe out the bridgehead had been cut to shreds by Bf 109s. On the following day German forces were assembling south of the river ready for a breakout to the west.

By 16 May German troops were pouring into northern France. The Stukagruppen were transferred to forward operating bases in Belgium and France, which reduced the flying time to reach their targets. In the days that followed, Stukas flew as many as three missions a day in support of the Panzer divisions as they pushed relentlessly onwards, towards the English Channel.

By 20 May Panzergruppe Kleist became the first German ground unit to reach the Channel coast, where Hitler ordered them to halt temporarily, allowing the hard-pressed infantry to catch up. The tanks resumed their advance on 26 May. The BEF and remnants of the French Army were now hemmed into the coastal strip around Calais and Dunkirk, from where evacuation by sea was being planned. On the 26th the British commander at Calais refused a German invitation to surrender, when his orders

ABOVE Stuka pilots from an unidentified unit receive a briefing from their Staffel commander (the Hauptmann on the right) before a mission in May 1940. Behind them can be seen a Ju 87 R. *(BA 101I-383-0338-03)*

LEFT Blitzkrieg – flat countryside with no natural obstacles around the Gembloux Gap in Belgium was ideal tank country, but on 15 May 1940 the German advance west was checked when its armour took heavy losses at the hands of French artillery. Stukas of StG 2 were among those supporting the 4. and 5. Panzer-Divisions around Gembloux by targeting the French positions, but they failed to turn the battle around. This is the scene at 11.30hrs on 15 May as the German advance was halted. *(BA RH 82 Bild-00059)*

ABOVE Lee Enfield rifles were a defiant but ultimately futile gesture against the hordes of Stukas that dive-bombed the BEF on the beaches of Dunkirk. *(Author's collection)*

BELOW Dunkirk burning – pillars of grey smoke rise into the atmosphere, seen at 3,000m (9,840ft) from the cockpit of a Ju 87 of IV./LG 3. *(Chris Goss collection)*

had been to stand fast in order to delay the German advance on Dunkirk. This resulted in the destruction of the port by StG 2 and StG 77.

Meanwhile, the Luftwaffe was briefed to force the Allied surrender by dive-bombing BEF and French troops crowded into the port of Dunkirk. Despite constant air attack by the Luftwaffe, including relentless dive-bombing by Stukas, it was indeed the 'miracle' of Dunkirk that 330,000 British and French troops were snatched off the beaches by an armada of vessels both great and small and repatriated to England. Hauptmann Helmut Mahlke again:

As we flew back to base I couldn't get the horrific spectacle that was Dunkirk out of my mind. An absolute inferno! Those poor beggars down there desperately fighting for survival. Just as well that at our height we were spared the gory details. But those men down there . . . didn't stand a chance if set upon by Stukas.

Altogether, some 241 Allied vessels were sunk at Dunkirk, out of which the Royal Navy lost 6 destroyers and 19 more damaged. Stukas were responsible for a great many of the overall losses, including the French destroyer *Adroit*, the paddle steamer *Crested Eagle* and the British destroyer HMS *Grenade*. The Belgian Army capitulated on 28 May and Dunkirk eventually fell to the Germans on 4 June.

The battle to subdue France began in earnest when the Germans launched 'Fall Rot' (Case Red) on 5 June, with Stukas continuing to fly missions to bomb enemy armour, communications targets and troop columns. On 22 June a Franco-German armistice was signed at Compiègne, with the defeated French signing the instrument of surrender in the same railway carriage and at the same spot where the Germans had been forced to do so by Marshal Foch in 1918. This symbolic act was not lost on the older generations of both sides who had experienced the First World War.

It was not long, now, before the attention of the Luftwaffe turned to England. The Stukagruppen of VIII. Fliegerkorps were transferred to airfields in Lower Normandy around Cherbourg in anticipation of missions against Channel convoys and land targets along the English south coast.

Clash of Eagles – the Battle of Britain

The first dive-bombing attacks of the Battle of Britain were made against British coastal shipping on 4 July, as a prelude to the main assault. By 20 July Luftflotten 2 and 3 had amassed 316 Ju 87 Bs and Ju 87 Rs, of which 248 were serviceable and ready for battle. Most of the dive-bombers were under the command of Generalleutnant Wolfram Freiherr von Richthofen's VIII. Fliegerkorps, which included seven Stukagruppen that comprised the Stab, I and III./StG 1, the Stab, I and II./StG 2 and the Stab, I, II and III./StG 77, with the newly formed I./StG 3 coming under the control of IV. Fliegerkorps, and the II Gruppe of StG 1 plus IV. (Stuka)/LG 1 providing the dive-bomber component of II. Fliegerkorps.

On 8 August the first concerted dive-bomber sorties of the battle were flown, five days before Adlertag (Eagle Day) on the 13th. Three waves of Stukas attacked Convoy CW9 in the Channel near the Isle of Wight, but in spite of massive top cover provided by Bf 109E and Bf 110 fighters, they suffered heavy losses from RAF fighters, with eight shot down and ten more damaged. This was a taste of things to come

ABOVE After playing a full part in the campaigns in Poland, France and the Low Countries under the command of Hauptmann Walter Sigel, I./StG 76 was disbanded in July 1940 to form I./StG 3 and III./StG 77. *(Chris Goss collection)*

BELOW Smoke billows from a British destroyer as it continues to manoeuvre after being dive-bombed and set on fire in the English Channel south of the Isle of Wight by Stukas of I./StG 77 in July 1940. At top left is what looks like a near miss. *(Chris Goss collection)*

ABOVE The unmistakeable sight and sound of a mass formation of Stukas would have been witnessed over southern England many times during July and August 1940. *(Andy Saunders collection)*

BELOW Some battle-damaged Stukas were able to limp back across the English Channel to make crash-landings in France. Attracting the attention of motorcycle troops is this Ju 87 B-1 of Stab StG 2, T6+FA. What appears to be battle damage can be seen on the leading edge of the tailfin, as well as a damaged starboard wingtip and collapsed undercarriage. Only one blade of the metal propeller is bent, indicating that the engine was not under power when the aircraft met the ground. The gunner's canopy has been removed and can be seen on the ground behind the port wing, which may suggest he was wounded and needed extrication from the aircraft. The smoke is probably exhaust from the motorcycle in the foreground. *(Chris Goss collection)*

for the Stuka units because over the next nine days 24 were lost over or off England.

On Adlertag itself a formation of 52 Ju 87s from StG 2 were heading to bomb the RAF fighter airfield at Warmwell in Dorset when it was intercepted by Spitfires of 609 Squadron. The fighter cover provided by Bf 109s from JG 27 and JG 53, and Bf 110s from ZG 2 and ZG 76, aborted due to bad weather and was turning for home when it was broken up by the Spitfires and the Ju 87s were quickly picked off, with five dive-bombers falling in flames while the rest scattered.

The last Stuka sorties in any number against

British targets took place on 16 and 18 August. On the 16th, I. and III./StG 2 lost nine aircraft attacking RAF Tangmere in Sussex, falling to the Hurricanes of 43, 111 and 601 Squadrons.

On the 18th an attack by 109 Ju 87s – the largest number of Stukas yet used – hit the airfields at Gosport, Ford and Thorney Island, and the radar station at Poling near Littlehampton. Escorted by no fewer than 157 Bf 109s, the entire strength of StG 77 was committed to the attack and crossed the Channel from their forward airfields near Cherbourg in one enormous formation. Each aircraft was carrying a 250kg bomb beneath the fuselage and four 50kg bombs under the wings: 28 Stukas of the I.Gruppe attacked Thorney Island; II.Gruppe with 28 Stukas hit Ford; III. Gruppe (31 Stukas) attacked Poling. The fourth unit involved was I./StG 3, which bombed Gosport with 22 Stukas.

The raids on the airfields at Gosport and Ford were particularly devastating, but during the attack on Thorney Island I./StG 77 suffered heavy losses with ten of its 28 Stukas shot down, while another four Ju 87s from StG 77 were lost to RAF fighters and one badly damaged Stuka crash-landed in France and was destroyed.

After 18 August the Stukagruppen were withdrawn from the Luftwaffe's battle order, but aviation historian and author Andy Saunders has questioned the received wisdom of why

this happened. The accepted version of events is that they suffered such a severe mauling by Fighter Command that the Stukas were taken out of the front line and never again committed in battle over England. Andy has noted that Stuka losses in July and August were probably no worse pro rata than any other front-line Luftwaffe flying unit in the battle at that time. He interviewed former Stuka crews and posed the question 'Were the Stukagruppen withdrawn because of unacceptably high losses?' They scorned this version of events and told him that after 18 August they were moved north from their airfields on the

ABOVE On 18 August, Major Helmuth Bode, Kommandeur of III./StG 77, led the massed formation of 109 Ju 87s that attacked airfields at Gosport, Ford and Thorney Island, and the radar station at Poling near Littlehampton. Displayed beneath the cockpit is the emblem of Stab III./StG 77, which was adopted from the coat of arms of the Bode family (Bode being the first commander of the Gruppe). *(Andy Saunders collection)*

Cherbourg peninsula up to bases in the Pas-de-Calais in anticipation of close-air support missions when Operation Sealion was launched against southern England. They expected to see imminent action above the beaches of Kent and Sussex, but when Hitler switched the Luftwaffe's attacks to London, the Stuka squadrons were not part of this plan and were held in readiness, resting and regrouping, awaiting the delayed launch of Operation Sealion, which never came.

Stukas made a brief and sporadic reappearance against Channel shipping in November. On the 1st, Ju 87 B-1 of 5./StG 1 was shot down into the Thames Estuary by AA fire from a small ship it had attacked, while on the 7th a Ju 87 of I./StG 3 was damaged by flak also over the Thames Estuary.

The next day Stukas made two large attacks on shipping targets near the Thames Estuary, from which three Ju 87s were lost, probably to Hurricanes of 17 Squadron – two from 3./StG 3 and one from 12./Lehrgeschwader 1 (LG 1). On 15 November two Ju 87 B-2s of 9./StG 1 were shot down off the North and South Foreland during an air battle over a convoy.

On 14 November Spitfire pilot Flight Lieutenant Hubert 'Dizzy' Allen of 66 Squadron shot down a Ju 87 and damaged another over Dover in the last daylight attack on the port by Stukas. He recalls:

We intercepted about forty Ju 87s accompanied by some escorting fighters, just before they reached their target, a coastal town. I was one of a section dispatched to intercept a single raider when we spotted them.

I rubbed my eyes when I saw these lumbering dive-bombers; I couldn't believe that it could be true. Then, with a howl of delight, I went straight into the middle. The next few minutes were spent by me in attacking and breaking up innumerable formations of these. I saw two break sharply and jettison their bombs, obviously hit. Then I made a longer attack on another who heeled over with oil pouring from his engine. I had not time to follow him down as I was too busy attacking the others. My technique was to go straight for the sections from every conceivable angle until they split up their formation. It was an impressive sight as we battled over the target. I could see the 87s go down vertically onto the target, and drop their bombs to the accompaniment of ack-ack of every calibre. Huge columns of water rose as the bombs exploded, and flashes and shell bursts could be seen everywhere. In the general mêlée I saw Spitfires attacking from everywhere, with their guns smoking as they fired. One man fired as he was on his back – or maybe I was on my back – I couldn't tell. . . . Aircraft disintegrated around me. I saw them catch fire, go straight down, smoking, into the sea. It was vivid.

Return by night

It was not until mid-January 1941 that Stukas returned to dive-bomb English targets, but this time by night, in what must have been tricky operations for the crews. On 15/16 January a pair of Ju 87s from StG 1, each carrying an SC 1000 (kg) bomb, ventured as far as South London under cover of darkness to make dive-bombing attacks on Deptford and Kidbrooke. Another Ju 87 dive-bombed Dover, also with an SC 1000. A second attack on targets in and around London was made two nights later, and a third on 19/20 January, but bad weather brought a temporary halt to Stuka night bombing ops over England until mid-February.

On the night of 5/6 February a Kette of three Stukas from II./StG 1 was attacked by Spitfires of 92 Squadron on convoy patrol. One Ju 87 B-1 was shot down by Pilot Officer R.H. Fokes after it attacked HMT *Tourmaline*, which was then sunk by a second Stuka.

Stuka night operations were gradually petering out. On 11/12 February Ju 87s of 5./StG 1 bombed the naval base at Chatham and once more a single Ju 87 B-2 was shot down, but this time by gunners on HMS *Eager*, with the aircraft blowing up and crashing into the sea. The following night a Ju 87 of 9./StG 1 crashed into the Thames Estuary, the cause unknown. A few isolated Stuka night-bombing raids were mounted in mid-September and early October 1941 against Dover, Margate and Ramsgate, but by then the end was truly in sight for Stuka bombing ops over England. By then, most Ju 87 units had already been transferred from France and Belgium to the Mediterranean, the Balkans and Greece – and of course to Russia for Hitler's great offensive in the east, Operation Barbarossa.

Malta

The island of Malta, lying in the centre of the Mediterranean shipping routes between Gibraltar and Port Said, and Sicily and Libya, was of key strategic importance to Britain as a naval base. Royal Navy forces from Malta harried Axis troop and armament convoys supplying the German and Italian armies in Libya. While Malta survived, it remained a threat to the power of the Axis forces in North Africa. The island was subjected to prolonged and heavy air attacks from June 1940.

Stukas of I./StG 1, II./StG 2 and the Stabstaffel StG 3 were sent to Italy for 'a limited period' by Hitler to help the struggling Italians. They arrived at Trapani on the western tip of Sicily in January 1941 with the aim of attacking British ships passing through the Strait of Sicily (the Narrows) between Sicily and North Africa.

The Royal Navy's first and newest armoured aircraft carrier, HMS *Illustrious*, was deployed as part of Force A to cover Operation Excess, a 'rush' of convoys through the Mediterranean's chokepoints in January 1941 to relieve Alexandria, Greece and Malta. Admiral Andrew Cunningham, C-in-C Mediterranean, commanded the operation from his flagship HMS *Valiant*.

Soon after midday on 10 January the 23,000-ton *Illustrious* came under heavy bombardment from 43 Stukas of I./StG 1 (Ju 87 R) and II./StG 2 (Ju 87 B) in a precision attack led by Hauptman Paul-Werner Hozzel and Major Walter Enneccerus. The carrier's Fulmar fighters, having already launched to deal with a decoy attack by Italian aircraft, were refuelling in Malta.

Watching from the bridge of HMS *Warspite*, Cunningham later recalled the attack on *Illustrious*:

We opened up with every AA gun we had as one-by-one the Stukas peeled off into their dives, concentrating the whole venom of their attack upon the Illustrious. *At times she became almost completely hidden in a forest of great bomb splashes. One was too interested in this new form of dive-bombing attack really to be frightened, and there was no doubt we were watching complete experts. Formed roughly in a large circle over the fleet, they peeled off one-by-one when*

BELOW A Ju 87 R of I./StG 3 returns to its base at Trapani in Sicily after bombing Malta. *(Bundesarchiv)*

HMS *Illustrious* comes under a determined dive-bombing attack from Ju 87s of I./StG 1 and II./StG 2 on 10 January 1941. A fountain of water from a near miss can be seen off the carrier's port bow, while puffs of grey smoke from exploding AA shells hang in the sky overhead. *(Copyright unknown)*

reaching the attacking position. We could not but admire the skill and precision of it all. The attacks were pressed home to point-blank range, and as they pulled out of their dives some of them were seen to fly along the flight-deck of the Illustrious *below the level of her funnel.*

In the space of 10 minutes six direct hits were scored and three damaging near misses, wreaking serious damage on the carrier which, by a miracle, managed to limp to the relative safety of Valletta dockyard, despite a second attack by Stukas between 16.00 and 17.00hrs. Some 6 or 7 Stukas were shot down during this action by Fulmars from *Illustrious*, having just refuelled and rearmed in Malta.

Cunningham went on to say:

In a few minutes the whole situation had changed. At one blow the fleet had been deprived of its fighter aircraft, and its command of the Mediterranean was threatened by a weapon far more efficient and dangerous than any against which we had fought before. The efforts of the Regia Aeronautica were almost as nothing compared with those of these deadly Stukas of the Luftwaffe.

Not content with this performance, Enneccerus took off the following afternoon with 10 Ju 87 Bs to hit another naval force spotted heading east towards Malta. In a surprise attack from out of the sun in a clear blue sky, the Stukas' bombs fatally damaged the 9,057-ton cruiser HMS *Southampton* operating with Force B. She was abandoned by her crew and finished off by her escorts.

Over the next week or so the Stukagruppen launched a series of determined strikes on *Illustrious* while she was laid up in the naval dockyard, and on the RAF fighter airfields at Hal Far and Luqa. Further damage was inflicted on the ailing carrier, but under cover of darkness on 23 January she raised anchor and made a dash for Alexandria, which she reached on the 25th and where she spent a year undergoing major repairs.

With the Royal Navy left licking its wounds, the Luftwaffe switched its attention to Malta in a concerted attempt to bomb the island fortress into submission. The two Stukagruppen at Trapani played a brief part in this renewed action, but within weeks they were posted away with their units to North Africa in support of Rommel's land forces in Libya, where they were joined by Italian Ju 87s (the 'Picchiatelli') of 96° Gruppo.

Their replacements were the other two

Gruppen of StG 1 (II and III), which flew down to Trapani from their bases in northern France and Belgium with their Ju 87 Bs and Rs, arriving on 23 February.

On 26 February III./StG 1 took off from Comiso escorted by Bf 109s of 7./JG 26, their target the airfield at Luqa. Led by its Gruppenkommandeur Hauptmann Helmut Mahlke, the Stukas took a pasting from light and medium AA fire and RAF Hurricanes of 261 Squadron; III Gruppe reported four aircraft lost, many more damaged and crews wounded. Stukas helped keep up the Luftwaffe's pressure on Malta over the coming weeks, suffering moderate casualties along the way, but by early May the aerial assaults against the island were petering out. A final burst of activity took place between 6 and 12 May when StG 1 and the Ju 87s (Picchiatelli) of the Regia Aeronautica carried out a series of unsuccessful attacks on British supply Convoy 'Tiger' carrying vital supplies for Malta and tanks for the British Army's campaign against Rommel in the Western Desert.

Towards the end of May, the Stukas of StG 1 had moved on from Trapani to north-eastern Poland when the Luftwaffe began transferring much of its strength from Sicily to prepare for the imminent invasion of Russia – Operation Barbarossa.

LEFT Walter Enneccerus was a dive-bomber man from the very beginning when he was first assigned to I./StG 165 in 1936. As a Hauptmann he took command of II./StG 2 on 16 December 1939, which he led until he was made Kommandeur of III./StG 3 on 13 January 1942. As a Major, he led II./StG 2 in the attack on HMS *Illustrious* along with Hauptmann Paul-Werner Hozzel, commanding I./StG 1. *(Copyright unknown)*

The task of subduing Malta was now left largely to the Regia Aeronautica and after the departure of the Germans from Sicily British power in the central Mediterranean saw an almost immediate resurgence.

LEFT Ju 87 Rs overfly Malta on 12 March 1941, with Valletta and the Grand Harbour spread out beneath them. During the 2½-year siege between June 1940 and November 1942, Malta held the unenviable record for enduring the heaviest, most sustained bombing attacks over some 154 days and nights, when 6,700 tons of Axis bombs rained down on the island. *(Chris Goss collection)*

The Regia Aeronautica and the 'Picchiatello'

Before the war Italy had developed its own dive-bomber, the Savoia-Marchetti SM85, but it had proved a dismal failure. The Italian Duce, Benito Mussolini, was determined that his air force, the Regia Aeronautica, was to have a dive-bomber, and so he negotiated the purchase of enough Ju 87s to equip two complete Gruppi. Training of Italian pilots by the Luftwaffe at Stuka-Schule 2 in Graz-Thalerhof in Austria began in July 1940. Mussolini's urgent need for dive-bombers meant the first aircraft delivered had been acquired from the Luftwaffe, so the Balkan cross and swastika were hurriedly over-painted with the Regia

Aeronautica's markings. The Italians renamed their Stukas 'Picchiatello' (plural Picchiatelli) which, translated, means 'a good thrashing' and 'slightly crazy' – a whimsical-sounding word that evokes a completely different image to the Teutonic 'Stuka'.

First unit to equip and see action with the new Picchiatello was 96° Gruppo based at Comiso in southern Sicily under the command of Capitano Ercolano Ercolani. On 2 September 13 Picchiatelli attacked the British aircraft carrier HMS *Illustrious* in the Mediterranean in what proved to be an inconclusive engagement. Over the next few weeks the Picchiatelli of 236a and 237a Squadriglie raided Malta on several occasions and suffered their first combat losses raiding Luqa airfield on 17 September. Mussolini, determined to expand Italy's influence in the Mediterranean and the Balkans, then turned his attention away from Malta.

In the early hours of 28 October, Il Duce issued Greece with an ultimatum as a precursor to launching an unprovoked attack on the country at dawn. In a triple-pronged offensive into Greece towards Salonika and Yanina, and along the coast towards the island of Corfu. Ercolani's 96° Gruppo with its Ju 87 Bs and Rs was moved south to Comiso to support ground operations in Greece. The Italians made good progress in the first few days of the campaign, but their fortunes quickly turned on

1 November when the Greek Army launched a counter-offensive and pushed the invaders back across the Albanian border. Despite vigorous air support along the Greek–Albanian border from 96° Gruppo's Ju 87s and the drafting in of a second (97°) Gruppo of Picchiatelli, the Italian offensive had unravelled and by December Mussolini was forced to call on the Germans to bail them out of the mess they found themselves in. The Greeks, too, called upon Britain for help and a military expeditionary force ('W' Force) was sent to their aid as well as a handful of RAF fighter squadrons with Hurricanes, Gladiators and Blenheims, but none at full establishment.

No. 96° Gruppo was withdrawn from Lecce on the heel of Italy and transferred to Comiso in January 1942 to tackle increased Allied convoy movements in the Mediterranean, while 97° Gruppo remained to continue with dive-bombing operations in Albania. From Comiso, 96° Gruppo's two squadrons resumed attacks on Malta and the interdiction of Allied shipping in the Mediterranean, including air strikes against the carrier *Illustrious* as she made for Malta after her mauling at the hands of the Stukas of StG 1 and 2. In early February, Ercolani's Gruppo crossed the Mediterranean to Castel Benito in Libya to support I./StG 1 and II./StG 2 in the war in North Africa, but the Italians with their Picchiatelli played second fiddle to the Luftwaffe's Stukas.

In Albania, organisational changes to the Picchiatelli units saw 97° Gruppo receive some additional resources for their ground-support missions when a new Gruppo (101°) was formed in March. The 97° Gruppo also had some limited success in anti-shipping strikes off Corfu, when their bombs were released in extremely low-level attacks causing the weapons to skim across the surface of the sea and striking the hulls of their targets before exploding. Two Greek vessels were sunk in this way on 4 April, but the independent action of the Picchiatelli units was quickly overshadowed by events unfolding in the Balkans, when German forces invaded Yugoslavia in the early morning of 6 April.

The Picchiatelli units of the Regia Aeronautica had never enjoyed the numbers or the successes of their Luftwaffe Stuka counterparts and forever lived in the shadow of the Germans.

Yugoslavia, Greece and Crete

Yugoslavia

The Italian failure in Greece raised the possibility of a prolonged conflict in the Balkans, with British intervention on the side of the Greeks. This instability severely threatened German interests in the region on the eve of their invasion of Russia, so Hitler resolved to support Mussolini by ordering a German invasion of Greece through Bulgaria, and by coercing neighbouring Yugoslavia into joining the Axis powers.

When Hitler's alliance with Yugoslavia failed two days after it was signed on 25 March, the Führer suspected a British plot and his plans to invade Greece were expanded to include the conquest of Yugoslavia in a dual attack.

The six Stukagruppen still based in northern France were moved to bases in southern Europe for the twin invasions as part of Fliegerkorps VIII's air component. German troops began to cross the Bulgarian border at 05.15hrs on 6 April and advanced into Yugoslavia. Only a few hours later waves of bombers proceeded to rain destruction on the capital, Belgrade, as punishment for the country's defiance of Hitler. In Operation Strafgericht (Retribution), which was implemented by the commander of Luftflotte IV, Generaloberst Alexander Löhr, Stukas of StG 77 accounted for almost a quarter of the bombers in the first wave of 300 aircraft, which also included He 111s and Dornier Do 17s. During three days of raids the bombing destroyed much of the city, killed thousands of civilians, paralysed the Yugoslav military and led to the rapid collapse of resistance. (Löhr was captured after the war, tried by a Yugoslav military court and executed.) Stukas of StG 2 covered the advance of the 12. Armee across southern Yugoslavia to join with the Italian forces in Albania, while Picchiatelli of the 97° and 101° Gruppos struck at land and sea targets along the Dalmatian coast. Yugoslavia was besieged from all quarters and finally the government surrendered on 17 April.

Greece

Attention swiftly turned to Greece, where the German 12th Army invaded the eastern part of the country in Operation Marita, cutting off enemy troops in this area before marching west to trap most of the Greek Army between themselves and the Italians in Albania.

It fell to the Stukas of StG 2 to destroy the fortifications of the 200km-long Greek Metaxas line that followed the border with Bulgaria and overlooked the Panzers' advance through the valleys below. Protecting the only main road through the mountains was Fort Istibei, the largest of the forts, which was renamed Fortress Mountain by the Germans.

RIGHT Ju 87 B-2s of StG 77 on a forward airfield at Prilep in Yugoslavia during the Balkan Campaign in 1941. *(Andy Saunders collection)*

An unnamed Luftwaffe Kriegsberichter (war reporter) flew a sortie in the rear seat of a Ju 87 belonging to StG 2 when the Staffeln attacked Fortress Mountain. This is the vivid account of his experience:

Now it was our turn to take off. As we climbed I could make out those behind us – small dots trailing long banners of dust behind them as they accelerated across the surface of the field. As they gained height to formate on us they looked like dark fishes swimming through the morning haze. Closing up in Ketten formation, we continued to climb. Spread out ahead of us were the mountains of Macedonia. We set course for Fortress Mountain. Rising from it, a long grey-blue column of smoke was spreading northwards, blown by the wind. Large fires were burning in the enemy positions and a bright red wall of flame was eating through the thick undergrowth on the Greek side of the mountain.

I did not have time to notice much else. 'Dive', yelled the pilot. I quickly grabbed the cabin cross-struts in both hands and braced my feet. The aircraft was already standing on its nose, tail pointing up into the blue sky. For a second we seemed to hang there in space. Then the force of the dive pressed me hard into the seat. In front of us, framed

ABOVE Ju 87 Rs of II./ StG 1 picketed around the perimeter of Argos airfield on the Peloponnese peninsula in southern Greece, where they had been transferred from Trapani and Comiso for Operation Merkur, the airborne invasion of Crete on 20 May 1941. Hurricanes from sections of 33, 80 and 208 Squadrons operated from this Greek training airfield from 22 to 24 April to protect the evacuation of Allied troops by sea from Greece. Stukas and Bf 109s bombed the airfield destroying many of the Hurricanes, although six or seven survived and managed to get away. In the foreground one of the wrecked Hurricanes lies in a dried-up riverbed. *(Bundesarchiv)*

in the windscreen and growing larger every second – Fortress Mountain.

We hurtled downwards towards some small grey squares. These must be bunkers. My whole body was quivering, the wings of the aircraft vibrated with a noise like ghostly metal drums, and my ears were filled with a high-pitched screaming and whistling. Suddenly a tremendous jolt and I felt a wave of dizziness – the pilot was pulling out of the dive. The pressure in my head and ears slowly eased – I could breathe freely again. Below us the bombs streaked towards their target. We were already several hundred metres away when they exploded, sending huge fountains of earth and debris high into the air between the bunkers.

Like the BEF in France in 1940, 'W' Force had been sent to Greece to help the Greeks defend their country against German and Italian invasion. But with the unstoppable Blitzkrieg through Yugoslavia and onwards into Greece, the decisive and rapid advance of the German Army caused the under-resourced 'W' Force to beat a hasty retreat south,

When faced with the numerically superior Luftwaffe, British air power in Greece achieved little in its attempts to turn around the desperate situation, although the RAF fought with great valour against a determined enemy.

Overwhelmed by the same speed and ferocity of the German attack as the Poles and

the French, the Greek Army surrendered on 20 April and asked the British to withdraw; by the 24th the Allied evacuation by sea had begun from ports and beaches in southern Greece. Stukas of Luftflotte IV harried the retreating troops during their desperate trek south, with orders to destroy them before they could be evacuated by sea. They dive-bombed Allied shipping around the Greek coast and sank two Greek destroyers on 22 April. On the 24th three large merchant vessels were sent to the bottom outside the port of Nauplia in full view of the troops waiting to be evacuated.

Further attempts to disrupt the Allied evacuation took place on the 26th when the Germans launched an airborne operation to seize the bridge spanning the Corinth Canal, which was being used by Allied troops to reach evacuation beaches to the west, being the only bridge linking mainland Greece with the Peloponnese. Up to 30 Stukas of I./StG 3 suppressed anti-aircraft gun positions, with Ju 88s of I./KG 51 and Bf 110s of I./ZstG 26, to support the assault force of 800 paratroops dropped from Ju 52s and carried in 12 DFS 230 gliders. The bridge was successfully taken, but it was destroyed minutes later in an unexplained explosion that not only cut off the Allies' escape route but also ruined any chance of the Germans being able to pursue them.

Saturday 27 April was disastrous for Allied forces in the Mediterranean for it was the day when Athens fell to the Germans, and the day on which two British destroyers (HMS *Diamond* and *Wryneck*) and a former Dutch passenger liner (the 11,800-ton *Slamat*, requisitioned as a troopship) were sunk by the Luftwaffe with massive loss of life. In the climate of confusion that had followed the German invasion three weeks previously, British warships and transports were being used to hurriedly evacuate Allied and Greek forces to Crete and Egypt. German bombers and fighter-bombers including Stukas from III./StG 2 and III./StG 77 flying from Almyros on mainland Greece, were responsible for sinking the three vessels. The loss of the *Slamat* represented the worst maritime disaster in Dutch history.

The desperate evacuation of 'W' Force was completed by 28 April, first to Crete and then to Egypt, with some 60,000 eventually making good their escape. At a cost of fewer than 6,000 casualties, the Germans had defeated armed forces of more than 1 million men in less than a month.

Crete

Although most of the success in the taking of Crete in Operation Merkur was down to General Kurt Student's Fliegerkorps XI, the three dive-bomber Geschwader of Fliegerkorps VIII with their Ju 87 Rs (StG 1, 2 and 77) were highly effective in grinding down Allied ground forces on the island and limiting the effectiveness of the Royal Navy. The loss of Crete after only a few days' fighting came as a shock to the Allies who paid a heavy price in men and materiel, including the loss of three cruisers, six destroyers and serious damage inflicted by Ju 87s upon the only aircraft carrier in the eastern Mediterranean, HMS *Formidable*.

After the capture of Crete on 31 May, resistance on mainland Greece and its islands finally buckled under the weight of the Axis occupation. Luftflotte 4 was withdrawn from the Balkans and Fliegerkorps X, formerly based on Sicily, moved to Crete and Greece. Targets in Egypt and the Levant were attacked occasionally while Tobruk bore the brunt of Fliegerkorps X's attacks. The task of subduing Malta was now left to the Italian Air Force and the departure of the Germans from Sicily saw an almost immediate resurgence of British power in the central Mediterranean.

Now, with a completely secure Balkan flank, the Germans were in a position to launch Operation Barbarossa. Before we look at how Stukas played a key role in Hitler's Blitzkrieg in Russia, across the Mediterranean in North Africa the Ju 87 was making an important contribution to the ground campaign of Field Marshal Erwin Rommel and his Afrika Korps.

North Africa

When Mussolini tried to emulate the Germans and their conquests in Europe by attempting to do the same in North Africa, his troops were thwarted by much smaller British and Commonwealth forces that drove out the Italian invaders and captured their entire 10th Army in the process. As with Mussolini's failed venture in the Balkans, Hitler was forced to send in troops and aircraft to assist his inept Axis partner. The Deutsches Afrika Korps, under the command of General Erwin Rommel, arrived in North Africa in April 1941 where the 'Desert Fox', supported by the Luftwaffe, fought many battles across the unforgiving deserts where, over the next two years, the fighting ebbed and flowed as first one side and then the other gained the upper hand.

The only aircraft immediately available to the Fliegerführer Afrika (Air Officer Commanding, North Africa) were 60 Ju 87s of I./StG 1 and II./StG 2 and as such they were soon in action against enemy ground positions and ports

ABOVE The former Dutch liner turned troopship *Slamat* was carrying 700 Allied soldiers to safety from Greece on 27 April 1941 when she was bombed and set on fire by Stukas. Her size and distinctive appearance made her an easy target for the attackers. *Slamat*'s loss was the worst maritime disaster in Dutch history.
(Copyright unknown)

along the coast of Cyrenaica in eastern Libya in preparation for Rommel's coming offensive. In shades of things to come, RAF Hurricanes of 3 Squadron shot down eight Stukas of StG 1 on 18 February 1941, but on the 22nd the monitor HMS *Terror* was badly damaged at Benghazi by Stukas and the destroyer *Dainty* sunk.

On 31 March Rommel launched his counter-attack with land targets softened up by Ju 87s in the days beforehand and soon most of Libya was back under Axis control, except for the small port of Tobruk that refused to surrender. Defended by a contingent of British, Australian and Indian forces, the strategically vital port held by the Italians had fallen to the Australians in January and held out for eight months in a siege that has become an epic of the Second World War.

On land at the end of May the unstoppable advance of the 'Desert Fox' and his Panzer force was held up at Bir Hacheim in the desert, but relentless dive-bombing by Stukas of StG 3, flying up to three missions a day against determined Allied fighter opposition, eventually subdued the fortress. The British Eighth Army's attempts to relieve Tobruk were repulsed by the Germans and they withdrew to the east.

ABOVE Still wearing their original European camouflage scheme colour of dark green, these Ju 87 B-2 trop of StG 2 have been over-sprayed with sand-yellow for service in North Africa. *(Copyright unknown)*

RIGHT Having just dropped its bombs on a British supply depot near Tobruk in October 1941, this unidentified Ju 87 B makes good its escape from the target area at low level to avoid AA fire. *(AP Photo)*

Stukas of StG 1, StG 2 and the Italian 96° Gruppo played an essential part in attempts to grind down Tobruk's defenders. With the end of hostilities in Albania and mainland Greece, two Italian Picchiatello units (97° and 101° Gruppo) were redeployed to Sicily and North Africa in May. No 97° Gruppo took part in shipping strikes off Tobruk to try to cut off the Allied attempts to resupply the garrison by sea.

The minefields that stood between Rommel and Tobruk were blasted by Stukas to clear the way to the port, which he besieged again from 18 June, but still its garrison held out. There was no let-up in Rommel's advance on Egypt, with Stukas and Picchiatelli maintaining their attacks on land targets and against Allied shipping.

In August Oberstleutnant Walter Sigel, Kommandeur of Geschwaderstab StG 3, took command of the two Stukagruppen in the desert – I./StG 1 (based at Derna) and II./StG 2 (Tmimi). Ignominy befell the Italian 209a Squadriglia on 14 September when 12 Picchiatelli on a sortie to provide air cover to an Axis operation around Sidi Barrani lost their bearings as well as their Bf 109 escort before running out of fuel. Ten Ju 87s force-landed in the desert and eight crews were captured.

The tides of war changed again on 18 November when British and Commonwealth forces under General Claude Auchinleck launched Operation Crusader which, after intense fighting lasting until the end of December, resulted in the relief of Tobruk and the first Allied victory by Allied ground forces over Axis forces of the war.

However, Crusader also witnessed the beginning of the end for the Stukagruppen in North Africa. Allied air power was starting to turn the fortunes of war and Stuka losses began to mount at the hands of enemy fighters. On 18 November I./StG 1 lost 6 Stukas while later in the day 18 aircraft of II./StG 2 were shot up on the ground at their base, Tmimi. Casualties continued to mount and at the end of the month 15 Stukas were shot down followed by 13 more on 4 December. Now, Ju 87s were often failing to reach their targets, instead dropping their bombs in the open desert and running.

Increasing numbers of enemy fighters and the emergence of the Bf 109 and Fw 190 as fighter-

ABOVE Stukas escorted by Messerschmitt Bf 109 fighters were a formidable combination in the early stages of the desert war in 1941. Here, a Ju 87 B-2 trop returning from a mission is shadowed by a Bf 109 E flown by Oberleutnant Ludwig Franzisket, the Gruppen-Adjutant of I./JG 27. Like many of the Stuka crews he escorted, Franzisket was a veteran of the Blitzkrieg campaigns in 1939 and 1940 and the Battle of Britain. He finished the war with 43 victories. *(Bundesarchiv)*

BELOW Ju 87 B-2 trops of 3./StG 1 operating from Gambut in Libya peel off as they begin their dive to attack a target. Note the roughly applied desert camouflage. *(Copyright unknown)*

bombers contributed to the Stuka's relative decline, which was helped on its way on New Year's Day 1942 when 16 Ju 87s were bounced by Kittyhawks of 3 Squadron RAF south-east of Agedabia – four of the dive-bombers and one Bf 109 escort fighter were shot down.

In mid-January I./StG 1 and II./StG 2 were amalgamated with StG 3 and became II. and III./StG 3 respectively, creating a single Stuka unit in North Africa. On 21 January Rommel launched a counter-attack north of El Agheila and his Panzers continued to beat a path towards Egypt, spearheaded by the Stukas of StG 3. In May, Ju 87s were in the vanguard of the action that saw the Gazala Line pounded relentlessly by dive-bombing before it was finally overrun and the Axis forces recaptured the port of Tobruk on 21 June. The Eighth Army fell back to El Alamein and in the Battle of Alam Halfa in July Rommel was checked at the gates of Cairo and the Suez Canal.

In August, I./StG 3 was transferred temporarily from Libya to Trapani in Sicily from where its Stukas flew in Fliegerkorps II's attacks on the 'Pedestal' relief force and convoy sailing through the Mediterranean from Gibraltar to Malta. Its

Ju 87s scored hits on the aircraft carrier *Indomitable* on 12 August, but lost two Ju 87 Ds shot down by the carrier's defences. Two Picchiatelli from 103° Gruppo were also lost.

Back in North Africa, it was at El Alamein that the Eighth Army made its famous stand in October under the leadership of its new commander, Lieutenant General Bernard Montgomery. The Battle of El Alamein became the turning point in North Africa, with Rommel and the Afrika Korps routed and forced into a long and protracted withdrawal westwards towards Tunisia. With the Allied Operation Torch landings in French North Africa (Morocco and Algeria) on 8 November 1942, the Germans were forced to fight on two fronts as they became trapped between the converging armies.

On 11 November I./StG 3 was almost wiped out when 15 Ju 87 Ds were despatched from their operating base at Qasaba to attack advancing British armour in the Gambut area east of Tobruk. Jumped by SAAF Kittyhawks who were joined later by USAAF P-40s, only one Stuka is believed to have escaped the mauling. Gruppenkommandeur Hauptmann Martin Mossdorf was among those captured. The tattered remnants of the Gruppe were withdrawn to Germany for rest and re-equipment.

Reacting to the shock of the Torch landings, the Luftwaffe hurriedly brought in units to counter the invasion forces. Among them was II./StG 3, which was rushed to Tunisia from Sicily with its Doras. Apart from losses to enemy fighters, the Gruppe suffered the destruction of 36 of its Stukas on the ground on 26 November when American tanks ran amok on Djedeida airfield.

In early 1943 the final gasps of the Ju 87 in North Africa saw II. and III./StG 3 fighting a valiant retreat back across Libya towards Tunis, facing constant losses from the swarms of Allied fighters that had gained almost complete command of the air. On 12 April, those Stukas which had survived withdrew across the narrow straits separating Tunisia from Sicily, leaving behind the German Army to its eventual fate.

Russia

Operation Barbarossa, 1941

At 03.15hrs on Sunday 22 June 1941, Hitler made his biggest gamble of the war when he launched Operation Barbarossa – the German invasion of Russia. With it commenced a war of racial annihilation, perpetrated by the Nazis in pursuit of Lebensraum (living space) for the German people in the vast lands of the east. At the same time, Hitler committed to destroying the 'Jewish-Bolshevik' political system, which he saw as an abomination, and securing resources to protect Germany from blockade. Another hope was that in robbing Britain of her last potential European ally, he would force Churchill and his government to make peace and recognise Germany's pre-eminence on the continent.

Germany committed some 4 million troops to battle along a 1,800-mile front. Four Stuka dive-bomber wings comprising some 290 aircraft were on the Luftwaffe's battle order – under VIII. Fliegerkorps were Stab, II. and III./StG 1, and Stab, I., II. and III./StG 2 'Immelmann'; attached to II. Fliegerkorps were Stab, I., II and III./StG 77; and operating from northern Norway under Luftflotte 5 was IV. Gruppe (St)/LG 1.

Before daybreak on 22 June, Stukas were airborne to spearhead the greatest land battle in history. Only two Ju 87s failed to return that day out of 35 German losses, but it was a very different story for the Soviet Air Force in western Russia, which was virtually wiped out at the hands of the Luftwaffe – with some 1,800 aircraft destroyed. Stukas exacted a heavy toll on enemy ground forces, helping to repel counter-attacks by Soviet armour,

LEFT More than 3,000 German tanks were unleashed against the Soviet Union with the launch of Operation Barbarossa on 22 June 1941. Stukas provided dive-bombing and close air-support for the armies on the ground and by the end of the first week of campaigning the Luftwaffe had achieved air supremacy over the battlefields. Here, a mixed force of Panzer IVs and Panzer IIs pause in the rolling Russian grasslands during the opening days of the invasion. (BA 101I-265-0040A-22A)

destroying strongpoints and disrupting supply lines.

At the end of June, Stukas were instrumental in closing the Minsk pocket – the first of a number of successful encircling operations – where 32 Russian divisions were wiped out, 2,400 tanks, 1,400 guns and 240 aircraft were captured or destroyed.

However, the appearance of the Soviet T-34 and the heavy KV tanks in the early days of Barbarossa came as a profound shock to the German invaders, and was a portent of bad things to come. For the moment, though, fortune smiled on Hitler.

When his armies were within 200 miles of Moscow, on 3 August Hitler surprised his generals by ordering Army Groups Centre and South to sweep south into Ukraine towards Kiev, while Army Group North headed towards Leningrad. Beginning on 9 September, the destructive siege of the city lasted until 27 January 1944.

Much of the city's defence came from the big-gun warships of the Russian Baltic Fleet holed up in the naval base at Kronstadt on the island of Kotlin, facing Leningrad. In a dramatic and highly publicised attack on 23 September, the battleship *Marat* was sunk in Kronstadt harbour by the future Stuka ace Hans-Ulrich Rudel from StG 2 'Immelmann', with a direct hit from a single 1,000kg bomb. During the same action the destroyers *Minsk* and *Steregushchiy* were also sunk, along with a submarine, and three other warships that were badly damaged, for the loss of two Ju 87s shot down.

In his autobiography *Stuka Pilot*, Rudel described his destruction of the Soviet battleship *Marat*:

I must surely be 90 degrees – sat tight as if I were sitting on a powder keg. Shall I graze Steen's aircraft, which is right on me, or shall I get safely past and down? I streak past him within a hair's breadth. Is this an omen of success? The ship is centred plumb in the middle of my sights. My Ju 87 keeps perfectly steady as I dive; she does not swerve an inch. I have the feeling that to miss is now impossible. Then I see the Marat *large as life in front of me. Sailors are running across the deck, carrying ammunition. Now I press the bomb-release switch on my stick and pull with all my strength. Can I still manage to pull out? I doubt it, for I am diving without brakes and the height at which I have released my bomb is not more than 275 metres [900ft]. The skipper has said when briefing us that the two thousand-pounder must not be dropped from lower than 900 metres [3,000ft] as the fragmentation effect of this bomb reaches 900 metres and to drop it at a lower altitude is to endanger one's aircraft. But now I have forgotten that! – I am intent on hitting the* Marat. *I tug at my stick, without feeling, merely exerting all my strength. My acceleration is too great. I see nothing, my sight is blurred in a momentary blackout, a new experience for me. But if it can be managed at all I must pull out. My head has not yet cleared when I hear Scharnovski's voice: 'She is blowing up, sir!' Now I look out. We are skimming the water at a level of 10 or 12ft and I bank round a little. Yonder lies the* Marat *below a cloud of smoke rising to 1,200ft; apparently the magazine had exploded.*

Meanwhile, Generalfeldmarschall von Kleist's 1. Panzergruppe wiped out three Russian armies between Kiev and Odessa in the Crimea, but more were to fall to the seemingly unstoppable German Panzer divisions. Stalin had ordered his armies to stand fast at Kiev. The 4. Panzer-Division pushed down from the north on 9 September, supported by wave after wave of Stukas, to link up with 1. Panzergruppe and 2. Panzergruppe (Guderian) and force bridgeheads over the River Dniepr before closing in on Kiev. Stukas were constantly in action during the heavy fighting that followed,

but by 26 September victory belonged to the Germans: five Soviet armies and 1 million men had been snuffed out. (From 22 January 1942 the Panzergruppen were redesignated Panzerarmee, i.e. 1. Panzergruppe became 1. Panzerarmee.)

When Army Group Centre resumed the advance on Moscow on 2 October, Ju 87s were at the forefront of the advance. Between 13 and 22 December the Stukas of the seemingly invincible StG 77 were responsible for the destruction of 420 vehicles and 23 tanks, which was a morale boost to the hard-pressed German infantry who were now battling against their greatest enemy, the bitter Russian winter, as well as a determined foe that was beginning to turn the tables.

Major Paul-Werner Hozzel, Kommodore of StG 2 'Immelmann', recalled the onset of winter and its effects on the German offensive:

All of a sudden Russia's 'General Winter' came over us. It was getting colder and cooler, the mud froze, vehicles got stuck and could no longer move in any direction. It started snowing. The units of the VIII. Fliegerkorps had to camp, unprotected. The advance of our troops came to a halt. It soon changed into a Napoleonic retreat, as we could recognise from the air during our last

ABOVE With engines and cockpits tightly wrapped in tarpaulins to ward off the ice, these Bertas of StG 1 with their air and groundcrews face their first Russian winter in 1941. *(Chris Goss collection)*

LEFT Ju 87 D-3, T6+AK, of 2./StG 2 'Immelmann', ready for combat during the Battle of Morosovskaya in November 1942, when the German 6th Army was locked in a vicious battle to halt Red Army forces charging toward Rostov. Note the MG 81Z 'Zwilling' gun installation with internal armour plate and the pair of 100kg bombs under the wing with Dinorstab and tail-screamers. *(BA 101I-393-1402-06A)*

RIGHT Stuka pilots of II./SG 1 receive a mission briefing from their commander on a snow-bound airfield at Rovaniemi, Finland, in April 1944. In the background can be seen a pair of Ju 87 D-5s. *(Copyright unknown)*

sorties in the Moscow area, much to our dismay. Our Geschwader could only get a small number of planes into the air per day.

At the end of Barbarossa in early December 1941 the Stukagruppen had notched up an impressive tally of destruction. As the Luftwaffe's top-scoring dive-bomber Gruppe in Russia, StG 77 had wiped out 2,401 vehicles, 234 tanks, 92 artillery batteries and 21 trains, all for the loss of 25 Ju 87s to enemy action. As for the other Stuka units, StG 1 had lost 60 Ju 87s in action, StG 2 – 39, and IV. (St) LG 1 lost 24 aircraft to enemy action.

Stuka units were now beginning to re-equip with the Ju 87 D – the Dora – and the first to see action with its new aircraft in January 1942 was I./StG 2 in Staraya Russa on the north-west Russian front, scene of heavy fighting the previous summer. The Staffel was commanded by Hauptmann Bruno Dilley, who had flown the first Stuka operation of the war in Poland on 1 September 1939.

Replacing Stukas – with Stukas

Luftwaffe plans to replace the ageing Stuka with newer and more capable dive-bomber aircraft were long overdue by 1942. It had been mooted as far back as 1938 that the twin-engined Messerschmitt Me 210 dive-bomber would eventually replace both the Ju 87 and the Messerschmitt Bf 110 'Zerstörer', but the new aircraft proved an unmitigated disaster and it never supplanted either type with the Luftwaffe, although the Axis ally Hungary used it on the Eastern Front. The other replacement aircraft was the twin-engined Henschel Hs 129, which saw limited service in the east. Armed with a 30mm Mk 103 cannon it was an effective tank killer, but unreliable engines and too few aircraft too late to make any difference put paid to its future. So, the Ju 87 was left to soldier on into 1943 and 1944, though attempts were made to improve its design and performance with the introduction of the Dora and Gustav models, the Dora seeing widespread use on the Eastern Front.

Kerch peninsula, 'Fall Blau' and the road to Stalingrad

After the Soviet 44th Army landed on the Kerch peninsula in the eastern Crimea on

ABOVE Hauptmann Rudolf-Heinz Ruffer was the first Henschel Hs 129 pilot to receive the Knight's Cross and he was probably one of the most famous. He is pictured in the cockpit of an Hs 129 B-2 on 4 June 1944, a few examples of which carried the BK 37 3.7cm automatic cannon, also used in the Ju 87 G. Note the angle-armoured steel 'bathtub' cockpit, steel canopy frame and externally mounted gunsight. Ruffer was killed in action by flak over Lemberg, Poland, on 16 July 1944, when serving as the Staffelkapitän of 10.(Pz)/Schlachtgeschwader 9. His personal score stood at some 300 missions and about 80 tanks destroyed. *(BA 101I-505-0352-23A)*

29 December 1941 in a bid to break the siege of Sebastopol, in early May 1942 two Ju 87 D dive-bomber groups from StG 77 were sent with four other bomber groups to dislodge the force. Thanks to German air superiority the Doras were able to operate with virtual impunity and in the first ten days of the offensive half the Soviet landing force was destroyed, while Black Sea traffic was halted by Stukas, with heavy losses inflicted on Russian shipping. The town of Kerch itself and ten Soviet divisions fell to the Germans on 16 May.

The strong Russian offensive around Kharkov that began on 14 May threatened the German occupation of the city. Stukas of StG 77 were quickly moved north to assist the ground forces in pinching off the Russian salient, which they did with stunning success, wiping out Soviet armour and destroying key communications targets. On 31 May StG 77 flew south again to its base at Sarabus-South in the Crimea, ready for the next round of fighting at Sebastopol.

Several Stukagruppen, like StG 77, were employed in what was termed a 'fire brigade' role, rushing back and forth over hundreds of miles to lend their muscle in one trouble spot after another. This relentless campaigning inevitably took its toll on men and machines, both through enemy action and crew fatigue. (Across the Eastern Front 8.8cm Flak gun crews were similarly tasked, often finding themselves bearing the brunt of anti-armour combat in sectors that were collapsing.)

After their failed first attempt to take Sebastopol in late 1941, the Germans began a second siege of the port city and its fortress that began on 2 June 1942. With air superiority swiftly achieved by the Luftwaffe, Stukas played a decisive part in softening up the Red Army forces by flying up to eight missions a day for a full month. Among the 600 ground-attack and heavy bomber aircraft flying these round-the-clock sorties, StG 77 flew some 7,708 combat missions and dropped 3,537 tons of bombs on beleaguered Sebastopol, which eventually surrendered to German ground forces after bitter fighting on 4 July.

In a continuation of Barbarossa, 'Fall Blau' (Case Blue) was the German summer offensive in southern Russia that saw an advance on the oilfields of Baku and a drive towards Stalingrad along the River Volga to cover the flanks of

FLIEGER VERBINDUNGSOFFIZIER – THE 'FLIVO'

Luftwaffe dive-bomber and ground-attack Gruppen played a vital part in the destruction of Soviet armour, particularly at the Battle of Kursk in 1943. By the time of Barbarossa the cooperation between German air and ground assets – especially the Stukagruppen – had become well established with the attachment of a Flieger Verbindungsoffizier (a Luftwaffe liaison officer) to armoured units. Known for short as 'Flivos', these were generally Stuka pilots who were in direct radio contact with the dive-bombers flying overhead, who could then be directed more quickly and efficiently on to enemy targets when they presented themselves.

Major Paul-Werner Hozzell recalls:

They [Flivos] used a scale of 1:300,000 with a grid net on it; the same as the armoured recce air liaison officer. We had contact; my crews heard it with me. They called out the targets to us and asked if we had it. They also shot flares to signal their own positions. They had panels to mark the forward lines, and our armour often had flags on the top – black, white, red. Easy to see.

A similar system known as 'cab-ranking' was used in Normandy in 1944, with RAF air liaison officers (usually pilots) who were attached to ground units calling down waiting Typhoons when they were needed to attack enemy targets.

RIGHT Stukas were never far away to lend firepower in support of their comrades on the ground. Here, a Panzer IVH medium tank in the foreground (with Schürzenarmour protection) heads a column of Tiger Is and infantry on the move through the bleak Russian winter landscape during January/February 1944. *(BA 101I-277-0843-06A)*

RIGHT Burning homes on the outskirts of Stalingrad show that Stukas have left their calling card in the summer of 1942. *(BA 101I-218-0526-37)*

the advance to Baku. For this great push the Luftwaffe amassed a force of 1,800 aircraft in Luftflotte 4, of which some 151 were Stukas.

The epic battle for Stalingrad began on 23 August 1942, but the German 6. Armee and elements of the 4. Panzerarmee became fatally bogged down as they fought to take the city, street by street. Fliegerkorps VIII was again at the sharp end, with StG 2 flying four or more missions a day against pinpoint targets in the city in an attempt to crush the fanatical Soviet resistance. Ju 87s continued to fly thousands of sorties against the city, with StG 1, StG 2 and StG 77 making 320 sorties on 14 October alone.

Günter Koschorrek was a Landser with Panzergrenadier-Regiment 21 (a motorised infantry regiment) in 24. Panzer-Division at Stalingrad. He remembers how the sight and sound of Stukas overhead boosted their morale, but he also recognises how the German dive-bomber was a frightening spectacle to friend and foe alike:

First there is a flight of three Stukas, which dive down; then three more follow. Their

LEFT This massive grain silo in Stalingrad was one of the main points of resistance in the city. It was only taken by the Germans on 21 September 1943 after fierce close-quarter combat. A small group of Russian troops held out against everything the Germans could throw at them, including tanks and Stukas. *(BA 00216-029)*

attack in front of us is a real spectacle but, even for us non-participants, it brings a cold creepy feeling to the spine. The fearsome shark mouths painted on the engine cowlings give the enemy a premonition of the catastrophe that is about to be visited on them. The aircraft first roll to the side, then with a deafening wail from their sirens getting louder and louder, swoop down on their target. As soon as they have released their bombs the planes climb steeply, only to dive again on another target. The effect on the morale of those on the receiving end must be terrible. It is just like the inferno of hell, even though the action is taking place far away from us.

ABOVE With the wide River Volga in the background, a Ju 87 B-2 flies over the burning city of Stalingrad in October 1942. *(BA 183-J20509)*

BELOW Stuka units were flying some five to six sorties per aircraft against targets at Stalingrad where they suffered their highest losses ever, but most were to Russian flak and not to fighters. This unidentified Ju 87 D has crash-landed in woodland somewhere on the Eastern Front. *(SA-Kuva)*

When the 6. Armee corralled Russian troops into a 1,000m^2 killing zone on the west bank of the River Volga, Stukas flew 1,208 sorties against this small piece of land, their dive-bombing decimating the Soviet ground forces, but they failed to destroy them. When the Russian forces counter-attacked from the north on 19 November they were unstoppable, surrounding the 6. Armee and parts of the 4. Panzerarmee in a pocket that was finally sealed and cut off.

Günter Koschorrek was one of the lucky ones when he was wounded on 15 December and evacuated to Germany for treatment. Panzergrenadier-Regiment 21 and 24. Panzer-Division were wiped out at Stalingrad. On 31 January 1943, General von Paulus surrendered the battered remnants of the 6. Armee to the Russians.

Stukas were operating at maximum effort during the Battle of Stalingrad, flying a high sortie rate and causing heavy losses to the Red Army, but these fever-pitch operations took their toll on crews with attrition due to exhaustion as well as enemy action.

Hozzel explains:

We suffered the highest losses ever in sorties against Stalingrad. It was incredible: I lost the mass of my Geschwader in a four-month period. Troops and planes were replaced at once, but those with prior experience in combat were irreplaceable.

Kursk

In the greatest tank battle the world has seen, before or since, Stukas were closely involved in Operation Zitadelle (Citadel) – the battle to 'pinch' out the salient around Kursk and cut off and destroy the Soviet forces trapped within. Launched on 5 July 1943, Stukas smashed their way through the enemy defences for the Panzer divisions and the newly formed Schlachtgeschwader (ground-attack) units with their ground-attack Fw 190s and Hs 129s to exploit.

Under the command of Luftflotte 6, I., II. and III./StG 1 and III./StG 3 were committed to battle, along with I., II. and III./StG 3 under Fliegerkorps VIII. It was at this time that the roles of close air-support and 'tank-buster' assumed more importance, with Ju 87s flying conventional dive-bombing roles as well as in mixed patrols with Kanonenvogel BK 37 Gustavs supported by Doras carrying 1,100lb bombs, SD 2 anti-personnel 'Butterfly' bombs and 'Gießkanne' WB 81 gun pods.

Large numbers of Soviet mobile flak units posed a serious problem for the Stukas. Bomb-carrying Ju 87s went in first to take out the flak batteries, followed by the Kanonenvogel to destroy the tanks, but the Russian gunners soon learned the trick and held their fire until the aircraft were committed.

Hans-Ulrich Rudel observed the fighting at Kursk:

Great tank battles rage below us during these operations, a picture such as we have rarely had the chance of witnessing since 1941. The tank masses face each other on open plains. The enemy anti-tank defences have sited themselves in the rear with their guns camouflaged. Sometimes also the tanks themselves are dug in defensively, especially when they have been immobilized but otherwise still retain their fighting efficiency.

When the Russians counter-attacked on the Orel front, Stukas were rapidly switched from one side of the Kursk salient to the other to firefight. BK 37-armed Ju 87 G Kanonenvogel of Rudel's StG 2 had a devastating effect on Soviet armour at Orel and Belgorod, but they failed to prevent the collapse of the last great German offensive in the east.

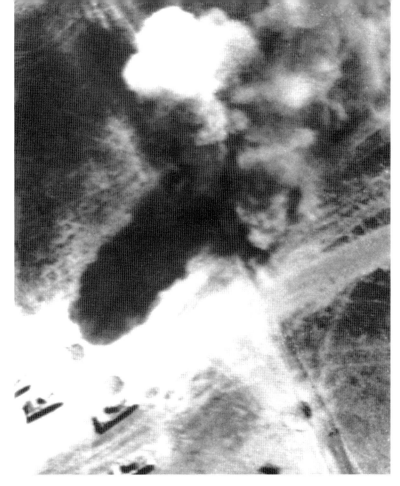

ABOVE From the lofty vantage point of his Ju 87 cockpit, Oberleutnant Erwin-Pieter Diekwisch, Staffelkapitän of 9./StG 1, looks down on a group of Russian tanks on the battlefield at Kursk in July 1943. Losses of Ju 87s and their crews were high at Kursk, with the Stuka arm losing eight of its Knight's Cross holders during the battle. *(Chris Goss collection)*

BELOW Diekwisch received the Knight's Cross in October 1942 and survived the war having flown 934 missions, destroyed 64 tanks, sunk 3 ships and 1 submarine, and scored 12 aircraft shot down. He is seen here as a Hauptmann with I./SG 8, celebrating his 700th mission at Alakurtii, Finland. *(Chris Goss collection)*

RUSSIAN WEATHER

ABOVE RUSSIAN MUD

In spring the snow-melt turned the ground into a sea of liquid mud, and when the autumn rains came the parched earth quickly became a quagmire again. This Ju 87 D-1, S2+NM, of StG 3, has had its wheel spats removed to avoid them becoming clogged with mud. *(BA 101I-630-3562-20A)*

LEFT SUMMER HEAT

Out on the exposed Steppe there was no hiding place from the heat of the sun. Engines and men could easily fall victim to overheating. On a field airstrip 'somewhere in Russia' during the summer of 1942, stripped to the waist, this Schwartzmann watches as the pilot of 'his' Ju 87 D-3 of II./StG 2 prepares to shut down the Jumo 211J after returning from a mission. Of note are the unit badge of the 'Bamberger horseman', Jericho trumpets on the undercarriage legs and the under-wing bomb-carrier. *(BA 101I-453-1042-34)*

LEFT WINTER SNOW

When operating from compacted snow runways and airstrips in the harsh Russian winter, Stuka crews termed it 'flying from the tablecloth'. This Ju 87 D-5 of StG 3 is taking off from Raadi airfield on the north-east edge of Dorpat in eastern Estonia on 9 March 1944, when the snow was still thick on the ground. Dorpat had been heavily bombed by the Soviet Air Force on 7–8 March and the Reds came again on 25–26 March. Most of the town was eventually destroyed in September that year when the embattled German Army pulled out. *(BA 101I-726-0223-13)*

On 14 July, Stukas were rushed in to hold a Soviet counter-offensive at Khotynets on the strategically important Bryansk–Orel highway. Until the Germans could bring up reinforcements, for two whole days all that stood between the Russian tanks and the vital railway line at Khotynets was Luftflotte 6 and its Stukas, which flew unrelenting low-level missions against troop concentrations and armour. They saved two German armies from encirclement and annihilation and reduced the Soviet 11th Guards Army to only 33 tanks by 20 July.

Kursk and Stalingrad marked the zenith of the Stuka as a weapon of war, but it also represented devastating defeats for the Germans, with a complete army destroyed. The growth in strength of the Red Air Force meant the initiative was at last taken from the Luftwaffe. From now on Stukas were fighting a defensive war in support of an army in retreat.

Winter weather began to close in from October. Aviation fuel shortages and the growing dominance of the Red Air Force were among the unrelenting pressures on the Stuka force, whose resources were spread ever more thinly.

Schlachtgruppe (ground-attack) Stukas

The German Army's failure at Kursk hastened changes in the Luftwaffe's command and organisation. Reflecting the constantly changing tactical situation in the east, on 18 October 1943 the Luftwaffe merged its existing Stukagruppen into a larger Schlachtflieger (ground-attack) force. This gathered together under a single commander all close-support dive-bomber, ground-attack and fighter-bomber units. Thus, StG 1, 2, 3, 5 and 77 were redesignated as Schlachtgruppen. (For example, Stukagruppe 1 was redesignated as Schlachtgruppe 1, abbreviated to SG 1.)

RIGHT Schlacht Stuka: Ju 87 D-5 of I./ Schlachtgeschwader 3, at Immola in Finland during the summer of 1944. Clearly visible in this photograph are the bomb trapeze beneath the fuselage, MG 151/20mm wing cannon, dive brakes and under-wing bomb-carrier with bombs attached. *(SA-Kuva)*

ABOVE On the opening day of the Battle of Kursk, Rudel flew his first combat missions with the BK 37 cannon-armed Ju 87 G against Russian tanks in the area of Belgorod. He was appointed Kommandeur of III./StG 2 in July 1943 and on 12 August Rudel and his gunner Erwin Henschel completed their 1,300th and 1,000th combat missions respectively. Henschel was the first gunner to achieve this number and Rudel opined that he was easily the best gunner in the unit: 'He is always furious if I leave him behind and someone else flies with me in his stead. He is as jealous as a little girl,' he wrote. *(Copyright unknown)*

Emphasising the continuing importance of dive-bombing to the Luftwaffe, an experienced Stuka man was appointed as General der Schlachtflieger, Oberst Dr Ernst Kupfer, erstwhile Kommodore of StG 2 'Immelmann'. When Kupfer was killed in a flying accident on 6 November, he was replaced by another old Stuka hand, Oberst Hubertus Hitschhold.

It was planned to convert the Stuka Schlachtgruppen to the Fw 190, but for several reasons this became a longer and more drawn-out process than expected, with one of the five former Stukagruppen (III./SG 2) only beginning to make the transition when the war ended. In the meantime, all units continued to operate the standard Ju 87 D-5 for dive-bombing and strafing attacks, although by the winter of 1943/44 the pilots were beginning to be returned to the Reich for conversion training on to the Fw 190.

One Stuka unit succeeded in avoiding the metamorphosis of the Luftwaffe's Stukagruppen into Schlachtgruppen and that was II./StG 2, which was redesignated II./StG 2(Pz). This small, specialised anti-tank Gruppe of (initially) little more than 20 Doras and Gustavs was committed straight away to hitting back at the westward advance of Soviet armour in pursuit of German forces under General von Manstein following the failure of the Kursk offensive in July 1943. Falling back behind the River Dnepr, the Germans were pursued into Ukraine where the capital, Kiev, was liberated by the Red Army on 6 November. The Gruppe suffered heavy losses in trying to slow the Russian advance, striking at the armoured thrusts through the winter of 1943/44.

In March 1944, the StG 2 was reorganised with the disbandment of its 6. Staffel and the redesignation of its 4. and 5. Staffels to become 10.(Pz)/SG 3 and 10.(Pz)/SG 77 respectively. Each of these Panzerstaffeln was equipped with twelve Gustavs plus four conventional Doras for flak suppression. At the end of the war just two Stuka Staffeln – 10.(Pz)/SG 2 and 10.(Pz)/SG 77 – remained fighting Soviet tanks on the Eastern Front, operating some 30 Doras and Gustavs between them.

Gefechtsverband Kuhlmey, Finland

When the Red Army launched their fourth major strategic offensive of the Soviet–Finnish Continuation War on 9 June 1944, Finland's president Gustaf Mannerheim asked Hitler for help in repulsing the attack on the Karelian Isthmus above Leningrad. A 70-strong Luftwaffe battlegroup was hurriedly assembled and arrived at Immola airfield in Finland on 17 June, comprising Ju 87s and Fw 190s under the command of Oberst Kurt Kuhlmey, the Kommodore of SG 3. Known as Gefechtsverband Kuhlmey (Battlegroup Kuhlmey), the group was made up from elements of I./SG 3, I./SG 5, II./JG 54 and NAG 1.

From 16 June to 20 July, Gefechtsverband Kuhlmey flew some 2,700 sorties against the Russians, dropping 770 tonnes of bombs and destroying more than 150 Soviet aircraft, some 200 tanks, as well as dozens of bridges. The unit suffered heavy losses that included 23 pilots killed and 24 wounded in action, as well as 41 of its aircraft to all reasons. The Ju 87 D-5s of I./SG 3 flew three missions with the battlegroup before returning briefly to Dorpat and then moving on again to Pardubitz/Bohemia, where the unit re-equipped with the Fw 190.

Operation Bagration and the beginning of the end in the East

The situation on the Eastern Front continued to worsen for the Germans as the Russian forces gained in their strength and resolve to push back the invaders. On 22 June 1944, the massive Russian offensive on the Central Front in Byelorussia began, three years to the day after Barbarossa. Codenamed Operation Bagration, the action was played out across many of the same battlefields as in 1941 and it came to a climax five weeks later with the Red Army at the gates of Warsaw. Ju 87 G tank-busters and Fw 190 fighter-bombers were among the aircraft fielded by Luftflotte 6, but they were too few in number to make a difference in the face of the numerically superior Soviet air force. Germany's Army Group Centre was routed, 17 Wehrmacht divisions were destroyed and more than 50 other German divisions were neutralised in the most serious defeat of the German armed forces of the war.

The Wehrmacht was now in full retreat, with the Red Army on the march into Poland, Romania, Slovakia, and by the end of 1944, the Baltic states. Stukas were rushed in to help stem the tide, but all to no avail.

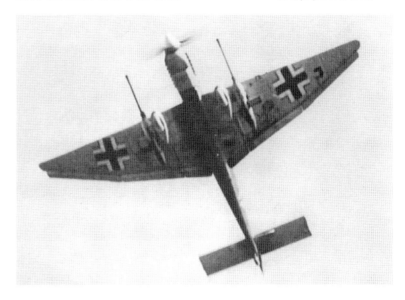

accompanying Stukas swooped in to make their attack.

Seven Nachtschlachtgruppen were equipped with Doras and each wing had some 60 aircraft, operating under cover of darkness on the Eastern Front, in northern Italy as well as over France, Belgium and Holland, and in the final last-ditch German offensive in the Ardennes in December 1944.

Nachtschlachtgruppen – the 'Night Attack Wings'

After the Normandy landings on 6 June 1944, the Stuka had become increasingly vulnerable to attack by Allied fighters when flying daylight operations, so the Luftwaffe created special Nachtschlachtgruppen (NSGr) or 'Night Attack Wings'. During the summer of 1944 three NSGr equipped with Ju 87 D aircraft were operating in western Europe. Designated D-7 and D-8, they were fitted with flame eliminators to mask their exhausts, ultraviolet lighting behind the instrument panel and special night reflector sights, or 'Nachtrevi'. The night tactics involved a lead aircraft dropping flares to illuminate a target while

The Battle of Leros – 8 September– 16 November 1943

When the Italians capitulated on 8 September 1943, the Italian garrison on the Dodecanese island of Leros was strengthened by British ground forces. The Germans were well prepared to counter this British attempt to regain a foothold in the Aegean and began bombing the island on 15 September. In the weeks that followed Ju 87 D-3s of I./ Schlachtgruppe 3 flying from Megara, and the II. Gruppe from Aros and later Rhodes, played a full part in the continuous and heavy air strikes against British and Italian ground and naval forces on Leros. With the Luftwaffe enjoying complete air superiority an amphibious landing was made on 12 November, which saw the Germans take the island, forcing the British and Italian garrisons to surrender on 16 November in what was the last significant defeat of the British Army in the Second World War.

Anti-partisan operations in Yugoslavia – 1943–45

Yugoslavia had first experienced the terror of the Ju 87 in April 1941, but with the rapid defeat of the country the Luftwaffe's Stukagruppen left for the Eastern Front. However, growing anti-fascist resistance in Bosnia, Herzegovina and Croatia saw the Stukas return again in 1943 when they flew intensive counter-insurgency missions against Tito's communist partisans who were supported by the Soviet Union. Between then and the end of the war two years later the Stukas caused widespread death and destruction, with the Germans working on the premise that everything

was a target – whether military or civilian. Only with the appearance later in the war of the Western Allies and, subsequently, the Red Army, was the Stuka's supremacy over Tito's poorly equipped partisans brought to an end.

Decline and fall

Towards the end of 1944 the Stuka was increasingly being replaced by the ground-attack Fw 190 and by 1945 a little over 100 Ju 87s remained in service. However, small numbers of NSGr Stukas continued to offer stubborn resistance to the advancing British and American forces – at Aachen (NSGr 1 on 29 October 1944), in the Ardennes during the 'Battle of the Bulge' over Christmas and New Year 1944/45 and in the spring some 100 Stukas were pulled together to contest the Allied crossing of the Rhine on 23/24 March 1945.

In the east, small numbers of Stukas alongside Fw 190s fought valiant battles to try to hold the Red Army as German forces were thrown back across the River Oder, which the Russians crossed on 31 January and there began its march on Berlin 50 miles away. In the Führerbunker, Hitler deluded himself that all was not lost and that the situation could be turned around, but those soldiers and airmen who were battling around the clock against the implacable Ivans knew differently.

Stuka sorties were hampered by the severe fuel shortage that was crippling the Luftwaffe. On 16 April the Soviets launched their final

assault on Berlin and a week later on the 24th the Red Army entered the German capital. Within weeks those Ju 87s that survived flew away to southern Germany and Austria where they were found by the advancing Americans along with large numbers of other Stukas (both flyable and wrecked) when the war ended.

It was a testimony to the valour and determination of the surviving Stuka air and groundcrews, who had flown and maintained the Ju 87 in combat, that they had fought the fight and stayed the course – some from the first days of the war, right up until the last desperate hours of the Third Reich in Berlin and elsewhere along the eastern front line. For an aircraft whose design was considered obsolete soon after the war had begun, the Ju 87 had given a good account of itself in some of the toughest battles of the war.

But in the end, even the appearance of a gaggle of Stukas over the battlefield was no longer able to turn around a seemingly hopeless situation on the ground.

ABOVE Ju 87 G-2, coded 6G, in a distinctive winter camouflage pattern. *(Copyright unknown)*

BELOW The end of the line: curious American troops crowd around a captured Ju 87 D-8, possibly of NSGr 10, at Fürth in Bavaria, May 1945. *(US National Archives)*

Chapter Five

Flying the Ju 87

'The Ju 87 did not appear to find its natural element until it was diving steeply. It seemed quite normal to stand this aircraft on its nose in a vertical dive because its acceleration has none of that uncontrollable runaway feeling associated with a 90-degree inclination in an aircraft like the Skua.' *(British test pilot Captain Eric 'Winkle' Brown, RN)*

OPPOSITE Ju 87 D-1s of StG 2 'Immelmann' show to good advantage the 'lean and mean' look of the Stuka. *(Copyright unknown)*

ABOVE Damage from anti-aircraft groundfire caused more damage and loss to Ju 87s than from fighter attacks. Here, a flak shell has punched right through the starboard wing of this Stuka, ripping open the skin and severing the rear spar, but the trusty 'Jolanthe' still made it back to base. *(Copyright unknown)*

BELOW Mahlke's Stuka. *(Chris Goss collection)*

Many Stuka pilots owed their survival in combat to the trusty Jolanthe. Although slow and not particularly well armed to defend themselves against the faster fighters of the day, the Ju 87 was a tough old bird that could absorb huge amounts of battle damage and yet still bring its crews home again after a mission. The big glazed canopy afforded pilot and gunner superb fields of view, but their high seating position inside the cockpit could sometimes give them a feeling of vulnerability.

That the Stuka was maligned by the Allied propaganda machine as a cumbersome unmanoeuvrable lump is contradicted by the experience of RAF fighter pilot Squadron Leader G.R.S. McKay DFC, who commanded 87 Squadron at the end of the Second World War. He had flown a captured Stuka on many occasions, describing its flying characteristics as excellent, with the controls so light that there was a distinct tendency to over-control. He considered that visibility from the roomy cockpit was excellent, the controls were simple to handle and overall he found the aircraft suggested power and strength.

The Stuka's distinctive trousered undercarriage was one of its prominent features, but in the age of the retractable landing gear it was looked upon by many as something of an anachronism and a cause of aerodynamic drag. However, the single-strut construction of the sprung oleo legs meant they were able to soak up the stresses of a heavy landing on difficult terrain without collapsing. This was particularly useful when operating from rough forward landing strips, which Stukas often did.

Later in the war the single-seat Focke-Wulf Fw 190s began replacing Ju 87s in the Stukagruppen. When the harsh Russian winter closed in across the Eastern Front, the more lightly built Fw 190 with its narrow main-gear tyres found it virtually impossible to operate in the treacherous snow and ice that covered runways and forward airstrips, whereas the robust old Stuka with its heavy-duty fixed undercarriage and fat tyres continued to fly.

The modernity of the 'Butcher Bird' and its extra speed came at the expense of bombing accuracy and efficiency – the gunner in the

Ju 87 had always been able to identify the target for his pilot and then record the results of their attack, but this was not possible with the '190.

German troops on the ground welcomed the regular close-support from the trusty Jolanthe, which was far more important to them than having no support at all from a modern, technically advanced aircraft like the Fw 190.

Recalling a forced-landing in Sicily in 1941 after an attack on Malta, Hauptmann Helmut Mahlke, Kommandeur of III./StG 1, describes how the Ju 87's strong undercarriage proved to be his salvation when he nursed his combat-damaged Stuka home to an emergency landing:

Both wings had been completely sieved by machine gun bullets. There was also a huge gaping hole in the right wing close to the starboard outer tank where the metal had been ripped to shreds. … Heading into what little wind there was I made my approach at low level and with the throttle wide open. … Over the edge of the field I chopped the throttle and switched off the ignition. Level out – now wait for the bang! The machine brushed the ground at high speed, jumped back into the air, tipped over onto its right leg

– just as I'd feared – but then bounced back onto the left leg and proceeded to career across the field, first on one wheel and then the other, before slowly beginning to lose speed. After covering a good two-thirds of its length I cautiously tried the brakes, gently at first, but then harder. The Ju 87 finally came to a stop only about 20 metres from the far end of the field. Despite all the flak and fighter fire we'd taken, the fuel tanks and the tyres had remained unscathed and we'd made it!

ABOVE The Ju 87's main wheelbrakes had a sharp bite and over-braking could easily result in the aircraft tipping up on to its nose, like this Ju 87 R, which has wrecked its wooden propeller blades as a result. *(Copyright unknown)*

LEFT Sometimes even the tough undercarriage could not ride out a bad landing or an overshoot, as witnessed with this early Ju 87 B-1 from 3./StG 77, where the port undercarriage leg has buckled under the strain. *(Copyright unknown)*

Flying the Ju 87 – the test pilot's view

When it came to recounting what the Stuka was actually like to fly, it fell to an English naval test pilot to describe it clearly and objectively. His name was Eric 'Winkle' Brown, a commander in the Fleet Air Arm, who was to become one of Britain's most celebrated post-war test pilots, with ultimately more than 250 aircraft types in his logbook. Brown got his hands on a captured Ju 87 D-3 at Husum in Schleswig-Holstein, on 23 August 1945, and this is his assessment of the Stuka:

'I clambered into the pilot's cockpit and settled down to look around, and my first impression of a very big aeroplane for one engine was reaffirmed. Following the Pilot's Notes I placed the fuel cock in the "both tanks" position, gave a few strokes of primer, switched on the fuel booster pumps, set the throttle to figure "1" on the quadrant, switched on both magnetos and energised the inertia starter and booster coil by pushing a handle on the lower left side for 10 seconds then pulling out the handle until the engine fired. Warm-up could be made up to 1,600rpm on the brakes but higher revs demanded that the tail be anchored in case the aircraft nosed over. After such anchoring, the engine was run up to 2,200rpm and 1.3 atas of boost [ata = atmospheres absolute, 1 ata being the equivalent of 14.696lb force/sq in] and then throttled back to 1.0 ata for magneto checks. After the engine checks the tail anchorage was released and the aircraft was taxied with the tailwheel lock in the free position. I found that the aircraft needed controlled braking to manoeuvre and was sensitive to any crosswind.

'Before taking off it was necessary to straighten out and lock the tailwheel, switch the fuel pumps on, set the flaps to take-off position, the trims to zero and airscrew pitch lever to START. The Ju 87 D-3 was fairly lightly loaded and with full power accelerated surprisingly well, unsticking at about 72mph [116km/h] in a distance of some 500 yards [457m]. The climb was made at 2,300rpm and 1.15 atas of boost, the flaps retracting meanwhile until two signal lamps indicated that they had reached the zero position. Climbing speed could then be increased to 133mph [215km/h] and was eased off 6mph [10km/h] for every 3,280ft [1,000m] of altitude gained. At an altitude of 11,480ft [3,500m] the supercharger was moved from low gear to the automatic position, but climb throughout was laborious.

'Once settled down to the cruise the feeling of vulnerability became almost oppressive, probably accentuated by the high position of the pilot's seat and the good visibility through the large glasshouse canopy. The Ju 87 D was big enough and slow enough to present an ideal target to the humblest tyro among fighter pilots and it must have come high in the popularity stakes with anti-aircraft gunners. Certainly its large ailerons failed to instil any liveliness into evasive manoeuvres, and although its elevators were reasonably light the aircraft was just too stable longitudinally to be very manoeuvrable. It was hardly surprising that once Soviet fighters of respectable performance began to put in an appearance in quantity over the Eastern Front the Ju 87 D-equipped Stukagruppen were decimated.

'There could be no doubt that the Ju 87

BELOW Captain Eric 'Winkle' Brown, Royal Navy test pilot. *(Copyright unknown)*

D needed fighter cover on its way to a target area as surely as a fish needs water. But my consuming interest was to learn how this aircraft, anachronism though it undoubtedly was, performed in the area in which it had displayed such astonishing bombing accuracy and precision in its heyday. So I flew out over the North Sea to put in some dive-bombing practice on the mud banks that lie off the coast.

'The check list for preparing the Ju 87 D to enter the dive was as follows:

- Landing flaps at cruise position.
- Elevator trim at cruise position.
- Rudder trim at cruise position.
- Airscrew pitch set at cruise.
- Contact altimeter switched on.
- Contact altimeter set to release altitude.
- Supercharger set at automatic.
- Throttle pulled right back.
- Cooler flaps closed.
- Dive brakes opened.

'The last action made the aircraft nose over into the dive under the influence of the pull-out mechanism, which was actuated by the opening of the dive brakes, which also activated the safety pilot control. The most difficult thing in dive-bombing training is overestimating the dive angle, which invariably feels much steeper than it actually is. Every dive bomber of WW II vintage featured some form of synthetic aid to judging the dive angle, and in the Ju 87 this consisted simply of a series of lines of inclination marked on the starboard front side screen of the cockpit.

'These marks, when aligned with the horizon, gave dive angles of 30 degrees to 90 degrees. Now a dive angle of 90 degrees is a pretty palpitating experience for it always feels as if the aircraft is over the vertical and is bunting, and all this while terra firma is rushing closer with apparently suicidal rapidity. In fact, I have rarely seen a specialist dive-bomber put over 70 degrees in a dive, but the Ju 87 was a genuine 90 degrees screamer! For some indefinable reason the Ju 87 D felt right standing on its nose, and the acceleration to 335mph [540km/h] was reached in about 4,500ft [1,370m]. Speed thereafter crept slowly up to the absolute permitted limit of 373mph [600km/h] so that the feeling of being on a

BELOW A loaded Ju 87 D taxies out for take-off from an airfield on the Eastern Front. *(Copyright unknown)*

ABOVE The distinctive silhouette of a Ju 87 D-5 in flight. *(SA-Kuva)*

runaway roller-coaster experienced with most other dive bombers was missing.

'As speed built up, the nose of the Ju 87 was used as the aiming mark. The elevators were moderately light in the initial stages of the dive but they heavied up considerably as speed built up. Any alterations in azimuth to keep the aiming mark on the target could be made accurately by use of the ailerons. These also heavied up as speed increased but always remained very effective. Use of the elevator or rudder trimmers in a dive or pull-out was strictly forbidden. During the dive it was necessary to watch the signal light on the contact altimeter, and when it came on the knob on the control column was depressed to initiate the automatic pull-out at 6-g, a 1,475ft [450m] height margin being required to complete the manoeuvre. The automatic pull-out mechanism had a high reputation for reliability, but in the event of failure the pull-out could be effected with a full-blooded pull on the control column aided by judicious operation of the elevator trimmer to override the safety pilot control.

'The sequence of events on selecting the dive brakes was most interesting. On extension of the brakes, red indicators protruded from each wing upper surface. This action automatically brought into play the safety pilot control and the dive-recovery mechanism. The object of the latter was to return the elevator trimmer flaps to their normal position after release of the bomb, thus initiating pull-out from the dive which had been started by the elevator trim being brought into action to nose the aircraft over. The safety pilot control was a restriction introduced into the control column movement whereby this was limited by means of only 5 degrees from the neutral position, thus obviating excessive g loads in pulling out. In an emergency this restriction could be overridden to give a 13 degrees movement. Once the aircraft had its nose safely pointed above the horizon from the pull-out, the dive brakes were retracted, the airscrew pitch set to take-off/climb and the throttle opened up 1.15 atas of boost, although in conditions of enemy flak it was recommended that the full 1.35 atas be used. The radiator flaps were then opened.

'When I finally turned for Schleswig, to where I was supposed to deliver the Ju 87 D-3, I must confess that I had had a more enjoyable hour's dive-bombing practice than I had ever experienced with any other aircraft of this specialist type.'

Flying the Ju 87 – the combat pilot's view

The Ju 87 had two principal combat roles – as a dive-bomber and in providing close air-support for the Army against targets that were in close proximity to friendly ground forces. In the first years of the war Stukas were at their most effective when delivering set-piece attacks on clearly defined targets in the enemy rear areas, such as bridges, rail targets, supply depots, barracks and troop concentrations. These operations were against what are now called 'air interdiction' targets, but it was after the German invasion of Russia on 22 June 1941 that the role of close air-support against enemy tanks and troop concentrations assumed an importance on a par with the Stuka's original dive-bombing brief.

Dive-bombing

While serving with I./StG 1 in the Norwegian Campaign, Hauptmann Paul-Werner Hozzel became the first Stuka pilot to be awarded the Ritterkreuz (Knight's Cross) on 8 May 1940. Later, as a Major, Hozzel was promoted to Kommodore of StG 2 'Immelmann' on 1 October 1941. At the young age of 31 he was an 'old school' commander who led the 'Immelmann' Geschwader according to the traditions handed down from the earlier days of the Prusso-German military. Hozzel and his subordinates led by example – from the front. Strict discipline was maintained and observed in the air and on the ground, with no toleration of poor conduct or sloppy dress.

As an experienced dive-bomber pilot, Hozzel describes the procedure that was followed in making a dive-bombing attack on a land target:

'We approached our target at an altitude of 5,000 metres, extended the hydraulic speed brakes shortly before the target, then making the target move into the bottom window in the cockpit below our feet. When it disappeared at the back edge we turned the plane down at a dive angle of 70 degrees.

'To go into a 70-degree dive it was first necessary to press the plane nearly into a back position, into a negative, about 100 degrees,

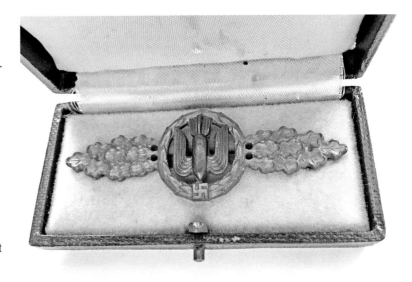

ABOVE The Bomber Clasp, as worn by Ju 87 pilots and gunners. The winged bomb signified the award for crews of heavy, medium and dive-bombers. As with all Luftwaffe 'Frontflugspange' (literally 'Front Flight Clasp') the colour of the clasp, with the exception of the centre, which is usually blackened, denoted the number of flights achieved: the bronze clasp was awarded for 20 flights, silver for 60 flights and the gold clasp was awarded for 100 flights. This example is in gold. *(Author's collection)*

BELOW A Ju 87 pilot carries out his final cockpit checks before extending the dive brakes, whereupon the automatic dive mechanism takes over and pitches the aircraft into a steep dive. *(Copyright unknown)*

ABOVE **The view from the pilot's cockpit as a Kette of Ju 87 As peels off above a wintry landscape to make its attack.** *(James Payne/ Through Their Eyes)*

pulling it by and by into a 70-degree dive. But experienced pilots could dive with 90-degree dive bombing, which increased the velocity in the dive.

'With the power shut off the plane quickly gained speed by its own weight, whilst the dive brakes kept it at a steady pace of 450km/h. We aimed through a reflector sight keeping

the whole plane in the centre of the target and allowing for velocity and direction of the wind, with the aid of the right lead angles. A continuously adjustable red marking arrow was mounted on the altimeter, set to local altitude above mean sea level, whereby the required bomb-releasing altitude could be set. When passing that altitude in the dive, a loud and clear horn signal was sounded, warning the pilot to press the bomb-release button on the control stick and to pull out the plane. By pressing the release button we also automatically actuated the hydraulic recovery device, which aided the pilot under the heavy g-load encountered in steep dive recoveries in pulling out of the dive.

'The normal bomb-release height was close to 700 metres. Experienced pilots would also venture down to 500 metres in order to increase the bombing accuracy. This, however, was the absolute minimum pulling-out radius to clear the ground in time. Below that there was no hope left as shown by the sadly remembered Stuka disaster of Neuhammer [in 1939, see pages 97-98] where a practically

RIGHT **In a near-vertical dive, the airspeed builds to 280mph [450km/h] before a klaxon sounds in the cockpit and the pilot presses the bomb-release button on his control column (this is a still from the wartime propaganda film *Stuka*).** *(Copyright unknown)*

complete Ju 87 Staffel crashed into the ground because of late recovery.

'The accuracy depended on the training … we had the goal at the time of training to drop our bombs within a 10-metre circle around the target's middle point. I must honestly confess that this was not achieved every time in the course of the war. It is another thing, dropping bombs in a training time without fear of being shot, or doing this in war. It depends on the individual pilot and how his nerves were. Was he strong enough to keep the target in sight up to the last second before dropping the bomb? It is natural in humans that some pilots – I couldn't observe everybody – dropped the bomb too high and their accuracy was not as high as it was expected to be.

'In order to egress the target area with its anti-aircraft defences as quickly as possible, Stuka pilots used the surplus speed they had built up by the end of the dive to make their getaway at treetop height where AA defences couldn't touch them. This was the reason we stayed down, not high. The first Stuka idea was to climb again, but this caused us heavy losses.'

ABOVE Bomb-release: a 250kg bomb hurtles earthwards moments after its release from the trapeze mechanism on a Ju 87 D, probably over the Eastern Front. Tanks or armoured vehicles can just be made out on the ground below. *(Andy Saunders collection)*

BELOW LEFT With dive brakes still open and its full load of a single 250kg plus four 50kg bombs falling away, this Ju 87 B is on the point of pulling out of its dive. *(Author's collection)*

BELOW The gunner reports that the target (a river bridge) has been hit as the pilot, helped by the automatic dive-recovery mechanism, flares the Stuka out of its dive. *(James Payne/Through Their Eyes)*

Ground-attack – close air-support

Stukas rarely made horizontal or level attacks against enemy armour, but they did attack from a slant angle of 30–40°, as Hozzel explains:

In this close air-support we never flew at 5,000 metres. We came in, for example, at 1,000 metres or it could be 500. In slant angle we tried to throw the bomb into the belly of the tank.

When we attacked tanks we had to approach the target very near, and drop the bomb in the 30 to 40-degree angle into the belly of the tank, and to have a direct hit it was necessary to fly over the tanks at a few metres' height, and then it happened that we were in danger of our own bomb exploding.

We released bombs individually, the heavy bomb on the first pass, each of the lighter bombs on subsequent passes. Then if we were to attack trucks or troops in assembly,

RIGHT Air-to-Ground Support Squadron clasp of crossed swords – for the Schlachtflieger crews that included pilots and gunners of the Ju 87. *(Author's collection)*

we used the machine guns, making five to seven passes per aircraft. We never used machine guns in classic dive-bombing attacks and made only one pass at the target, exiting then to escape anti-aircraft fire.

Auftragstaktik or 'mission command'

One of the key factors that enabled the German Panzer divisions to win battles in the rapid advances of the early war years was the military doctrine of Auftragstaktik. Roughly translated as 'mission command', it empowered commanders on the ground to show initiative, flexibility and improvisation which, when combined with speed and manoeuvre, were often the deciding factors in who won. Ju 87 unit commanders in the Stukagruppen and Schlachtgruppen were encouraged to employ Auftragstaktik when flying their close air-support missions, as Hozzel explains:

Our intensity of attacking from the air was so great, it was so effective, that our unit leader decided whether to attack new targets. He was free to attack on his own decision, having the combat situation before his eyes. This made a lot of success – individual responsible decisions from the unit commander in combat.

RIGHT Ju 87 Ds of StG 77 return from a mission over Russia in 1943. Note that the wheel fairings have been removed to avoid them clogging with mud. *(BA 101I-630-3561-27A)*

Hans-Ulrich Rudel

Stuka pilot Hans-Ulrich Rudel was the man of whom the last commander of the Oberkommando des Heeres in 1945, Generalfeldmarschall Ferdinand Schörner, said: 'Rudel alone is worth an entire division!' He was also the man who Adolf Hitler wanted to succeed him as Führer of the German Reich.

Born on 2 July 1916 in Konradswaldau, Silesia, the son of a Lutheran minister, Rudel became the most famous Luftwaffe combat pilot of the Second World War. His achievements became a propaganda gift to the Nazis: by the war's end he had flown an astonishing 2,530 combat missions and claimed one battleship, one cruiser, a destroyer and 70 landing craft destroyed, as well as some 800 vehicles, 150 gun positions, prodigious numbers of armoured trains and bridges, some 519 tanks and 9 aircraft. Most of his tank kills were made while flying the Ju 87 G 'Kanonenvogel' equipped with the BK 37 under-wing cannon. This staggering personal achievement confirms Rudel as the world's most successful ground-attack pilot ever.

Rudel was posted to I./StG 2 'Immelmann' in Greece at Easter 1941, but the unit was soon transferred to the Russian Front where Rudel was to fly most of his wartime sorties in the Ju 87, almost exclusively with the 'Immelmann' Geschwader. In his first 90 days of operational flying he completed 500 missions and sank the Soviet battleship *Marat*.

During his subsequent combat career he was recognised by his peers and superiors as an exceptional airman and inspirational warrior who always went far beyond the call of duty and took risks that no one else dared. However, these risks were not without danger; he was shot down or crash-landed more than 30 times and was injured on several occasions, the last time so badly (on 8 February 1945) that his right leg had to be amputated below the knee.

Rudel was awarded the Knight's Cross with Oak Leaves, Swords and Diamonds on 29 March 1944, as only the tenth German serviceman to receive the award. On 1 January 1945 he was personally invested by Adolf Hitler with Golden Oak Leaves to his Knight's Cross, a prestigious award that was originally intended by the Führer to be limited to 12 recipients, but in the end (because war events had overtaken actions) only one was ever awarded, and that was to Rudel. The 'Eagle of the Eastern Front' died on 18 December 1982 aged 66.

Anton Hübsch

Anton 'Toni' Hübsch was the second highest-scoring Stuka ace of the war. He was born in

FAR LEFT Hans-Ulrich 'Uli' Rudel. *(Coyright unknown)*

LEFT Anton 'Toni' Hübsch. *(Coyright unknown)*

Rottach-Egern in southern Germany on 16 March 1918. Enlisting in the Luftwaffe he trained as a pilot and as an NCO he was posted in June 1942 to 2./StG 2 'Immelmann' where he remained, except for a few brief interruptions, until the end of the war.

Hübsch flew the Ju 87 with StG 2 on the Eastern Front, supporting the German advance on Stalingrad. From the summer of 1941 he took part in many battles and honed his skills as a tank hunter and destroyer, which saw him complete 500 combat missions by June 1943. Between September and December Hübsch served as a flying instructor. He returned again to the fighting on the Eastern Front in January 1944, where Stuka crews were desperately trying to stem the relentless Soviet advance. By February he had raised his mission total to 600, which climbed to 700 in April and reached a total of 800 in May 1944.

During an attack on Soviet positions on 3 July he was seriously injured and spent two months in hospital convalescing. It was during this time that on 8 August he received the Knight's Cross. Returning to operations in September he continued to fight tirelessly, and

RIGHT Gerhard 'Stutz' Stüdemann.
(Coyright unknown)

as a commander of an Fw 190 unit he reached the milestone of 1,000 combat missions. By the war's end he had completed 1,060 missions (190 on the Fw 190, as well as 140 in the Battle of Stalingrad), he had destroyed more than 120 tanks – mainly with bombs (compared to Rudel, who preferred to use his guns), achieved eight air victories, sank two cargo ships, and damaged a battleship. He died aged 55 on 31 October 1973.

Gerhard Stüdemann

'Stutz' Stüdemann was the third top-ranked Luftwaffe ground-attack ace with 996 operational sorties and 117 tanks destroyed. Born in Rom-Parchim, Mecklenburg, on 19 June 1920, Stutz joined the Luftwaffe in October 1939, and on completion of his training as a Stuka pilot in February 1941 he was posted to II./StG 77 as a 'green pilot' on the Channel Front. He saw no combat there, but things soon changed when his Gruppe took part in the Balkan Campaign. He saw action during the Battle for Crete, during Barbarossa (on the first day, 22 June, he flew seven combat sorties, the first at 03.40hrs) and at the siege of Sebastopol, followed by the Battles of Stalingrad and Kursk. On 16 February 1943 he was appointed to command 7./SG 151, followed soon afterwards as Staffelkapitän of 9./StG 77. It was on 17 August 1943 that he flew his 500th mission on a sortie over Orel, followed on 26 March 1944 by his 700th and the award of the Knight's Cross (as an Oberleutnant), and 800 missions just over three weeks later on 20 April. Stutz was promoted to Hauptmann on 1 December 1944 and in February 1945 he was appointed Kommandeur of III./SG 77. Oak Leaves were added to his Knight's Cross on 28 March. He died at Trier on 6 December 1998.

Karl Henze

Henze was one of those rare combat pilots on both sides who flew and fought from the beginning to end of the war in Europe. He was shot down several times, completed an incredible 1,098 missions (most of them with the Stuka), and was the holder of the Knight's Cross with Oak Leaves.

Born in 1916, Karl Henze joined the

ABOVE **Karl Henze.** *(Coyright unknown)*

Luftwaffe as an officer cadet in 1936 and
learned dive-bombing with 1./StG 165,
before joining 2./StG 77 as a Leutnant in
1938 on completion of his training.

He flew in the invasion of Poland in 1939
and in the Battle of France, before becoming
a 'Channel Pilot' (and Gruppenadjutant)
with I./StG 77, seeing action in the Battle
of Britain. He was wounded after combat
with Spitfires over Ford airfield on 18 August
1940, but despite serious injury he made
it back to France at wave-top height in
his badly damaged Ju 87 B-1 to make a
crash-landing. He fought in Yugoslavia and
Greece, during the launch of Barbarossa
on 22 June 1941 and he saw combat at
the siege of Sebastopol (1941–42) and at
Kursk in 1943. Henze enhanced his already
legendary reputation in 1943 when he
rescued a wounded downed comrade of
his Gruppe in the Crimea, west of Taganrog,
while under heavy enemy fire. He was later
appointed Gruppenkommandeur of I./
Schlachtgeschwader 77 on 1 December
1943. Henze's last command may have been
Schlachtgeschwader 103 and 151 in April
1945, flying the Ar 96, Fw 190 F and G and
the Ju 87 D, G and R. He died on
25 September 1985.

Ground-attack – BK 37 cannon-armed 'Gustav' versus T-34 tank

The Versuchskommando für
Panzerbekämpfung (anti-tank unit) had been
formed at Rechlin late in 1942 under Hauptmann
Hans-Karl Stepp to test the effectiveness of the
new Ju 87 G variant in the anti-tank role when
fitted with a pair of under-wing Bordkanone (BK)
37mm auto-cannon. In February 1943, Stuka ace
Oberleutnant Hans-Ulrich Rudel joined the unit
when it was despatched to the Kuban and Kerch
peninsulas, where its 'Kanonenvogel' were used
to hit the Red Army's tanks in the former and its
landing craft in the latter as Russian forces tried
to push back the Kuban front with an amphibious
landing behind German lines in the Gulf of
Temryuk.

Each BK 37 weighed in at over 355kg,
making a combined weight for the pair of
cannon as being some 710kg – almost ¾ of
a tonne or 1,600lb – which took its toll on the
Stuka's performance, most notably its speed
and manoeuvrability. Rudel, commanding III./StG
2, recognised that Gustavs fitted with the heavy
BK 37 were not able to carry bombs as well:

*It is obvious that we must always carry
bombs to deal with the enemy defence, but*

ABOVE **A Ju 87 G-2
'Kanonenvogel' from
the Panzerjägerstaffel
of SG 2 with its twin
Bordkanone BK 37
37mm cannon, its
unit indicated by the
silhouette of a tank
on the upper engine
cowling. The aircraft
is believed to be that
of Hans-Ulrich Rudel.**
(Alamy DD2012)

we cannot carry any on our cannon-carrying aircraft as the bombload makes them too heavy. Besides, it is no longer possible to go into a dive with a cannon-carrying Ju 87 because the strain on the plane's wings is too great. The practical answer is therefore to have an escort of normal [ie, bomb-carrying Ju 87 D] Stukas.

Rudel described his method of attacking Soviet tanks when flying a BK 37-armed Gustav:

Sometimes we dive onto the steel monsters from behind, sometimes from the side. The angle of attack is not too steep to prevent us flying in quite close to the ground, and so also when pulling out from getting into any trouble in case the aircraft overshoots. If it overshoots too far it is hardly possible to avoid contact with the ground with all its dangerous consequences.

Each time before coming in to the attack I climb to 2,400ft as the flak cannot follow me to this altitude. From 2,400ft I scream down in a steep dive, weaving violently. When I am close to the tank I straighten up for an instant to fire, and then streak away low above the tank with the same evasive tactics until I reach a point where I can begin to climb again – out of range of the flak. We have always to try to hit the tank in

one of its most vulnerable places. The front is always the strongest part of every tank; therefore every tank invariably tries as far as possible to offer its front to the enemy. Its sides are less strongly protected. But the best target for us is the stern. It is there that the engine is housed, and the necessity for cooling this power centre permits only a thin armour plating. In order to further assist the cooling this plating is perforated with large holes. This is a good spot to aim at because where the engine is there is always petrol. When its engine is running a tank is easily recognisable from the air by the blue fumes of the exhaust. On its sides the tank carries petrol and ammunition. But there the armour is stronger than at the back.

Anti-shipping strikes

Although the Stuka is best known for its deadly dive-bombing attacks on enemy tanks, vehicle convoys and ground troops, arguably its greatest successes were achieved when it was pitted against enemy shipping.

During the Norwegian Campaign in the spring of 1940, Ju 87 Rs of StG 1 sank the Royal Navy destroyers HMS *Gurkha* on 9 April and HMS *Afridi* on 3 May, while during the Allied evacuation from Dunkirk in May and June dive-bombers were responsible for the destruction of dozens of marine craft, ranging from small boats and paddle steamers to destroyers.

In the early stages of the Battle of Britain, Stukas famously played havoc with British convoys in the English Channel and along the North Sea coast. The following year in the Mediterranean, Ju 87s proved their worth when they put the carrier HMS *Illustrious* out of action on 10 January 1941, badly damaged the cruiser *Southampton* the next day and sank HMS *Gloucester* on 22 May. The 23,000-ton aircraft carrier HMS *Formidable* was seriously damaged in a dive-bombing attack by Stukas four days later and put out of action for six months.

S.W.C. Pack was a Royal Navy officer on HMS *Formidable*. He recalls the action of 26 May that left the carrier fighting for its survival against repeated Stuka attacks:

We could see the swarm of Stukas in the clear blue sky silhouetted against the bright sunlight. They were already peeling off undaunted by the gunfire. Their target was obviously the carrier. Violent avoiding action was now taken in answer to the captain's orders for 'Hard a-port' followed next by 'Hard a-starboard'. The Formidable *responded instantly, heeling sharply to starboard as her head turned to port: then seconds later to port as her head came back again. But all of us on the bridge could*

see the relentless approach of the Stukas. And now we could hear the whistle of the bombs. A mountain of filthy black water shot up close on our starboard bow and rose to eighty feet. Five seconds later there was another mountain, even closer and higher. Millions of crystals of water glittered in the sunlight as they fell.

Then there were two in succession. We continued to weave. The next one hit. We were immediately on fire on the starboard side forward. A bomb had penetrated one of the 4.5in gun turrets. The explosion had blown out the ship's starboard side below the fo'c'sle causing damage, and the fire appeared to be spreading. The sea was calm and the hull was still sound below the water-line, so little water was being shipped into the great gaping hole as we tore along.

The firing from the fleet continued; and still the bombers peeled off to dive. There were further near-misses, and then a gigantic jolt in the Formidable *when the whole ship seemed to lift from aft. A 1,000lb bomb had gone right through the after starboard 4.5in gun sponson and exploded under the starboard quarter. It was an uncanny sensation feeling the stern violently lifted and then falling, shuddering like a tuning fork vibrating through its fixed end. It was all terrifying but in some odd way exhilarating.*

BELOW HMS *Formidable* **fell victim to a Stuka attack in the Mediterranean on 26 May 1941 that put the aircraft carrier out of action for six months.**
(Copyright unknown)

On 15 June Ju 87s sank HMS *Airdale* and the destroyer *Nestor*, and damaged the cruiser *Birmingham*. The carrier *Indomitable* was badly damaged by dive-bombing on 11 August 1942. Royal Navy warships continued to suffer loss and damage at the hands of Stukas through 1943.

On the Eastern Front Stukas dealt crippling blows to both the Soviet Black Sea and Baltic fleets. On the Leningrad Front, the Soviet Baltic Fleet was subjected to a series of heavy attacks by StG 1 and StG 2 in September 1941 – the battleship *Oktyabrskaya Revolutsiya* was hit four times and seriously damaged on the 23rd at Tallinn; the cruisers *Maksim Gorky*, *Kirov* and *Petropavlovsk* and destroyer *Silny* were each hit by bombs and suffered serious damage, while the submarine depot ship *Smolny* and submarine *Shch-306* were also hit.

The battleship *Marat* was sunk in shallow water inside the Russian naval base at Kronstadt on 23 September 1941 by two bomb hits, one of which was claimed by the future Stuka ace Hans-Ulrich Rudel of III./StG 2 flying a Ju 87 B. Rudel describes the tactics he used in this dive-bombing attack:

Both harbour and town are heavily defended; and, besides the whole Russian Baltic fleet is anchored in the immediate vicinity, and outside the harbour. We in the leading Staffel aircraft always fly at an altitude between 9,000 and 10,000ft; that is very low but, after all, we want to hit something. When diving on to the ships we use our dive brakes in order to check our diving speed. This gives us more time to sight our target and correct our aim. The more carefully we aim, the better the results of our attack, and everything depends on them. By reducing our diving speed we make it easier for the flak to bring us down, especially as if we do not overshoot we cannot climb so fast after the dive. But, unlike the flights behind us, we do not generally try to climb back out of the dive. We use different tactics and pull out at low level close above the water. We have then to take the wildest evasive action over the enemy occupied coastal strip. Once we have left it behind we can breathe freely again.

In the Crimea the Luftwaffe's principal target was the Russian Black Sea Fleet, which was supplying the besieged Soviet garrisons in Odessa and Sebastopol. Later they evacuated many of the exhausted soldiers and civilians (more than 250,000) from Sebastopol at the end of October 1941, but in the process Stukas managed to catch and sink the destroyer *Frunze* and a gunboat. Stukas of III./StG 3 badly damaged the battleship *Kharkov* and sank the destroyers *Sposobny* and *Besposchadny* on 5/6 October 1943 while raiding the Crimea.

Soviet vessels unloading supplies at besieged Sebastopol were also hunted down and sunk by Stukas and Ju 88s.

Ultimately, it was down to the consummate skill of the Stuka pilots with their nerves of iron that made the Ju 87 such a deadly assailant when pitted against naval targets.

The quality of mercy

In what is more of a reflection on the personal integrity of some who flew the Ju 87 than on the act of flying the dive-bomber itself, the following extract from the autobiography of Focke-Wulf Fw 190 pilot Norbert Hannig makes illuminating reading. It bears out the seventh commandment governing the conduct in war of the German soldier, which was printed inside the cover of the Luftwaffe pay-book – 'The civil population is inviolable. A soldier is not permitted to plunder or deliberately to destroy.'

On 11 October 1944, four Fw 190 A-6s of 5./JG 54 flying from Insterburg in East Prussia provided a fighter escort to a Staffel of Ju 87s from I./SG 4, briefed to attack a column of Russian tanks reported to be approaching the border.

Norbert Hannig was one of the fighter pilots. He recalls:

At 10.00hrs the next morning [the 11th] the Stukas took off. I led my four Fw 190 A-6s into the air shortly afterwards and quickly caught up with the dive-bombers. I waggled my wings and the Ju 87 leader responded. Contact established. I took up position with my katschmarek [wingman] to the right of the formation, Kroschi and his wingman to the left.

The Stukas droned eastwards, over Kroschi's hometown of Gumbinnen towards the Lithuanian border. Above us at 1,200 metres the cloud base was solid, but visibility was good. The road the Ju 87s were following was lined on either side by an avenue of old trees, their gnarled branches clearly visible. The open fields bordering the road were covered in a blanket of snow. On the road itself long lines of horse-drawn farm wagons, piled high with people and their possessions, plodded along. Interspersed among them were other figures on foot, some pulling handcarts or sledges. These were refugees from the border area fleeing westwards to escape the Red Army.

Suddenly the road ahead was empty. The Stukas slid into attack formation, line ahead. Still following the road, the leader appeared to be searching. In the distance another caterpillar-like line of refugees appeared. But they were rapidly being overhauled by a column of Russian tanks charging across the snow covered fields to the left of the road. The Stuka leader wheeled his machines into a circle above the enemy armour and prepared to attack.

ABOVE Ju 87s of SG 3 head out over a wintry Estonian landscape on a bombing mission in 1944. *(BA 101I-726-0224-09A)*

ABOVE Refugees,
their worldly
possessions piled on
horse-drawn wagons
and sleds, flee across
the ice at Pillau, East
Prussia, in the face
of the advancing Red
Army during December
1944. It would have
been a scene like this
which Norbert Hannig
witnessed.
(BA 183-R77440)

But he had been spotted. Before he could start his dive the Soviet tanks had turned sharply left, their churning tracks sending up flurries of snow as they charged straight into the refugee column packed tightly along the thin ribbon of road. Panic broke out. Horses bolted, wagons overturned, people ran into the open fields. The Stukas circled helplessly. The enemy tanks were using the refugees as a living shield. The snow was stained red where they ploughed unheedingly over man and beast. The Stuka leader called off the attack. He could not add to the carnage by bombing the tanks and spreading more death and destruction among the civilians below.

The Ju 87s returned to Insterburg and landed with their bombs still aboard. It was the one and only occasion throughout my entire time on the Eastern Front that a Stuka formation I was escorting had been unable to carry out its mission as ordered.

The refugees fleeing the Soviet advance into East Prussia were probably Volksdeutsch (ethnic Germans). This assault was temporarily halted after two weeks of vicious fighting, but in early 1945 the exodus westwards became a torrent when the Red storm broke over East Prussia on 12 January and between then and mid-February 1945 almost 8.5 million Germans fled the eastern provinces of the Reich in the face of the marauding Red Army.

The Stuka's legacy – the Fairchild Republic A-10 Thunderbolt II

In an interview with the *Daily Beast*, the American news and opinion website, engineer Pierre Sprey, a former Pentagon procurement official who in the 1970s helped design the US Air Force's A-10 Thunderbolt ground-attack jet, confirmed that Colonel Hans-Ulrich Rudel was consulted in the development of the 'Hog' (as it is popularly known):

While we were readying the airplane and gun for full-scale production, the 30mm gun program manager, Col Robert Dilger, invited Rudel to lead a symposium in [Washington] DC attended by several hundred engineers, analysts, tacticians and intel types on all aspects of CAS [close air-support] operations in combat. For lots of them it was eye-opening. I translated for Rudel who spoke very little English.

Rudel was certainly the expert on killing Soviet tanks – 519 of them. But he was also brilliant on tactics – both ground and air, training, C3 [Command, Control and Communication], reconnaissance and squadron leadership. During our concept design phase, I required every member of the team to read Stuka Pilot, *Rudel's superbly detailed recounting of his combat experiences, in order to understand the most crucial combat effectiveness characteristics of a CAS fighter.*

Many of the characteristics of the Hog – arguably the finest ground-attack jet ever built – were directly influenced by Rudel's experience flying the Stuka and the ground-attack version of the Focke-Wulf Fw 190 (the D-9) against the Red Army. Sprey continued:

The book most certainly influenced me, particularly regarding how critical it was to incorporate in any effective CAS design such things as cockpit armour, fire suppression, need for ultra-tight turn radius manoeuvring performance, ability to fly under 500ft,

weather, getting 3–5 sorties per day per plane, large calibre cannon, ability to move a squadron overnight, and ability to operate sustainably from unprepared fields – grass, dirt, mud, gravel, etc.

So, in some respects the spirit of the Stuka lives on in an American ground-attack jet designed in the 1970s, still in service in the 2010s, but considered by some US generals and politicians as an anachronism that needs retiring. There are certain uncanny parallels here with the Stuka and its putative replacements in the early 1940s – the Henschel Hs 129 and Messerschmitt Me 410. The pressure to replace the Hog with something more modern and high-tech is based largely on prejudice against an ageing and low-tech (but capable) aircraft, as well as political considerations, in a story that mirrors the experience of the Stuka. In the end it became plain that the Stuka was very good at doing what it did, in much the same way as the Hog does more than 70 years later.

BELOW The spirit of the Ju 87 lives on in the Fairchild A-10 Thunderbolt II – the US Air Force's legendary and feared 'Hog' ground-attack jet. *(USAF)*

Chapter Six

Maintaining the Stuka

Built with ease of maintenance and repair in mind, the Stuka was an ideal aircraft to take on campaign. Operating from rough airstrips far away from the engineering facilities of established airfields, the Ju 87's sensible design meant groundcrews were not only able to carry out basic servicing promptly, but they were also able to replace engines and access vital systems with comparative ease.

OPPOSITE **Schwarzmänner from Gefechtsverband Kuhlmey (Battlegroup Kuhlmey) bomb-up a Ju 87 D-5 of I./SG 3 at Immola in Finland on 28 June 1944.** *(SA-Kuva)*

RIGHT Hangar maintenance of a Ju 87 B (T6-GM) of StG 2 'Immelmann' during the winter of 1939/40. Working inside was clearly no guarantee of warmth as these Schwarzmänner are well wrapped up against the cold. *(BA 101I-378-0037-22)*

BELOW Pilots relied on the Schwarzmänner to keep their aircraft flying. When a Stuka Staffel was operating away from the technical facilities of an established airfield, the pressure was on them to maintain aircraft serviceability. This is Oberleutnant Martin Schmidt, Staffelkapitän of 5./ StG 51, with two groundcrew in spring 1940. StG 51 was redesignated StG 1 on 9 July 1940. *(Chris Goss collection)*

Like squadron groundcrews in most other air forces of the Second World War period, those who served in the Luftwaffe's Stuka Staffeln were among the forgotten many who ensured their aircrews had serviceable aircraft, armed and fuelled and ready to fly into battle.

In the months before the outbreak of war in 1939, Erhard Milch and Ernst Udet had introduced a system that was predicated on the Luftwaffe fighting a series of small campaigns interspersed with long periods of downtime in between. Investment in aircraft repair facilities and the stockpiling of spares was kept intentionally low, with the emphasis on replacing broken or damaged parts with new ones, but this was only possible for

short spells. With the outbreak of war this all changed and as the conflict continued it quickly became an unsustainable model. This is in contrast to the RAF, for example, where the civilian 'make-do-and-mend' mentality extended to the groundcrews working in the hangars and dispersals on operational airfields at home and overseas.

Schwarzmänner – the Blackmen

Popularly known by the nickname Schwarzmänner (or Blackmen) – a term dating from the days of the Legion Kondor during the Spanish Civil War, owing to their dark-coloured oily overalls – men in the Luftwaffe groundcrew (Bodenpersonal) trades often came from civil engineering backgrounds or had previously worked in the aircraft industry. A good number of the NCOs were experienced career servicemen who had joined the fledgling Luftwaffe during the 1930s when it was being grown by stealth against the terms of the Versailles Treaty. By the time the war came, however, most Schwarzmänner were wearing dark blue or green cotton twill overalls, but the nickname stuck. These were the men who toiled to keep their Ju 87 charges fit for operations at all times, in all weathers and in all theatres of operations.

JU 87 STAFFEL AIR AND GROUNDCREW ESTABLISHMENT, 1942

In the summer of 1942 the air and groundcrew establishments for a typical Ju 87 Staffel (or squadron, in this instance of StG 77) with nine aircraft would have been as follows:

- 1 Staffel commander (Hauptmann – flight lieutenant)
- 1 Officer for Special Purposes (Oberleutnant – flying officer)
- 11 Pilots (3 Leutnants – pilot officers, 8 Oberfeldwebel – flight sergeant)
- 12 Radio operator/rear gunners (Oberfeldwebel)
- 1 Flying personnel Oberfeldwebel
- 18 Aircraft mechanics (8 Unteroffiziere – corporal, 10 Flieger – aircraftman)
- 6 Engine fitters (4 Unteroffiziere, 2 Flieger)
- 2 Electricians (2 Flieger)
- 1 Precision engineer (Flieger)
- 1 Air weapons Oberfeldwebel

- 14 Air weapons armourers (1 Feldwebel – sergeant, 4 Unteroffiziere, 9 Flieger)
- 1 Radio Oberfeldwebel
- 3 Radio mechanics (1 Unteroffiziere, 2 Flieger)

ABOVE Engine maintenance outside for this Ju 87 B-1 of StG 77. *(James Payne/ Through Their Eyes)*

Schwarzmänner on campaign

Alongside their aircrew comrades, Schwarzmänner plied their groundcrew trades in some of the most extreme and inhospitable climatic conditions known to man – from sub-zero frozen landscapes in Norway, Finland and Russia, to the waterlogged airstrips of southern Italy and the scorching sun and blistering sands of North Africa. Each location called for its own particular adaptations to aircraft and revisions to servicing routines in order for a Staffel to operate effectively – or in some instances, operate at all.

In the early days of Blitzkrieg campaigning in France in 1940, the pace of the advance on the ground often outstripped the support echelons' capacity to bring up stores and equipment quickly enough by road transport to keep a Stuka unit at operational readiness. The lesson was quickly learned and from then on, when transferring from one airfield to another, the chief mechanic (or 'crew chief') of each Stuka would squeeze into the rear cockpit with the gunner for the transit flight (so long as the move did not involve a combat mission en route).

Essential tools were packed in a crate and secured to the aircraft's under-fuselage ETC weapons rack. Assuming the new airfield or operating base already had reserves of fuel and ammunition on site, the unit could be brought to operational readiness quite swiftly.

This practice breached regulations, but the powers that be turned a blind eye to the arrangement, although it soon became a standard operating procedure on all Stuka units

BELOW Groundcrew swarm around a Ju 87 B-1 (T6+GS) of StG 2's 8th Staffel in France during May 1940. The aircraft has been bombed-up and is ready for operations. *(Chris Goss collection)*

on whichever front they were fighting.

When a Stuka unit was stationed on a permanent airfield with its hangars, technical support and messing facilities, life was tolerable for the Schwarzmänner. But when it was deployed on campaign the picture could change dramatically, as it did when the Luftwaffe was fighting in Russia and North Africa, where extremes in temperature and weather were perhaps the most obvious causes of difficulty when it came to maintaining aircraft in a serviceable state.

The North African desert

Sand and dust storms were part of the desert war experience that ground troops and airmen on both sides had to endure. Pilots were forbidden from trying to take off or fly in a sand- or dust storm for the simple reason that they would probably never get out of it alive. If they were caught in the air when a dust storm blew up then they knew to head back to base as quickly as possible.

When the air was filled by a choking fog of flying sand and fine dust whipped up by a ferocious wind, it was virtually impossible to see or breathe properly. Ground staff hurriedly lashed down aircraft, pulled over the protective tarpaulin covers and packed away as many portable items of equipment as possible into whatever was handy, like empty wooden bomb crates. The only thing now was to get under cover and sit out the storm, which brought all activity to a standstill. It could be a matter of hours before it abated, but sometimes it could last for days. When the air finally cleared and the sun broke through, the job of clearing up began. However, sand and dust had a knack of penetrating into every conceivable crack and crevice of man and machine.

Hauptmann Helmut Mahlke remembers how, soon after his unit's (I./StG 1) arrival in Libya in April 1941, his ground staff were faced with a job after a sandstorm that was completely new and unfamiliar to them:

Using either their hands or empty ration tins, they began scooping incredible quantities of sand out of the innermost recesses of

RIGHT Freezing conditions could not be allowed to interfere with the operational readiness of a Stuka Staffel. In a scene repeated endless times and in countless places along the Eastern Front a Ju 87 D-5 of StG 3 is readied for a mission on 9 March 1944, at Dorpat in eastern Estonia. *(BA 101I-726-0223-02)*

our machines. They had to make sure that all moveable parts still actually moved, that all air intakes were free of sand and that the aircraft were fully operational again.

After a spell of intensive operations against Tobruk, the Gruppe was stood down for a day to carry out essential maintenance on aircraft. Mahlke again:

For the first time since arriving in Africa we were finally allowed a breathing space to undertake all the servicing work that was crying out to be done on our machines. The groundcrews soon had the engine cowlings off and began by shovelling out all the fine desert sand that had found its way back into every nook and cranny. There was sand everywhere! It was a miracle our engines were still running. It was almost as if they were actually benefitting from the constant sand-blasting they were getting!

In Russia

Russia is a vast country with mountains and areas of desert, tundra, steppe and plateaux, all with their own climate. Almost everywhere in Russia the winters can be very cold with harsh frosts and heavy snowfall, with the first snows often arriving in October and hanging around on the ground until March. Spring and autumn can be very unsettled with frequent rain, snowfall and strong winds. In summer the temperature can vary from comfortably warm along the Baltic coast to searingly hot and dry on the south-eastern Steppes. For the Stukagruppen on campaign along the Eastern Front, the Russian weather became as implacable a foe as the Ivans.

Research has shown that in the first winter following Barbarossa, 1941/42, the weather

in Russia and central and eastern Europe is believed to have been the coldest in more than 250 years. During the three bitter winters when the Stukagruppen were operating on the Eastern Front, Ju 87s flew out of ice-bound airfields and rough landing strips, hampered by snow drifts and with nothing in the way of creature comforts like heated accommodation or facilities for personnel or aircraft.

Winter temperatures frequently plunged below freezing, sometimes to as low as −30°C. The Schwarzmänner were obliged to start up and run their Stukas' engines half-hourly during the long nights to keep them from freezing solid and to make sure they were fit for operations at first light. The sub-zero temperatures not only caused frostbite, but they also made engine oil and fuel lines crack and starter motors quickly became unreliable. As a consequence, over the winter of 1941/42 Ju 87 serviceability fell off to under 30% of unit strength.

BELOW Groundcrew at work in the Russian snow manhandle bombs for loading on to a Ju 87. *(Copyright unknown)*

In many instances the appalling weather
conditions meant that supply echelons carrying
essential ground staff and equipment by motor
transport became bogged down when the
summer dust of the Steppes was turned into
thick mud by the autumn rains, and then when
the winter freeze set in they were stuck fast
in the snow and ice. Supplies of fuel, spares
and ammunition were interrupted, which
meant operational flying was suspended until
conditions improved. Those Bodenpersonal
who were flown in by air in Ju 52 transport
aircraft did not always fare any better.

So, improvisation became the
Schwarzmänner's best tactic: protective tents to
enclose the Stukas' engines; or wood foraging
to build open fires that were lit under the
engines to enable at least three or four aircraft
to be serviceable in the morning.

In the hot summers on forward operating
bases out on the Ukrainian Steppe, the barren
landscape had no trees or bushes to give
shelter from the sun's rays. Tarpaulin covers
were pulled over the cockpit glazing to give
some heat protection to the interior, while the
physical nature of the Schwarzmänner's job
meant they needed to guard against heat
exhaustion and dehydration.

Hans-Ulrich Rudel described the landscape
in his autobiography, *Stuka Pilot*:

*The country is perfectly flat and offers no sort
of obstacles in the way of terrain. Everything
is Steppe as far as the eye can reach. The
only possible cover is in so-called Balkas,
clefts in the surface of the earth, or gulleys,
the bottoms of which lie some 30 feet below
the surrounding plain. They are relatively
wide so that vehicles can be parked in them,
not only one behind the other but also side
by side. The whole country stretches like this
for many hundreds of miles from Rostow to
Stalingrad. If the enemy is not encountered
on the march, he is always to be found in
these hiding places.*

Stukagruppen in retreat

The Battle of Stalingrad that lasted for
just over five months in 1942–43 was a
watershed in the fortunes of the Luftwaffe,
compounded in July 1943 by the Battle of
Kursk (Operation Zitadelle) where the Red
Army continued to push back against the
German invaders. During the first half of 1943
the attrition levels in aircraft and crews, as
well as among ground staff, were losses from
which the Luftwaffe never recovered. They
were high among experienced technicians
and engineers – the Schwarzmänner – and
these losses were made worse from late 1942

onwards by Reichsmarschall Goering's policy of wanting to make infantry soldiers out of 'underemployed' (as he mistakenly believed) ground staff. The result was the creation of 22 Luftwaffe Field Divisions, which he raised from between 200,000 and 250,000 ground support personnel, most of whom spent their time on the Eastern Front.

Major Paul-Werner Hozzel recalls the fate that befell many of the groundcrew from StG 2 'Immelmann' after Stalingrad:

Winter was near at hand. So came the end. Today we know the prescience of imminent disaster would come true, even surpass all expectations. … The Geschwader 'Immelmann' flew out the mass of its groundcrews from the pocket by transporting them in the wings and rear cockpits of the planes. As many as about 700 men were ordered to be left behind. They were integrated into the Luftwaffe Field Battalion 'Immelmann'. We never heard of them again.

With their numbers not only depleted by heavy losses on active service, but also due to Goering's plunder to fill his Field Divisions, the demands placed on the remaining Schwarzmänner to maintain aircraft capable

of going to war was further compromised by economic factors way beyond their control. As a result of Allied strategic bombing on German industry and the loss of oil production in Romania and the Middle East, shortages of everything worsened – from spare parts and materials to consumables like fuel, lubricants and rubber for tyres, pipes and seals. Buna rubber, of course, was still available, but that too was reliant on the chemical industry for its production.

When the end came in 1945, the Schwarzmänner who had survived the final desperate months of war went into the PoW bag. Those who surrendered to the British or the Americans fared better than the men who became prisoners of the Russians. Of the three million Germans taken prisoner by the Soviets during the war, more than a third died in captivity. Hatred of Germany and the Germans was endemic in Soviet society during the war and this, combined with a burning desire to repay the barbarity shown to their own prisoners by the Germans, meant the Russians felt they had the right to repay them in kind.

Some lucky prisoners were sent home as early as 1947, but most remained in the brutal Soviet Gulags until the 1950s, when Stalin finally issued an amnesty.

BELOW **End of the line: Ju 87 D-3(N) (E8+Gl) of 3.Nsgr 9, abandoned by its unit and hidden in a shed on an airfield west of Innsbruck, Austria, in June 1945.** *(US National Archives)*

Operating instructions for cold-start preparation
Mixing of fuel and oil in the oil tank
Ju 87 B (Ju 87 A in brackets)

This instruction applies to all aircraft that are not yet fitted with a cold-start cock.

■ After returning from a sortie the aircraft should be refuelled.
■ Fill with 30 litres of oil (for Ju 87 A, 27 litres).
■ Using a funnel, or a funnel and hose, carefully and accurately add 7 litres of fuel to the 30 litres of oil (for Ju 87 A, 6 litres).
■ During mixing make sure the oil temperature is not more than 40°C and no lower than 20°C.

■ Start up the engine and run for 4 minutes at 900rpm.
■ The aircraft is now ready for the next cold start.
■ (It must be clearly indicated to the pilot that the engine has been prepared for a cold start.)

Remarks: if the aircraft has flown for less than 1 hour since the previous cold start the oil level in the tank should be topped up to 30 litres (27 litres for Ju 87 A) if required.

The fuel quantity to be added to the oil tank is shown in the table below:

Flight duration	Fuel	
	For Ju 87 B	For Ju 87 A
More than 1 hour	7 litres	6 litres
¾ hour	6 litres	5 litres
½ hour	5 litres	4 litres
¼ hour	4 litres	3 litres

Care must be taken that the fresh oil added to the oil in the tank is at not less than 0°C otherwise filling will be very difficult.

In winter engines need to be warmed up for longer because oil is more viscous and circulates more slowly. Dilute oil works just as well as warm oil and its lubricating properties are unaffected by the benzene additive in the fuel.

ABOVE Groundcrew use a funnel to top up the main engine oil tank of a Ju 87 B-2 of III./StG 51. *(Chris Goss collection)*

RIGHT Cold start: a Ju 87 R-2 of IV.(Stuka)/ LG 1 (minus its wing tanks) is refuelled in Norway in 1941. *(BA 101I-091-0195-17)*

STUKA TURNROUND

This collection of superb photographs was taken at Immola in Finland on one day, 28 June 1944, when Ju 87 D-5s of I./SG 3 – part of Gefechtsverband Kuhlmey (see pages 136-137) – were being readied for a mission against the bridges at Tallinn, the capital of Estonia.

1   An armourer carries on his shoulder a 50kg bomb fitted with tail-screamers. (SA-Kuva)

2   This SC 1000 bomb has been manoeuvred into position underneath the Stuka, the suspension band has already been fitted and its lugs have been located in the two forks of the swing-down trapeze mechanism... (SA-Kuva)

3   ... before being carefully raised into position underneath the aircraft for attachment to the bomb shackles. It takes four strong men to complete the activity. (SA-Kuva)

4   Under each wing a pair of SC 50 bombs is lifted manually into position and attached to the ETC 50/VIIIe ejectors. (SA-Kuva)

5   Meanwhile, the aircraft's internal wing tanks are filled with B4 (87-octane) synthetic fuel from a 200-litre drum using a Kraftstoff handpumpe KHP 4 (fuel hand pump). Up to 60 litres/min could be transferred using this method. Fuels refined from crude oil were becoming scarce by this time in the war and so synthetic aviation fuel derived from coal was used instead. *(SA-Kuva)*

6   Sitting on an SC 250 bomb, armourers find time for 'eine Zigarettenpause'. German soldiers and airmen loved British or American brands such as Lucky Strike or Players if they could get their hands on them, but it was usually the Third Reich's 'Glimmstängel' (German slang for fags) like Juno, Milde Sorte and Eckstein No 5. *(SA-Kuva)*

7   A fitter sits in the cockpit to run up the Jumo 211J, making sure that all is working according to the book after any repairs and adjustments. *(SA-Kuva)*

8   Oberleutnant Hans Töpfer, commanding I./SG 3, briefs his crews before they fly their mission. The unit left Finland for Germany in August where it relinquished its Ju 87s and re-equipped with the Fw 190. Töpfer was an experienced Stuka man who had flown more than 600 missions by the war's end, mostly in the Ju 87, during which time he was shot down twice and wounded twice. *(SA-Kuva)*

9   Töpfer pulls on his 'Channel' trousers while his crew chief waits in the background to start the engine. *(SA-Kuva)*

10 He is helped to strap in before donning his flying helmet, which can be seen resting on top of the cockpit canopy. Waiting to board the aircraft, his

gunner wears typical Luftwaffe aircrew flying kit of the period: model LKp S100 summer flying helmet and summer-weight 'Channel' flight jacket and trousers; his belt carries a leather drop-style holster for a side-arm; an Armbandkompass is looped around the belt. (SA-Kuva)

11 A starting handle is used to wind up the Bosch inertia starter that turns over the Jumo, which then bursts into life. (SA-Kuva)

12 Fully armed and ready to go, the Stuka strains against the brakes as the pilot runs up the engine. (SA-Kuva)

13 Take-off – the target for this mission was the bridges at Tallinn, 140km away to the south across the waters of the Gulf of Finland. The Stukas are trying to stall the Soviet attempt to retake Estonia. (SA-Kuva)

The following maintenance plan is a summary of all the scheduled maintenance checks required on the Ju 87 R-1. It is subdivided first by the maintenance frequency, followed by the design structures involved and then by the tests that were to be carried out, if necessary, after certain time intervals, as well as including partial and full overhauls.

When	Where	What
Fuselage		
Daily	Fuselage outer covering and centre section	Torn rivets, damaged paintwork, dents. Tight fit of all flaps and hatches.
	Canopy release	Sign 'secured' must be visible.
Every 4 weeks	Canopy jettison mechanism	
Landing gear		
Daily	Undercarriage fairing	Tight fit.
	Tyre creep, rims and tyre	Movement of red tyre creep mark.
	Tyre pressures	Check only on hot and very cold days, otherwise according to need.
	Operation of tailwheel	Free rotation, check tightness of securing nuts and screws.
	Rudder pedals	Check effectiveness of the brake pedals.
	Oleo struts	Check tightness of leather seals.
	Tailwheel lock	Check it can be locked in position.
After 400 operating hours	Main undercarriage and tailwheel	Remove. Check attachment points, bolts, wear and tear, fatigue cracks.
Tailplane		
Daily	Elevators and rudder	Check tight fit of all flaps and panels. Check for play in elevators.
	Plating	Torn rivets, damaged paintwork, dents.
	Wing flaps and dive brakes	Check tightness of nuts and bolts, ensure control surface bearings are well greased.
Controls		
Daily	Control column, rudder pedals	Check for free movement, swing and play.
Every 100 hours	Rudder and elevator trimmer cables	Check wear and tensioning of rudder and elevator trimmer cables. Do not grease cables.
	Dive brakes, elevator trimmers, control column	With dive brakes lowered, check if the two right-hand trim tabs are facing upwards, that dive brakes are not loose, and that control column movement is restricted to 5°.
After 400 hours – partial overhaul	Control surfaces, flaps, wings, fuselage interior	Removal and adjustment of control runs.
After 2,000 hours – full overhaul	Wing flaps	Removal and adjustment.
Wings		
Daily	Wing skins	Check for tight fit of all covers and flaps, torn rivets, damaged paintwork, dented areas, serious creasing to wing skins.
After first flight and after 40 hours	Ball joints to wing ribs	Tight and secure fit.
After 100 dive-bombing sorties	Wing spars	Check for cracks.

When	Where	What
Engine installation		
Daily	Removable cowlings	Check for proper fit and closure. Torn rivets, damaged paintwork, dents.
After the first flight and after 40 operational hours	Ball joints	Tight and secure fit.
After 10 operational hours	Removable cowlings	Check for wear of rubber seals and Neolite (synthetic rubber) strips.
After 100 operational hours – partial overhaul	Engine mountings	Distortions, damage, cracks.
	Engine attachment points	Bearing tightness, perfect condition of the rubber bushes.
Powerplant		
Daily	All levers	Check for full movement.
	Cold start equipment	Delivering correctly.
	Removable containers	Check seals are tight.
	Fuel, lubricant and coolant lines as well as radiators	Check for leaks.
	Ends of the exhaust pipes	Check they are not frozen over.
After 50 service hours	Starter system push-rod	Lubricate with aircraft blue grease.
	Cable brackets	Properly attached.
	Engine control linkages through the firewall	Check for tight fit of seals.
	Lubricating oil pressure line	Refill with a glycol/coolant mixture in the ratio 60:40 to 70:30.
After 100 service hours – partial overhaul	Inertia starter	Overhaul, in accordance with Bosch instructions.
	Fuel, lubricant and coolant system	Pressure test.
	Operating systems (linkages, lever rods and cable-pulls)	End positions of the actuating levers must correspond with those of the cockpit operating levers. Ease of operation.
Equipment		
Daily	Pilot's cockpit switches	Collector-voltage (when engine is stopped). Check generators are working (when warming up).
	Pilot's cockpit	Test magnetos.
	Hydraulic oil system, retraction struts and pressure fittings	Check for leaks.
	Hydraulic oil tank	Check oil level.
	Hydraulic oil system	If necessary, bleed the system.
Every 20 hours	Moving parts (rudder levers etc.)	Check for full movement.

Chapter Seven
Stuka survivors

The Ju 87 is a rare bird in the 21st century. What was once the scourge of the battlefield is now an endangered species. Out of more than 5,700 Ju 87s that were built, only a handful has survived that are substantially complete. Two essentially intact examples are on public display in museums in London and Chicago, while some salvaged but incomplete Stukas can be seen in collections elsewhere.

OPPOSITE In 2014 local fishermen alerted the Croatian Department of Underwater Archaeology to the wreck of a Ju 87 R-2 in the Adriatic off the coast of Croatia, close to the island of Žirje. *(Claudia Weber-Gebert)*

175

ABOVE It was found to be a Picchiatello of the 239th Squadrigila, 97° Gruppo of the Italian Air Force. In this view from above and behind the aircraft, the single-piece variable incidence tailplane can be clearly seen in the foreground. *(Claudia Weber-Gebert)*

BELOW Although encrusted with marine growth, the pilot's cockpit and instrument panel are still recognisable, in particular his control column (centre) and the propeller pitch control (left of centre). *(Claudia Weber-Gebert)*

BELOW RIGHT The Ju 87 was remarkably intact despite more than 70 years lying in 28m of water at the bottom of the Adriatic. This is the gunner's canopy (which has been slid back) showing the circular aperture that would have contained his MG 17 machine gun in its Linsen-Lafette mounting. The pilot's sliding canopy is not present. *(Claudia Weber-Gebert)*

Towards the end of September 2014, divers taking part in a harpoon competition near the Croatian island of Žirje on the Dalmatian coast came across the wreckage of an aircraft lying 28m down on the sandy seabed of the Adriatic. Its discovery caused a stir when it was confirmed by the Croatian Institute for National Heritage as being a Ju 87 R-2 'Picchiatella' of the Regia Aeronautica.

It was later found to be one of three Ju 87s of the 239th Squadriglia, 97° Gruppo Bombardamento, which had attacked a pair of Yugoslav warships sheltering in a bay near Šibenik on 12 April 1941, but two of the three

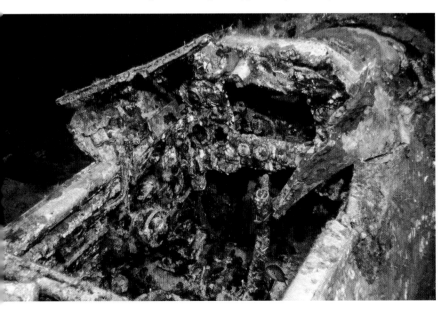

were shot down. The first aircraft had been destroyed and the crew killed, but the second had been damaged and made a forced landing on the sea. It is presumed the crew made good their escape because the cockpit canopy is missing from the wreck and no signs of human remains were found.

The wreck is remarkably intact and stands on its undercarriage on the sandy bottom among a meadow of Poseidon sea grass. The Stuka's Jumo 211 engine was thought to be lost, but it was discovered nearby, probably torn from its mountings by the impact with the sea or later caught up in the trawl nets of fishermen. It was subsequently moved by divers to be nearer the wreck.

At first the wreck was closed to divers, giving the institute's underwater archaeology team the opportunity to examine the aircraft and recover some significant parts for museum display. Included among the artefacts are the pilot's control column and the MG 17 machine gun from the rear cockpit.

Plans to salvage the Ju 87 for preservation as a museum exhibit were soon abandoned, but it was declared cultural heritage and given a listed monument status by the Croatian government. Organised dives to the wreck have been allowed since April 2015, but physical contact with the aircraft is prohibited in order to prevent further deterioration.

The Žirje Ju 87 R-2 is one of the best-preserved examples of a Stuka to be discovered in recent years, and with this in mind it is disappointing that more has not been done by officialdom to salvage the aircraft. And so it remains on the seabed.

Like many other aircraft types from the fighting powers of the Second World War, the Ju 87 is not alone in being virtually extinct except for a handful of rare survivors in museums. At the end of the war there were few people who gave a second thought to the preservation of combat aircraft or the notion of aviation heritage. However, with an eye to the future, the British Air Ministry were prescient in selecting 12 German aircraft of different types for museum display from among the hundreds that had been captured. One of these was a Ju 87 G discovered in Germany near the Russian border, wearing mottled grey camouflage and bearing the Werk Nummer (Wk Nr) 494083 with fuselage codes RI+JK. It is probably the most complete surviving example of a Ju 87 in the world today and can be seen in the RAF Museum at Hendon in north London.

The list that follows records most of the surviving Ju 87 airframes that are on public display, including of course the one survivor that cannot, as it remains at the bottom of the Adriatic near the island of Žirje.

United Kingdom

Royal Air Force Museum, London – Hendon
Junkers Ju 87 G-2, Wk Nr 494083, RI+JK, of 10. (Panzerjäger) Staffel, II./ Schlachtgeschwader 3

Ju 87 G-2, Wk Nr 494083, is thought to have been built during 1943–44 as one of 1,178 Ju 87 D-5 ground-attack variants, but was later modified to G-2 standard. This included fitting under-wing mounting points for the two 3.7cm BK 37 Bordkanone carried by this variant. It is possible that the Werke Nummer may have been changed from 2883 (D-5) to 494083 when the airframe was rebuilt as a G-2, of which 210 were eventually produced.

Wk Nr 494083 was one of 59 Ju 87s located and captured by the British Disarmament Wing at the end of the war. It was discovered in Germany, possibly at a factory near the Russian border, and was later recorded at

BELOW During 2017, 494083 was partly dismantled during a reorganisation of exhibits for the museum's RAF centenary exhibition in 2018. This afforded a rare opportunity for visitors to examine parts of the Stuka that are not usually seen.
(Richard Crockett)

ABOVE A pristine-looking 494083 at RAF St Athan in the late 1960s.
(PRM Aviation)

Eggebek airfield, Schleswig-Holstein, coded RI-JK (unidentified unit). It became one of 12 German aircraft of different types chosen by the Air Ministry for museum display, rather than as evaluation aircraft, and as such it never received an 'Air Min' number. Nine of these museum aircraft survive to this day.

On 4 September 1945 the aircraft left Eggebek by surface transport, retaining for exhibition purposes its original markings and mottled grey camouflage. It was subsequently moved between several RAF maintenance units with other captured Luftwaffe equipment until ending up the Air Historical Branch's (AHB) official store at RAF Fulbeck in Lincolnshire, from where it was allocated to RAF St Athan in August 1960 when the Fulbeck collection was dispersed. Wk Nr 494083 was still in a complete condition except for a few missing cockpit instruments.

RIGHT Now on public display at the RAF Museum, Hendon, 494083 is pictured at RAF Chivenor in 1970 wearing the fuselage code W8-A. *(Ruth AS/ Wikimedia Commons)*

In 1967 it was moved to RAF Henlow in Bedfordshire along with other AHB aircraft for possible use in the film, *Battle of Britain*. It was repainted with the fuselage codes W8+A (carried by a Ju 87 unit in Europe in 1940) and given dummy wooden dive brakes, undercarriage leg sirens, a fibreglass bomb and a modified rear gun position, which involved removing and replacing the original twin 7.92mm MG 81Z mounting.

Wk Nr 494083's Jumo engine was run at least once at this time and the distinctive sound was recorded for use on the film's soundtrack. The aircraft was probably taxied, too. Film maker United Artists eventually obtained MoD permission to restore the Ju 87 to airworthy condition, but further inspection of the airframe revealed that restoration to airworthiness would be a costly exercise. Instead, three Percival Proctors were modified as 'Proctukas' to resemble Stukas for the film, but when they were flight-tested they did not fly well and so were not used. Instead radio-controlled scale models were built to look like late-model Stukas (in order to match 494083 if it had flown for the film) and were eventually used to 'bomb' the Ventnor radar station film set that was constructed at The Mound near Dover.

After its abortive film debut, over the next few years 494083 appeared as a static exhibit at various Battle of Britain Open Days on RAF bases including St Athan, Chivenor and Colerne (where the author saw it in 1972). In 1975 the aircraft was repainted at St Athan as RI+JK and eventually returned to the RAF Museum, Hendon, for display in the new Battle of Britain Museum that opened to the public on 28 November 1978. In December 1998, 494083 was reunited with its original MG 81Z rear gun mounting, which had been recovered from the RAF Museum's Reserve Collection at Cardington. Since then this aircraft has been displayed in the markings of 10. (Pz) Staffel, II./Schlachtgeschwader 3.

Various locations
Ju 87 B-1, Wk Nr 5518, A5+DN, 2./StG 77
The former Front Line Aviation Museum, Sandown Airport, Isle of Wight, displayed the rear fuselage, engine propeller, canopy frame and undercarriage parts of Ju 87 B-1 A5+DN recovered from Fishbourne Creek in 1977 and 1979. These survive in private ownership and some are now on display at the Wings Museum at Balcombe, West Sussex.

Serbia

Aeronautical Museum, Belgrade
Ju 87 B-2, Wk Nr 0870406, 98+01
Restored tail section only, with other centre section, wing section parts and engine cowlings from three other Ju 87s in storage.

Ju 87 R-4, Wk Nr 1394, A5+DN, 5./StG 1
Privately owned in the UK, the rear fuselage, undercarriage and cockpit parts were recovered from a crash site.

Greece

Hellenic Air Force Museum, Dekhelia, Athens
Ju 87 D-3/Trop, Wk Nr 100375, S7+GM, of II./StG 3
In October 2006, II./StG 3's S7+GM was recovered from the seabed off the island of

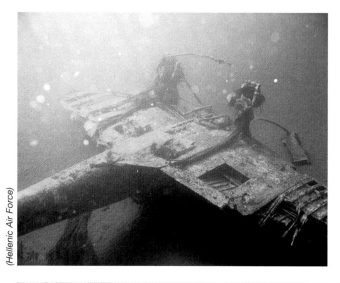

In October 2006 a Ju 87 D-3 trop was recovered from the Aegean near the Greek island of Rhodes. Its Luftwaffe markings and unit code (S7+GM) are still visible after almost 70 years underwater. It was found lying in 15m of water in the Prasonisi area, off the southern tip of the island.

Rhodes and is now displayed in the Hellenic Air Force Museum at Dekhelia, Athens.

Flying from their base at Argos on Crete on 9 October 1943, some 25 Stukas of II./StG 3 were the second wave of Ju 87s to attack a Royal Navy task force led by HMS *Carlisle* and HMS *Panther* passing through the Scarpanto Strait in the late morning. (The first attack wave was from I./StG 3 flying out of Megara.) When the Stukas were intercepted by P-38 Lightnings from 37th FS, 14th FG, flying from Gambut airfield in Libya, they jettisoned their bombs and made their escape towards the southern tip of Rhodes. In a running fight with the American fighters S7+GM was one of six Stukas that were by shot down at about 12.15hrs south-west of Rhodes. Pilot Leutnant Rolf Metzger and radio operator Unteroffizier Hans Sonnemann were both killed.

United States

Museum of Science and Industry, Chicago, Illinois

Ju 87 R-2 trop, Wk Nr 5954, A5+HL, I./StG 1
A5+HL was written off as 80% damaged after a crash-landing due to enemy fire on 22 November 1941 at Gambut, Libya, where it was abandoned. The aircraft was found by British forces and later donated by Britain to the USA as part of a drive to raise money for War Bonds. The Experimental Aircraft Association at Oshkosh restored A5+HL for the Museum of Science and Industry in 1974, where it was moved by 1988.

Flying Heritage Collection, Everett, Washington

Ju 87 R-2, Wk Nr 0875709, L1+KU, I./StG 5
The remains of Ju 87 R-2, Wk Nr 0875709, L1+KU, are undergoing long-term restoration in the USA for Microsoft billionaire Paul Allen's Flying Heritage Collection (FHC) at Everett, Washington.

Forced down in combat close to Motowski Bay near Murmansk on 28 May 1942, pilot Leutnant Eberhardt Klauck and gunner Obergfreiter Hans Hullen survived the crash and are listed as having returned to German lines. The airframe was discovered in 1996 and the remains were recovered to the UK in 1998. Traces of what are thought to be the

original factory radio code letters consisting of a black 'Z' are visible, along with the white 'K', denoting the individual aircraft callsign within the squadron.

The airframe was offered for sale for $50,000 via 'Royal Warbird Finders', based in the USA, and was purchased by the Flying Heritage Collection.

Germany

Deutsches Technikmuseum, Berlin

Ju 87 R-4, Wk Nr 6234, L1+FW, 4./LG 1
Ju 87 R-4, Wk Nr 5856, L1+BL, 3./StG 5
In 1997 the Museum für Verkehr und Technik in Berlin (renamed Deutsches Technikmuseum the same year) purchased two Junkers Ju 87 wrecks from the founder of the New Zealand Fighter Pilots Museum (now the Warbirds and Wheels Museum), Sir Tim Wallis. Both wrecks had been recovered from northern Russia.

Ju 87 R-4, L1+FW, was serving with 4./LG 1 in Russia when it crashed on 24 April 1942 near Murmansk and was recovered in 1990 by Jim Pearce. The salvaged parts included the engine, centre section and rear fuselage, tail unit, tailplane, port wing and badly damaged starboard wing. In 2004, L1+FW was registered as G-STUK to Glenn Lacey in Epsom, Surrey, but the registration was later cancelled and the aircraft remains with the Deutsches Technikmuseum in Berlin.

While operating with 3./StG 5, Ju 87 R-4, L1+BL was forced to make an emergency landing in Russian-held territory after it

ABOVE Chicago Museum of Science and Industry's Ju 87 R-2 trop is missing its under-wing fuel tanks and is fitted with non-Ju 87 main gear wheels. *(Wikimedia Commons)*

ABOVE Ju 87 R-2, 5856, was recovered from Russia in 1994 and is on display at the Deutsches Technikmuseum in Berlin. *(Wikimedia Commons)*

was attacked by enemy fighters on 2 July 1942 following a strike on the railway line between Murmansk and Leningrad. Leutnant

BELOW The front half of Ju 87 B-2, 1301643, was recovered from the seabed of the Mediterranean off St Tropez in 1989 and is displayed at the Sinsheim Auto und Technikmuseum. *(Wikimedia Commons)*

Karl-Heinz Herbst and Unteroffizier Alfred Nowitsch evaded capture and made it back to the German lines. (Herbst was later killed in action in January 1943.) Discovered in 1992, the wreck was initially found to be in good condition but during the two years that it took before recovery took place it was heavily vandalised. Recovered to the UK by Jim Pearce in 1994, it was later purchased by the Alpine Fighter Collection, Wanaka, New Zealand, before being acquired in 1997 by the Deutsches Technikmuseum, where it remains on display in the entrance hall of the museum in an unrestored condition.

Auto und Technikmuseum, Sinsheim
Ju 87 B-2, Wk Nr 1301643, 4./StG 77

The Auto und Technikmuseum displays the wings and front half of Ju 87 B-2, Wk Nr 1301643, which was recovered from 60m of water off St Tropez in 1989. This aircraft crashed in the Mediterranean near the French resort on 16 August 1944 while attacking the Allied invasion fleet during Operation Dragoon. It was raised from the seabed in 1989 and the museum displays the aircraft in an 'as found' condition, with no plans for a restoration.

Appendix 1

Luftwaffe unit organisation

Luftflotte

Numbered from 1 to 6, Luftflotten were organised to cover particular areas of combat within theatres of operations. They had no fixed strength but their establishment could vary from as few as 200 aircraft up to 1,500.

Fliegerkorps

Numbered I to X, Fliegerkorps operated as part of a Luftflotte, or as an independent unit like Fliegerkorps X. They comprised all types of aircraft and their strength could vary between 150 and 800 aircraft.

Geschwader (RAF/USAAF equivalent – wing)

This was the Luftwaffe's largest formation at a tactical level. It had a fixed establishment of aircraft, nominally 90 in three Gruppen, plus a Stabstaffel (staff flight). The Geschwader was named according to its purpose – in the case of a dive-bomber wing it was a Sturzkampfgeschwader, shortened to Stukageschwader. For example, Stukageschwader 1 was referred to as StG 1, or in common parlance as 'Stuka One'. A Geschwader was commanded by a Kommodore with a minimum rank of Major, but more often an Oberstleutnant or Oberst.

Gruppe

A Gruppe normally had a strength of some 40 to 50 aircraft typically in three Staffeln, plus a Stabstaffel. For example, the 1st Gruppe of Stukageschwader 1 was referred to in Roman and Arabic numerals as I./StG 1, or in common parlance as 'One Stuka One'. A Gruppe was commanded by a Gruppenkommandeur, who was usually an experienced Hauptmann or a Major with his own administrative staff (Gruppenstab). At this command level the Gruppenkommandeur was an active service officer, flying combat missions regularly.

Staffel (RAF/USAAF equivalent – squadron)

With a nominal strength of between 12 and 16 aircraft, there were three Staffeln to each Gruppe. Later, a fourth Staffel was added to tank-buster units in Russia. Later in the war a Staffel would be hard-pressed to reach an establishment of 12 aircraft. It was commanded by a Staffelkapitän, who was usually an Oberleutnant or a Hauptman.

> I. Gruppe – comprised of Staffel 1, 2 and 3.
> II. Gruppe – comprised of Staffel 4, 5 and 6.
> III. Gruppe – comprised of Staffel 7, 8 and 9.

Kette (RAF equivalent – flight)

A Staffel was subdivided operationally into several sections. In a bomber unit this was called a Kette and was the smallest flying formation, with three aircraft.

BELOW Souvenir hunters have started to pick clean this Italian Ju 87 that came to grief in North Africa. It might have been one of the ten Picchiatelli that force-landed in the desert on 14 September 1942. *(Andy Saunders collection)*

Comparative ranks

Luftwaffe	RAF	USAAF
Reichsmarschall	No equivalent	No equivalent
Generalfeldmarschall	Marshal of the RAF	General (5-star)
Generaloberst	Air Chief Marshal	General (4-star)
General der Flieger	Air Marshal	Lieutenant General
Generalleutnant	Air Vice-Marshal	Major General
Generalmajor	Air Commodore	Brigadier General
Oberst	Group Captain	Colonel
Oberstleutnant	Wing Commander	Lieutenant Colonel
Major	Squadron Leader	Major
Hauptmann	Flight Lieutenant	Captain
Oberleutnant	Flying Officer	1st Lieutenant
Leutnant	Pilot Officer	2nd Lieutenant
Stabsfeldwebel	Warrant Officer 1st Class	No equivalent
Oberfeldwebel	Flight Sergeant	Master Sergeant
Feldwebel	Sergeant	Sergeant
Unteroffizier	Corporal	Corporal
Obergefreiter	Leading Aircraftman	No equivalent
Gefreiter	Aircraftman 1st Class	Private 1st Class
Flieger	Aircraftman 2nd Class	Private

Sources

Books

Ailsby, Christopher, *Combat Medals of the Third Reich* (PSL, 1987)

Brown, Eric, *Wings of the Luftwaffe: Flying German Aircraft of World War II* (Hikoki, 2010)

Cull, Brian, *Gladiator Ace* (Haynes, 2010)

de Zeng IV, Henry L. and Stankey, Douglas G., *Dive-Bomber and Ground-Attack Units of the Luftwaffe 1933–1945, A Reference Source, Volume 1* (Classic, 2009)

Eisenbach, Hans Peter, *Fronteinsätzeeines Stuka-Fliegers* (Helios, 2010)

Forbes, Athol and Allen, Hubert, *Ten Fighter Boys* (Collins, 1942)

Green, William, *Aircraft of the Battle of Britain* (Macdonald/Pan, 1969)

Griel, Manfred, *Junkers Ju 87 Stuka* (Airlife, 2001)

Hannig, Norbert (ed. and trans. John Weal), *Luftwaffe Fighter Ace* (Grub Street, 2004)

Hozzell, Brig-Gen Paul-Werner, *Conversations with a Stuka Pilot* (Proceedings of a conference featuring Paul-Werner Hozzel, Brigadier-General Ret, German Air Force, at the US National War College, November 1978)

Koschorrek, Günter K., *Blood Red Snow: The Memoirs of a German Soldier on the Eastern Front* (Frontline, 2011)

Le Tissier, Tony, *With our Backs to Berlin* (Sutton, 2001)

Leonarde, Herbert and Jouineau, André, *Junkers Ju 87 from 1936 to 1945* (Histoire et Collections, 2003)

Merriam, Ray, *World War 2 in Review: German Airpower*, Issue 1 (Merriam Press, 2017)

Price, Alfred, *The Hardest Day: Battle of Britain, 18 August 1940* (Haynes, 2010)

Saunders, Andy, *Convoy Peewit: Blitzkrieg from the Air and Sea, 8 August 1940* (Grub Street, 2010)

Saunders, Andy, *Stuka Attack: The Dive-Bombing Assault on England during the Battle of Britain* (Grub Street, 2012)

Skaarup, Harold, *RCAF War Prize Flights, German and Japanese Warbird Survivors* (iUniverse, 2006)

Smith, Peter C., *The Stuka at War* (Ian Allan, 1971)

Smith, Peter C., *Impact! The Dive-Bomber Pilots Speak* (William Kimber, 1981)

Smith, Peter C., *Stuka Squadron: Stukagruppe 77 – the Luftwaffe's 'Fire Brigade'* (PSL, 1990)

Smith, Peter C., *Stukas over the Steppe, 1941–45* (Pen & Sword Aviation, 2015)

Trew, Simon and Sheffield, Gary (eds), *100 Years of Conflict 1900–2000* (Sutton, 2000)

Ward, John, *Hitler's Stuka Squadrons: The Ju 87 at War 1936–1945* (Brown Reference Group, 2004)

Weal, John, *Junkers Ju 87 Stukageschwader of North Africa and the Mediterranean* (Osprey Combat Aircraft No 6, 1998)

Weal, John, *Luftwaffe Schlachtgruppen* (Osprey, 2003)

Weal, John, *Junkers Ju 87 Stukageschwader of the Russian Front* (Osprey Combat Aircraft No 84, 2008)

Whealey, Robert H., *Hitler and Spain: The Nazi Role in the Spanish Civil War, 1936–1939* (The University Press of Kentucky, 1989)

Magazine articles

'Germany's dive-bomber: captured Ju 87 described – speed sacrificed for simplicity' (*Flight*, 17 October 1940)

'The dive bomber: reasons for dive brakes, some engine problems, history of German development' (*Flight*, 17 June 1943)

'The Junkers Jumo 211 Series' (*Flight*, 26 August 1943)

'Mediterranean Convoy Operations, Operation Excess' (*London Gazette*, 10 August 1948)

Websites

http://aircrewremembered.com

www.germanluftwaffe.com

www.ww2.dk/Airfields/lwairfields.html – Henry L. de Zeng IV, 'Luftwaffe Airfields 1935–45: Italy, Sicily and Sardinia'

www.axis.classicwings.com/Luftwaffe/junkers/junkers87

http://www.geocities.ws/hjunkers/ju_mus.htm– Junkers museum and survivor aircraft

Manuals

Ju 87 A Bedienungsvorschrift – Bewaffnung (1937)

Ju 87 B-1 Betriebsanleitung (April 1939)

Ju 87 B-2 Betriebsanleitung (June 1940)

Ju 87 B-1, B-2 Bewaffnung (1939)

Ju 87 D-1 Bedienungsvorschrift – Schusswaffenanlage (January 1942)

Ju 87 D-1 trop Flugzeug-Handbuch – Abwurfwaffenanlage (February 1942)

Ju 87 D-5 Flugzeug-Handbuch – Schusswaffenanlage (November 1943)

Ju 87 G-2 Flugzeug-Handbuch – Schusswaffenanlage mit zwei 3,7cm BK (October 1943)

Ju 87 R-1 Bedienungsvorschrift-Fl (March 1942)

Junkers Jumo 211A aero engine Series 1, preliminary operating instructions and maintenance (1939, Junkers Flugzeug und Motorenwerke)

Junkers Jumo 211F and J aero engines, Series 1 (extract from the engine manual, 1941, Junkers Flugzeug und Motorenwerke)

Junkers VS 11-Verstelluftschrauben-Anlage am Jumo 211 F u. J (1941)

MG81 – 7.9mm-Flugzeugmaschinengewehr 81 Waffen-Handbuch, Beiheft 1: WB81A und B (Waffen-Behalter 81A und B) (January 1943)
GSL-k 81Z – Gleitschienenlafetteklein 81Z mit VE 42, Waffen-Handbuch (December 1941) *Kurzbetriebsanleitung Junkers Ju 87 D-3 für den Flugzeugführer.*

Index